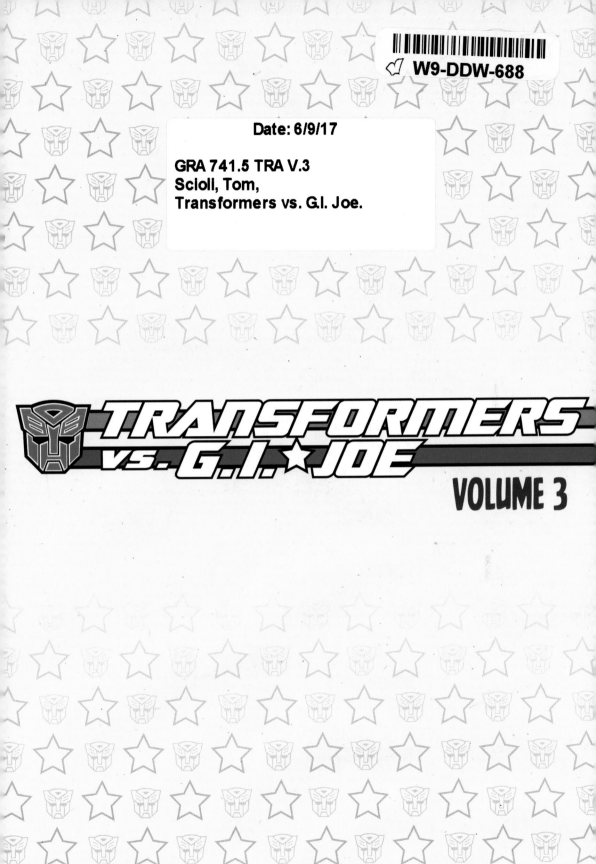

TRANSFORMERS vs. G.I. ☆ JOE

VOLUME 3

WRITTEN BY:
TOM SCIOLI AND JOHN BARBER

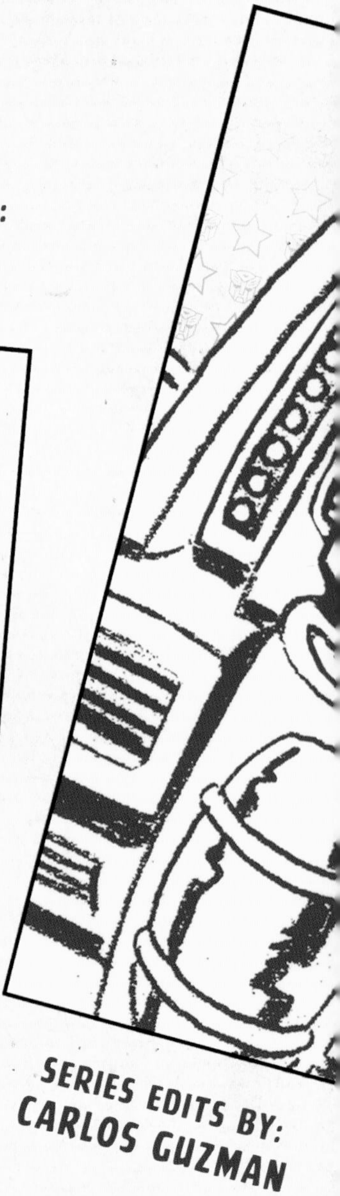

ART, COLORS, AND LETTERING BY:
TOM SCIOLI

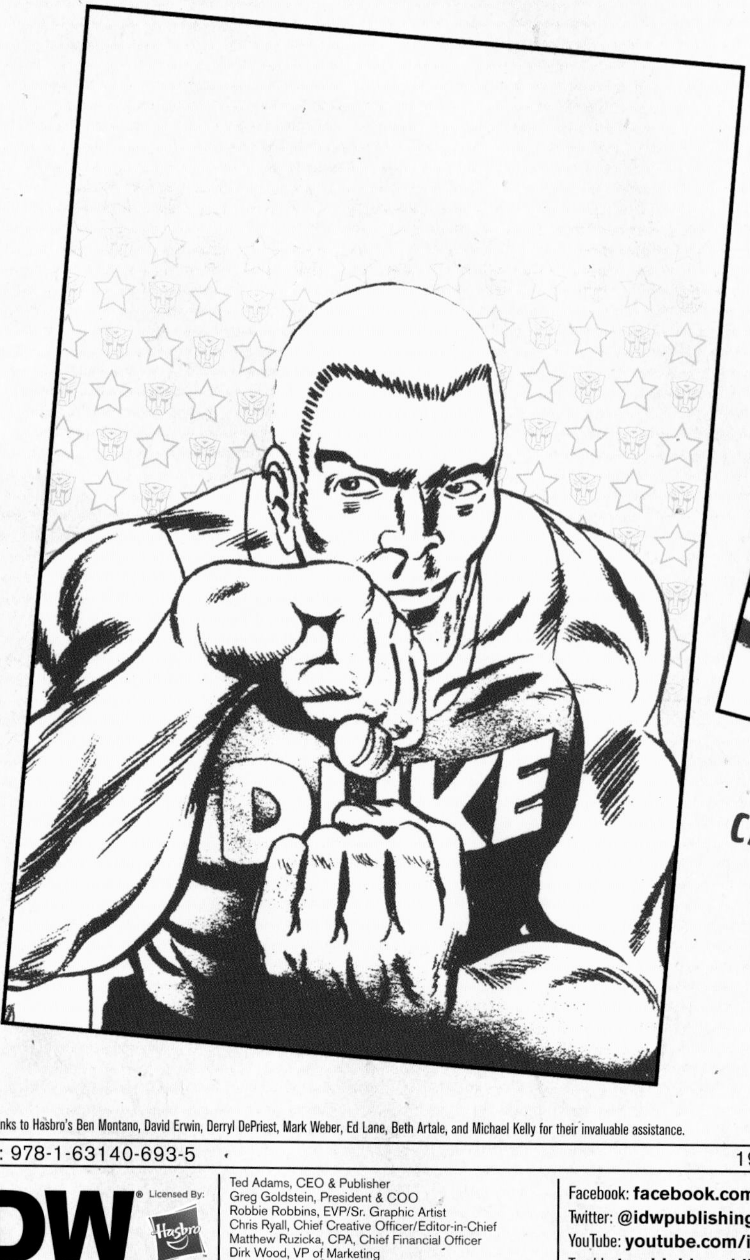

SERIES EDITS BY:
CARLOS GUZMAN

Special thanks to Hasbro's Ben Montano, David Erwin, Derryl DePriest, Mark Weber, Ed Lane, Beth Artale, and Michael Kelly for their invaluable assistance.

ISBN: 978-1-63140-693-5

19 18 17 16 1 2 3 4

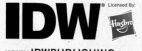

IDW® Licensed By: Hasbro

www.IDWPUBLISHING.com

Ted Adams, CEO & Publisher
Greg Goldstein, President & COO
Robbie Robbins, EVP/Sr. Graphic Artist
Chris Ryall, Chief Creative Officer/Editor-in-Chief
Matthew Ruzicka, CPA, Chief Financial Officer
Dirk Wood, VP of Marketing
Lorelei Bunjes, VP of Digital Services
Jeff Webber, VP of Licensing, Digital and Subsidiary Rights
Jerry Bennington, VP of New Product Development

Facebook: facebook.com/idwpublishing
Twitter: @idwpublishing
YouTube: youtube.com/idwpublishing
Tumblr: tumblr.idwpublishing.com
Instagram: instagram.com/idwpublishing

Originally published as THE TRANSFORMERS VS. G.I. JOE issues #10–13.

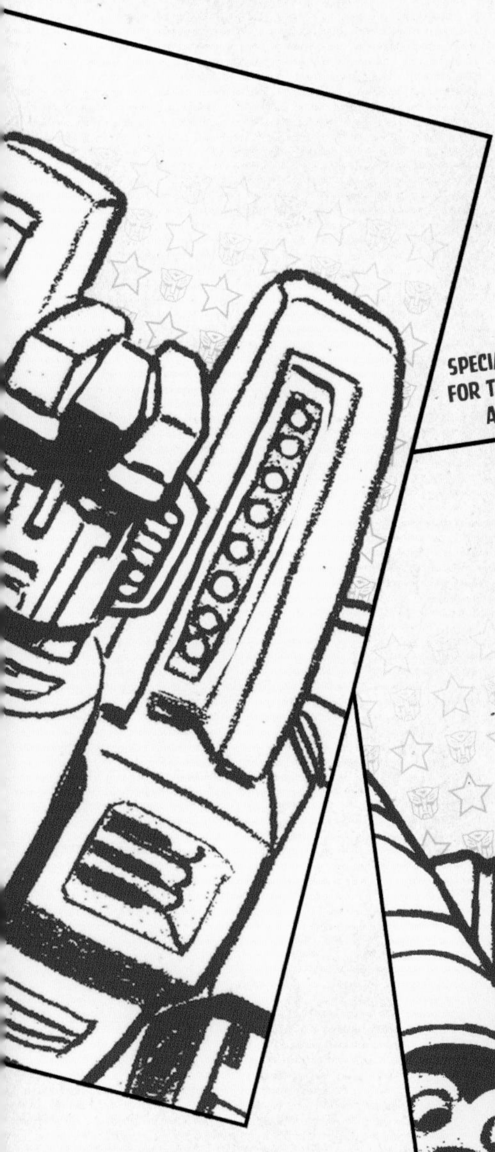

COVER ARTWORK BY:
TOM SCIOLI

SPECIAL THANKS TO ED PISKOR, JASEN LEX, AND AYCHBE FOR THE LOAN OF THEIR COLLECTIONS OF TRANSFORMERS AND G.I. JOE MEMORABILIA FOR ART REFERENCE.

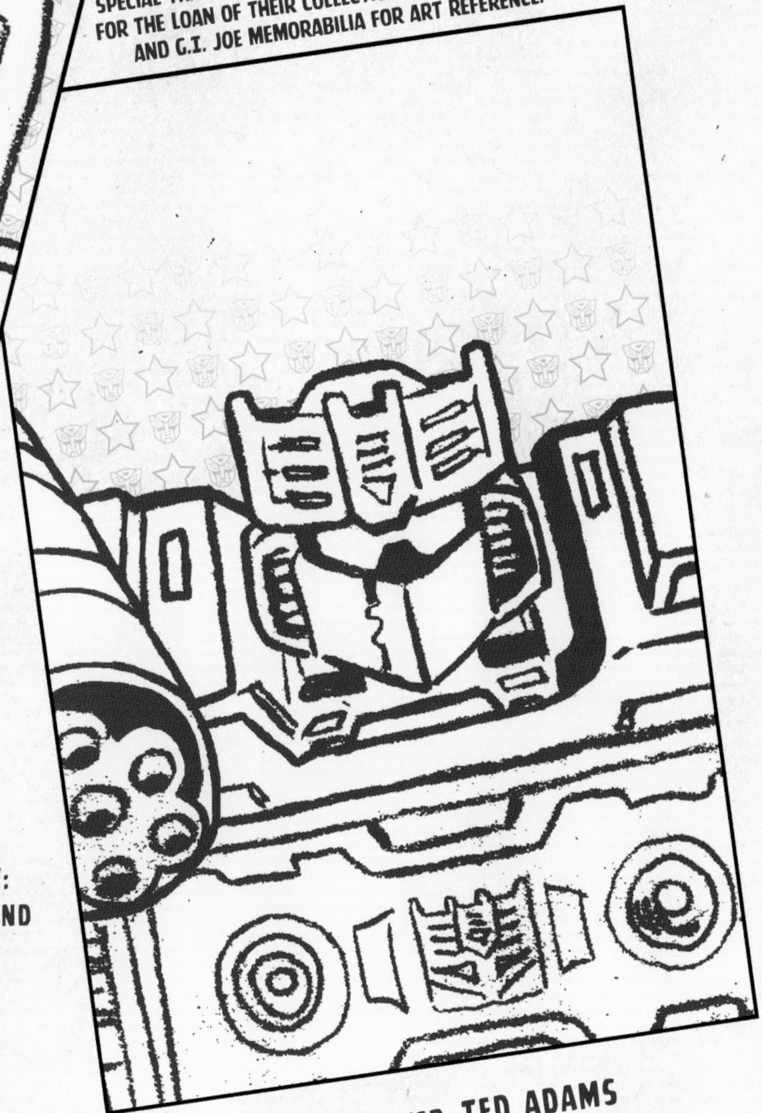

COLLECTION EDITS BY:
JUSTIN EISINGER AND ALONZO SIMON

COLLECTION PRODUCTION BY:
CLAUDIA CHONG

PUBLISHER: TED ADAMS

CHAPTER 10

ARTWORK BY TOM SCIOLI

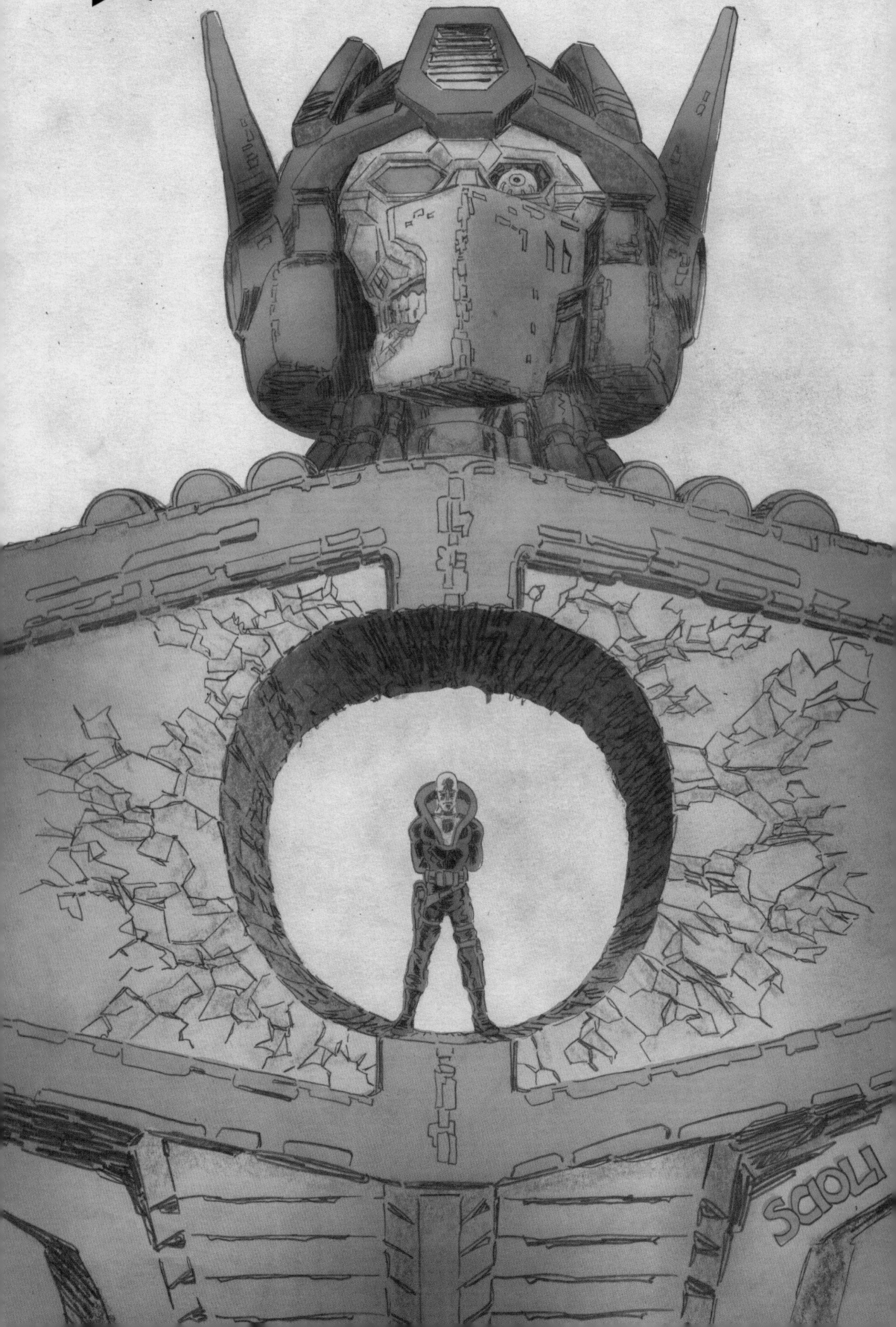
SCIOLI

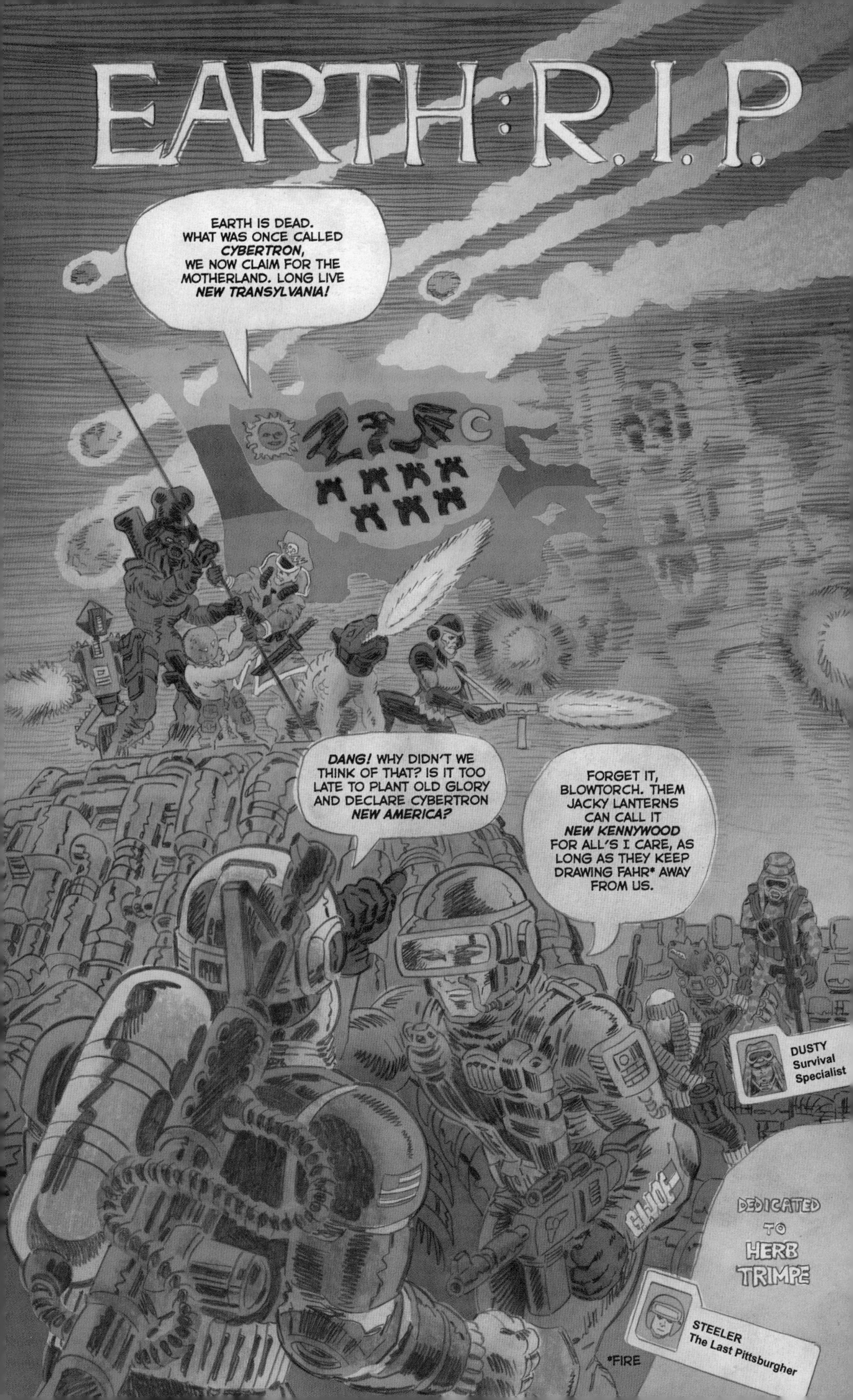
EARTH:R.I.P.
EARTH IS DEAD. WHAT WAS ONCE CALLED CYBERTRON, WE NOW CLAIM FOR THE MOTHERLAND. LONG LIVE NEW TRANSYLVANIA!
DANG! WHY DIDN'T WE THINK OF THAT? IS IT TOO LATE TO PLANT OLD GLORY AND DECLARE CYBERTRON NEW AMERICA?
FORGET IT, BLOWTORCH. THEM JACKY LANTERNS CAN CALL IT NEW KENNYWOOD FOR ALL'S I CARE, AS LONG AS THEY KEEP DRAWING FAHR* AWAY FROM US.
DUSTY Survival Specialist
DEDICATED TO HERB TRIMPE
STEELER The Last Pittsburgher
*FIRE

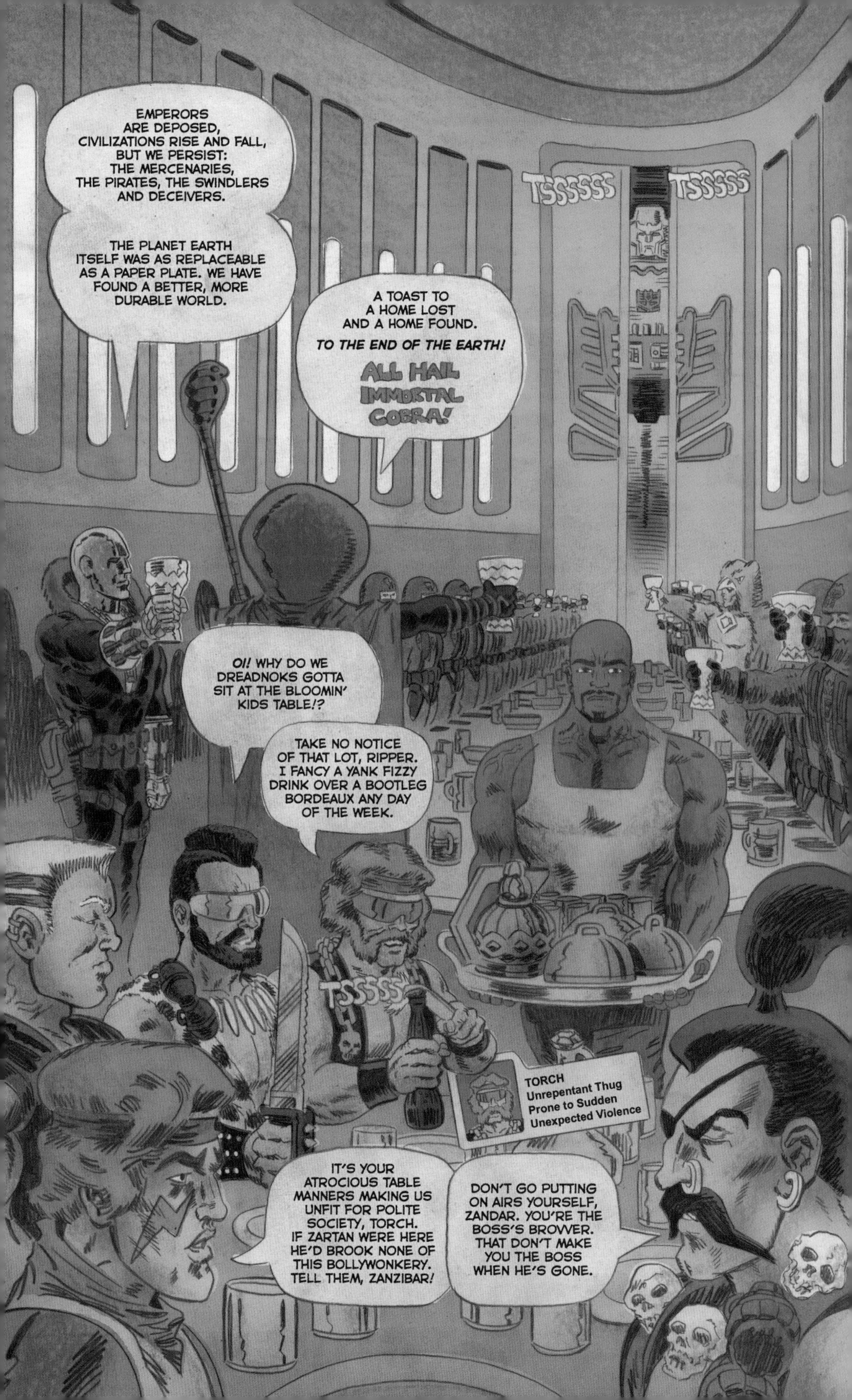
EMPERORS ARE DEPOSED, CIVILIZATIONS RISE AND FALL, BUT WE PERSIST: THE MERCENARIES, THE PIRATES, THE SWINDLERS AND DECEIVERS.
THE PLANET EARTH ITSELF WAS AS REPLACEABLE AS A PAPER PLATE. WE HAVE FOUND A BETTER, MORE DURABLE WORLD.
TSSSSSS
TSSSSS
A TOAST TO A HOME LOST AND A HOME FOUND.
TO THE END OF THE EARTH!
ALL HAIL IMMORTAL COBRA!
OI! WHY DO WE DREADNOKS GOTTA SIT AT THE BLOOMIN' KIDS TABLE!?
TAKE NO NOTICE OF THAT LOT, RIPPER. I FANCY A YANK FIZZY DRINK OVER A BOOTLEG BORDEAUX ANY DAY OF THE WEEK.
TSSSSS
TORCH
Unrepentant Thug
Prone to Sudden
Unexpected Violence
IT'S YOUR ATROCIOUS TABLE MANNERS MAKING US UNFIT FOR POLITE SOCIETY, TORCH. IF ZARTAN WERE HERE HE'D BROOK NONE OF THIS BOLLYWONKERY. TELL THEM, ZANZIBAR!
DON'T GO PUTTING ON AIRS YOURSELF, ZANDAR. YOU'RE THE BOSS'S BROVVER. THAT DON'T MAKE YOU THE BOSS WHEN HE'S GONE.

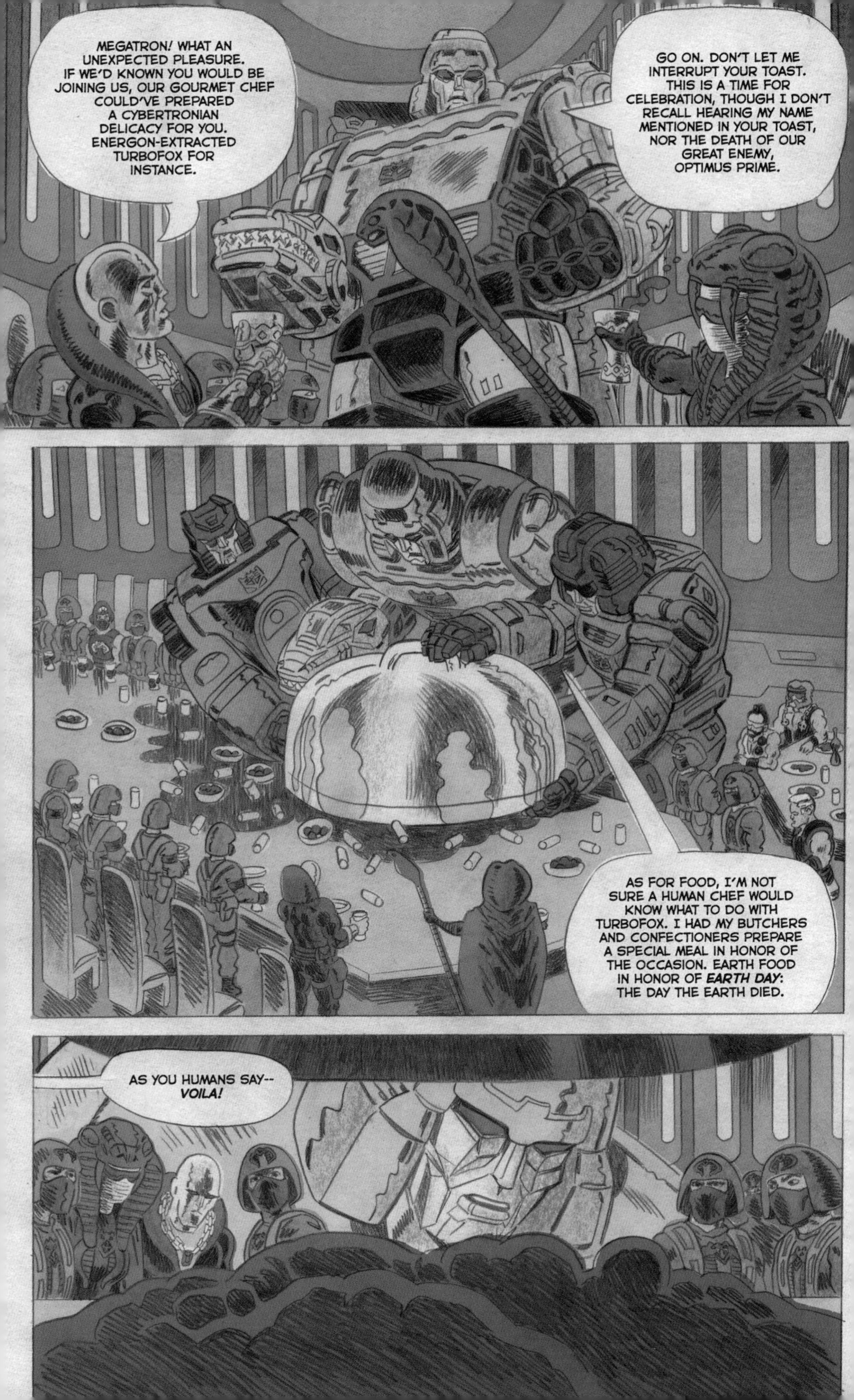
MEGATRON! WHAT AN UNEXPECTED PLEASURE. IF WE'D KNOWN YOU WOULD BE JOINING US, OUR GOURMET CHEF COULD'VE PREPARED A CYBERTRONIAN DELICACY FOR YOU. ENERGON-EXTRACTED TURBOFOX FOR INSTANCE.
GO ON. DON'T LET ME INTERRUPT YOUR TOAST. THIS IS A TIME FOR CELEBRATION, THOUGH I DON'T RECALL HEARING MY NAME MENTIONED IN YOUR TOAST, NOR THE DEATH OF OUR GREAT ENEMY, OPTIMUS PRIME.
AS FOR FOOD, I'M NOT SURE A HUMAN CHEF WOULD KNOW WHAT TO DO WITH TURBOFOX. I HAD MY BUTCHERS AND CONFECTIONERS PREPARE A SPECIAL MEAL IN HONOR OF THE OCCASION. EARTH FOOD IN HONOR OF *EARTH DAY*: THE DAY THE EARTH DIED.
AS YOU HUMANS SAY-- *VOILA!*

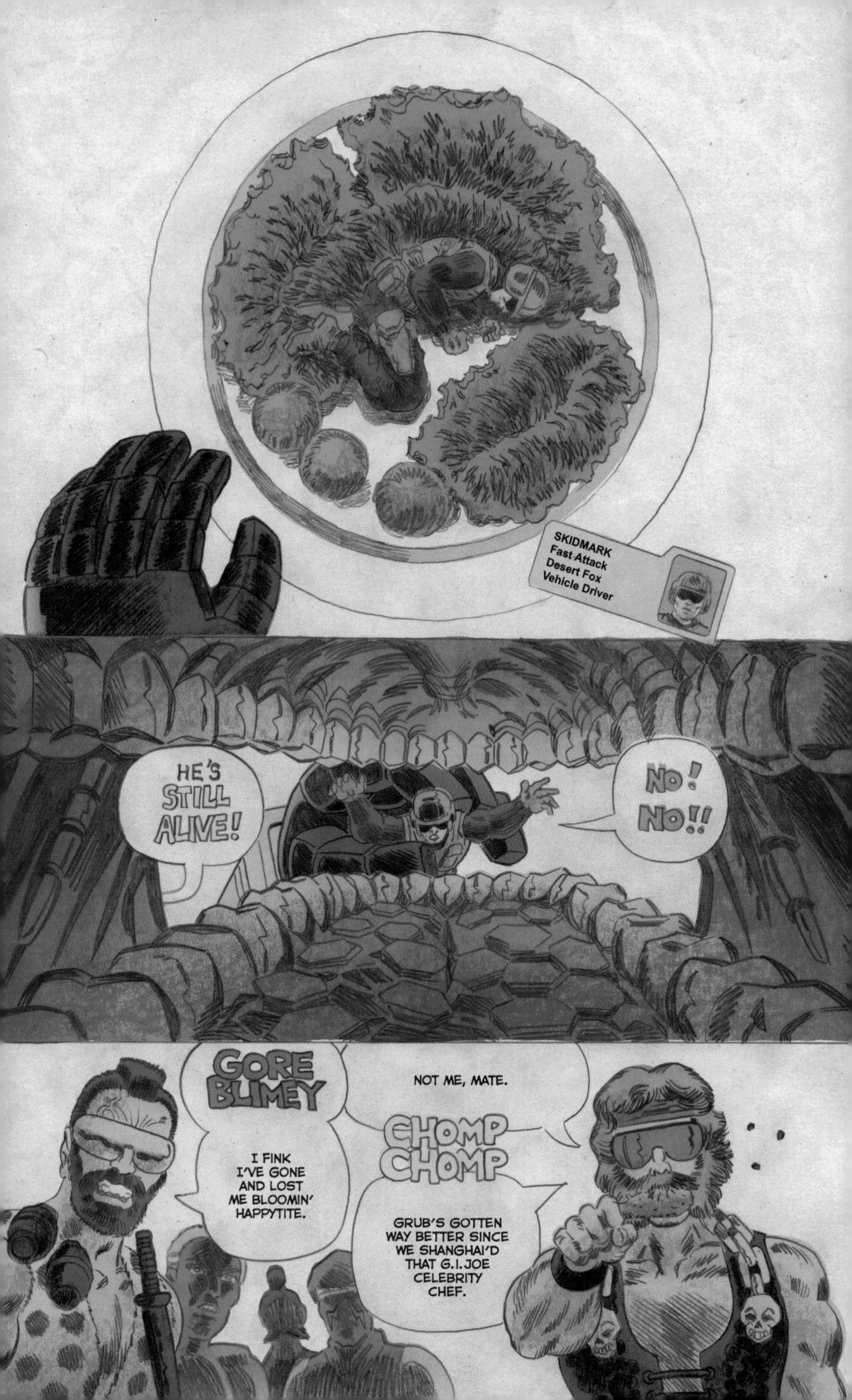
SKIDMARK
Fast Attack
Desert Fox
Vehicle Driver
HE'S STILL ALIVE!
NO! NO!!
GORE BLIMEY
NOT ME, MATE.
CHOMP CHOMP
I FINK I'VE GONE AND LOST ME BLOOMIN' HAPPYTITE.
GRUB'S GOTTEN WAY BETTER SINCE WE SHANGHAI'D THAT G.I.JOE CELEBRITY CHEF.

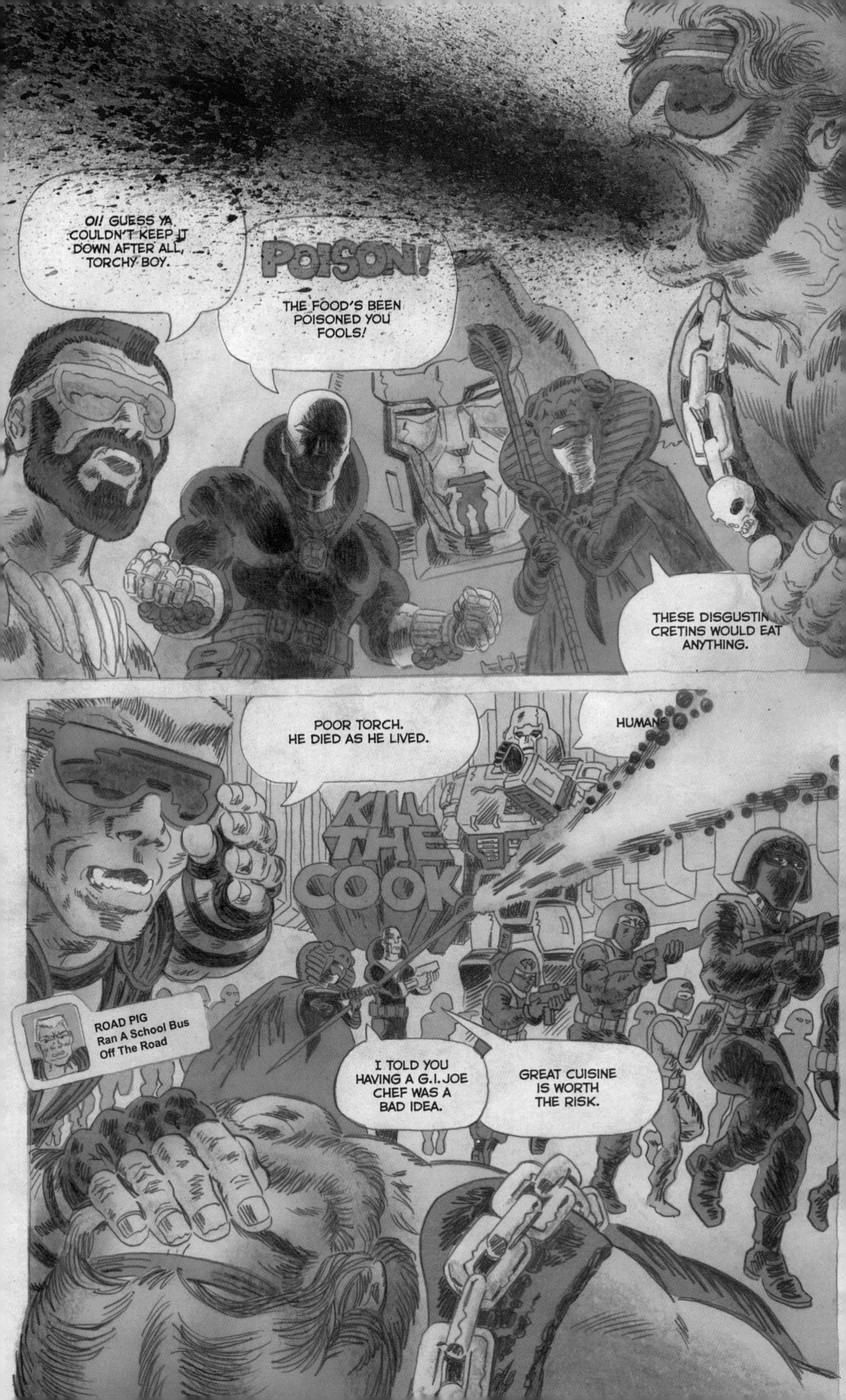
OI! GUESS YA COULDN'T KEEP IT DOWN AFTER ALL, TORCHY BOY.
POISON!
THE FOOD'S BEEN POISONED YOU FOOLS!
THESE DISGUSTIN CRETINS WOULD EAT ANYTHING.
POOR TORCH. HE DIED AS HE LIVED.
HUMANS
KILL THE COOK!
ROAD PIG
Ran A School Bus Off The Road
I TOLD YOU HAVING A G.I. JOE CHEF WAS A BAD IDEA.
GREAT CUISINE IS WORTH THE RISK.

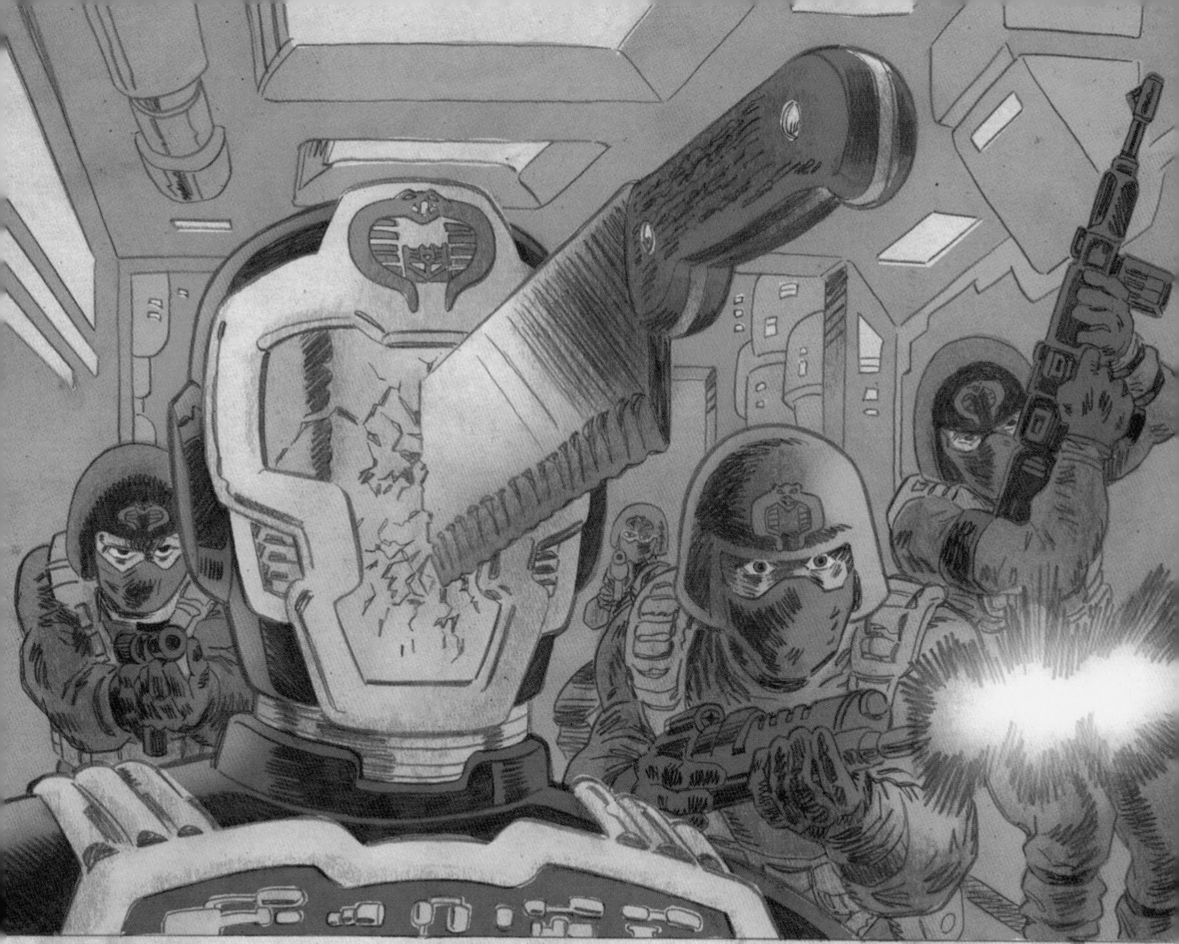

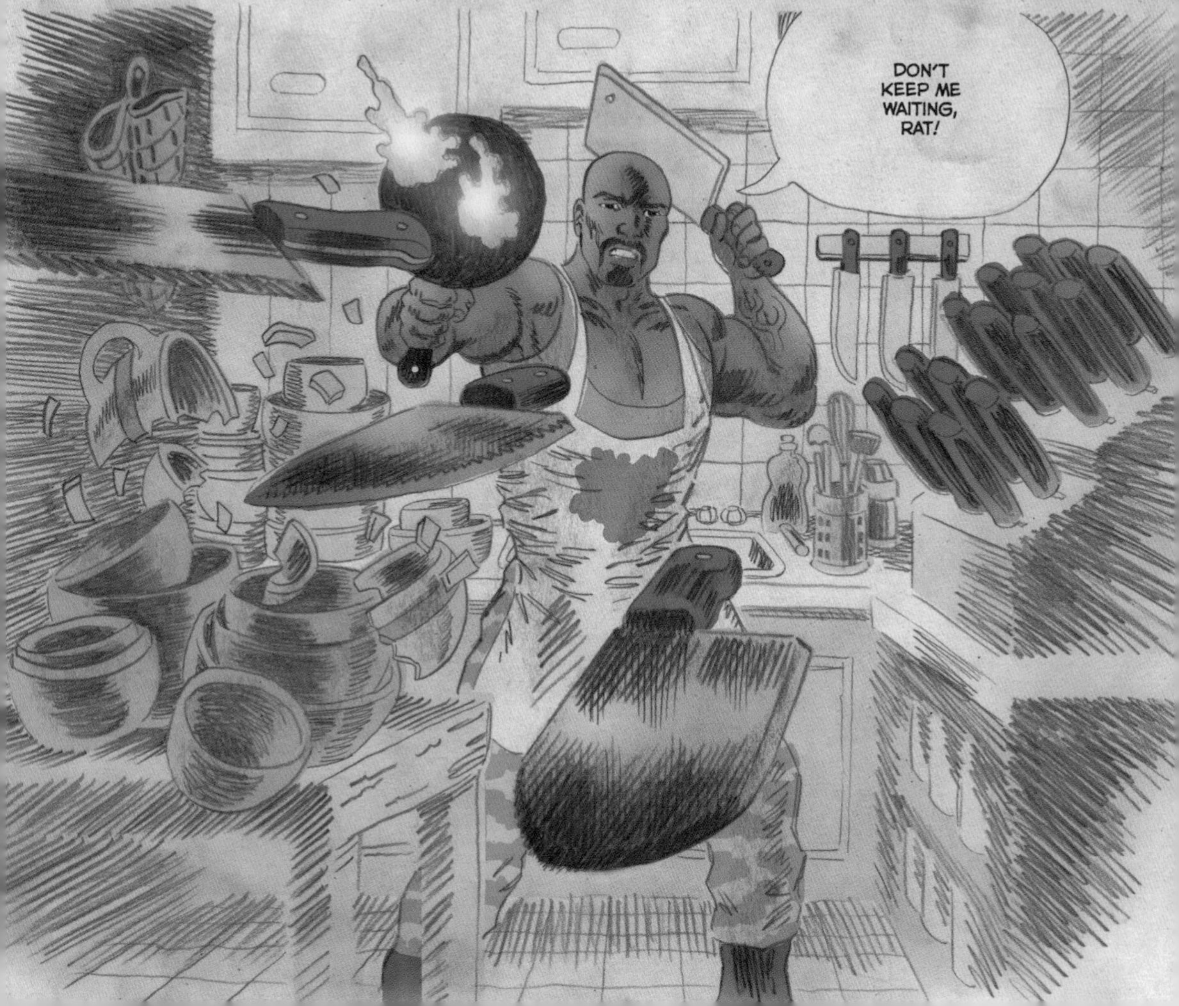
DON'T KEEP ME WAITING, RAT!

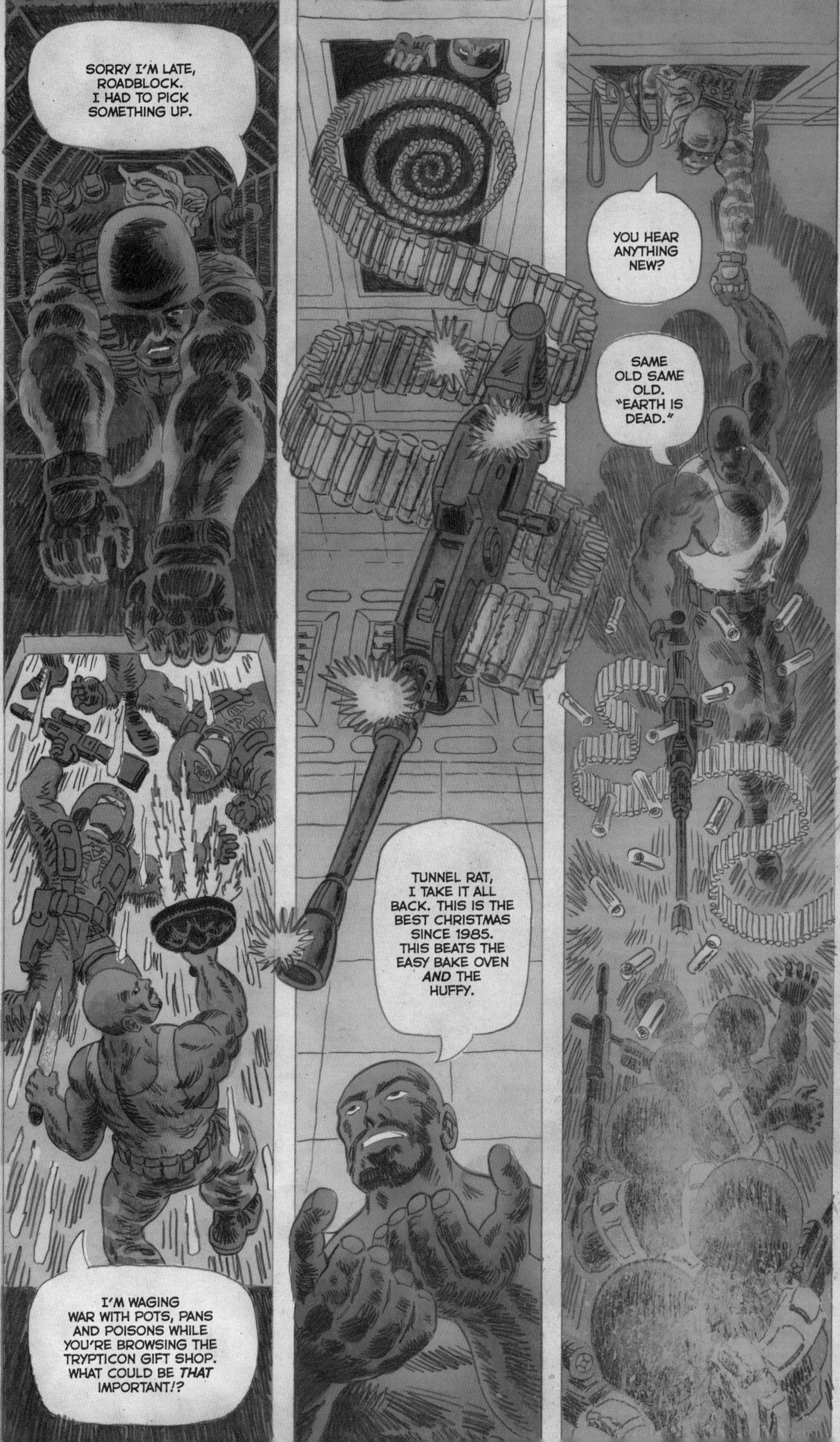
SORRY I'M LATE, ROADBLOCK. I HAD TO PICK SOMETHING UP.
I'M WAGING WAR WITH POTS, PANS AND POISONS WHILE YOU'RE BROWSING THE TRYPTICON GIFT SHOP. WHAT COULD BE *THAT* IMPORTANT!?
TUNNEL RAT, I TAKE IT ALL BACK. THIS IS THE BEST CHRISTMAS SINCE 1985. THIS BEATS THE EASY BAKE OVEN *AND* THE HUFFY.
YOU HEAR ANYTHING NEW?
SAME OLD SAME OLD. "EARTH IS DEAD."

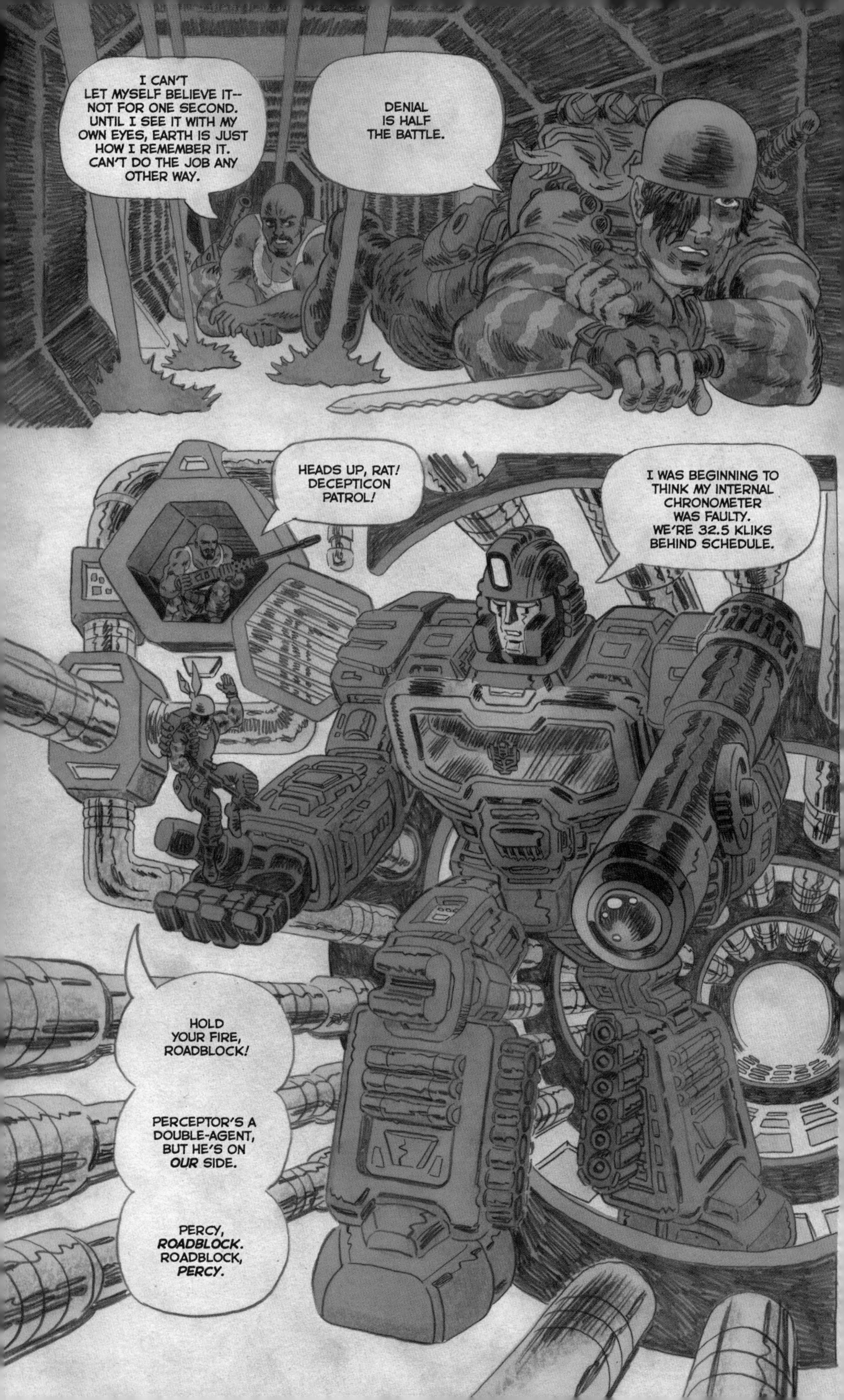
I CAN'T LET MYSELF BELIEVE IT-- NOT FOR ONE SECOND. UNTIL I SEE IT WITH MY OWN EYES, EARTH IS JUST HOW I REMEMBER IT. CAN'T DO THE JOB ANY OTHER WAY.
DENIAL IS HALF THE BATTLE.
HEADS UP, RAT! DECEPTICON PATROL!
I WAS BEGINNING TO THINK MY INTERNAL CHRONOMETER WAS FAULTY. WE'RE 32.5 KLIKS BEHIND SCHEDULE.
HOLD YOUR FIRE, ROADBLOCK!
PERCEPTOR'S A DOUBLE-AGENT, BUT HE'S ON *OUR* SIDE.
PERCY, ***ROADBLOCK***. ROADBLOCK, ***PERCY***.

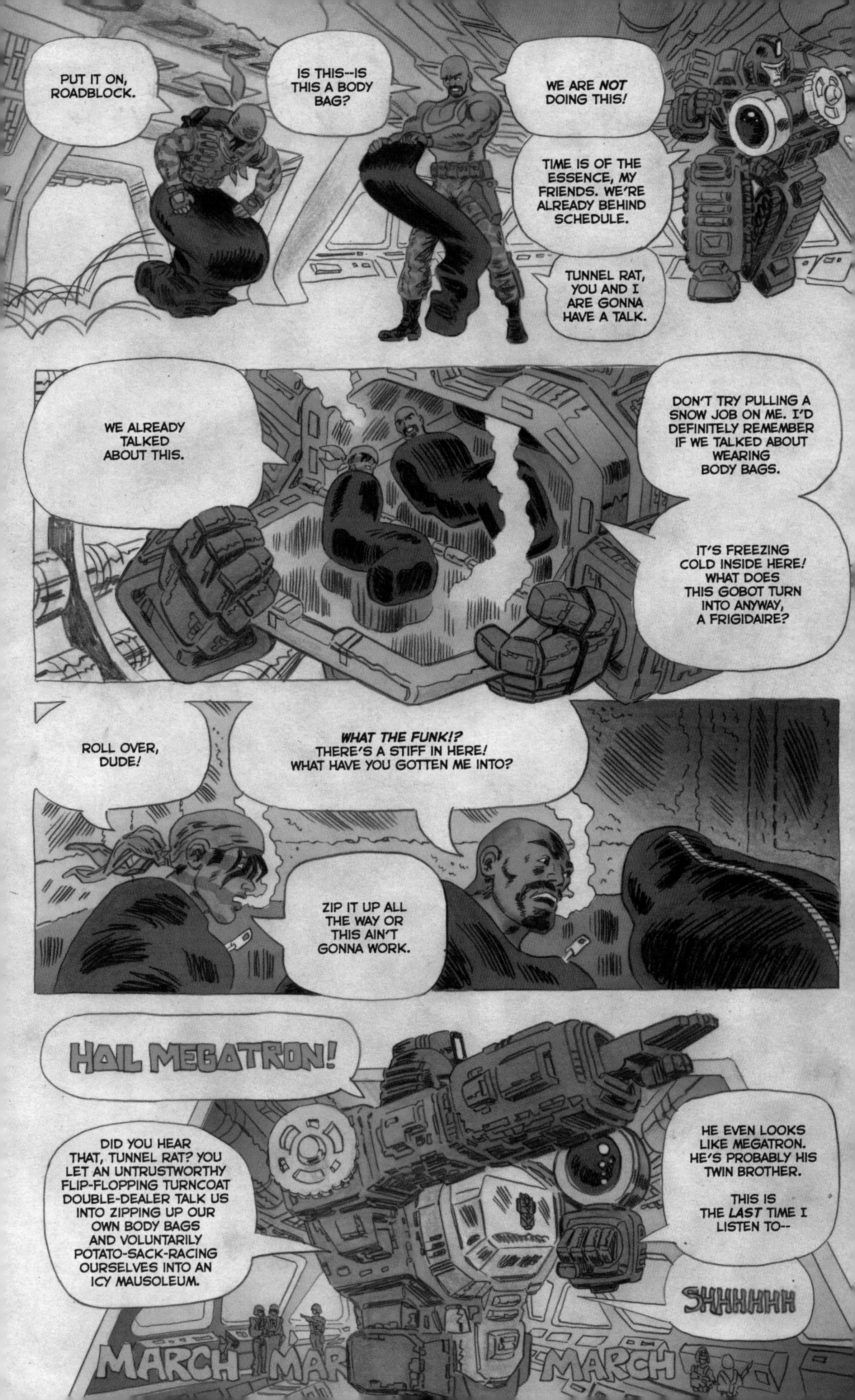
PUT IT ON, ROADBLOCK.
IS THIS--IS THIS A BODY BAG?
WE ARE *NOT* DOING THIS!
TIME IS OF THE ESSENCE, MY FRIENDS. WE'RE ALREADY BEHIND SCHEDULE.
TUNNEL RAT, YOU AND I ARE GONNA HAVE A TALK.
WE ALREADY TALKED ABOUT THIS.
DON'T TRY PULLING A SNOW JOB ON ME. I'D DEFINITELY REMEMBER IF WE TALKED ABOUT WEARING BODY BAGS.
IT'S FREEZING COLD INSIDE HERE! WHAT DOES THIS GOBOT TURN INTO ANYWAY, A FRIGIDAIRE?
ROLL OVER, DUDE!
WHAT THE FUNK!? THERE'S A STIFF IN HERE! WHAT HAVE YOU GOTTEN ME INTO?
ZIP IT UP ALL THE WAY OR THIS AIN'T GONNA WORK.
HAIL MEGATRON!
DID YOU HEAR THAT, TUNNEL RAT? YOU LET AN UNTRUSTWORTHY FLIP-FLOPPING TURNCOAT DOUBLE-DEALER TALK US INTO ZIPPING UP OUR OWN BODY BAGS AND VOLUNTARILY POTATO-SACK-RACING OURSELVES INTO AN ICY MAUSOLEUM.
HE EVEN LOOKS LIKE MEGATRON. HE'S PROBABLY HIS TWIN BROTHER.
THIS IS THE *LAST* TIME I LISTEN TO--
SHHHHHH
MARCH MAR MARCH

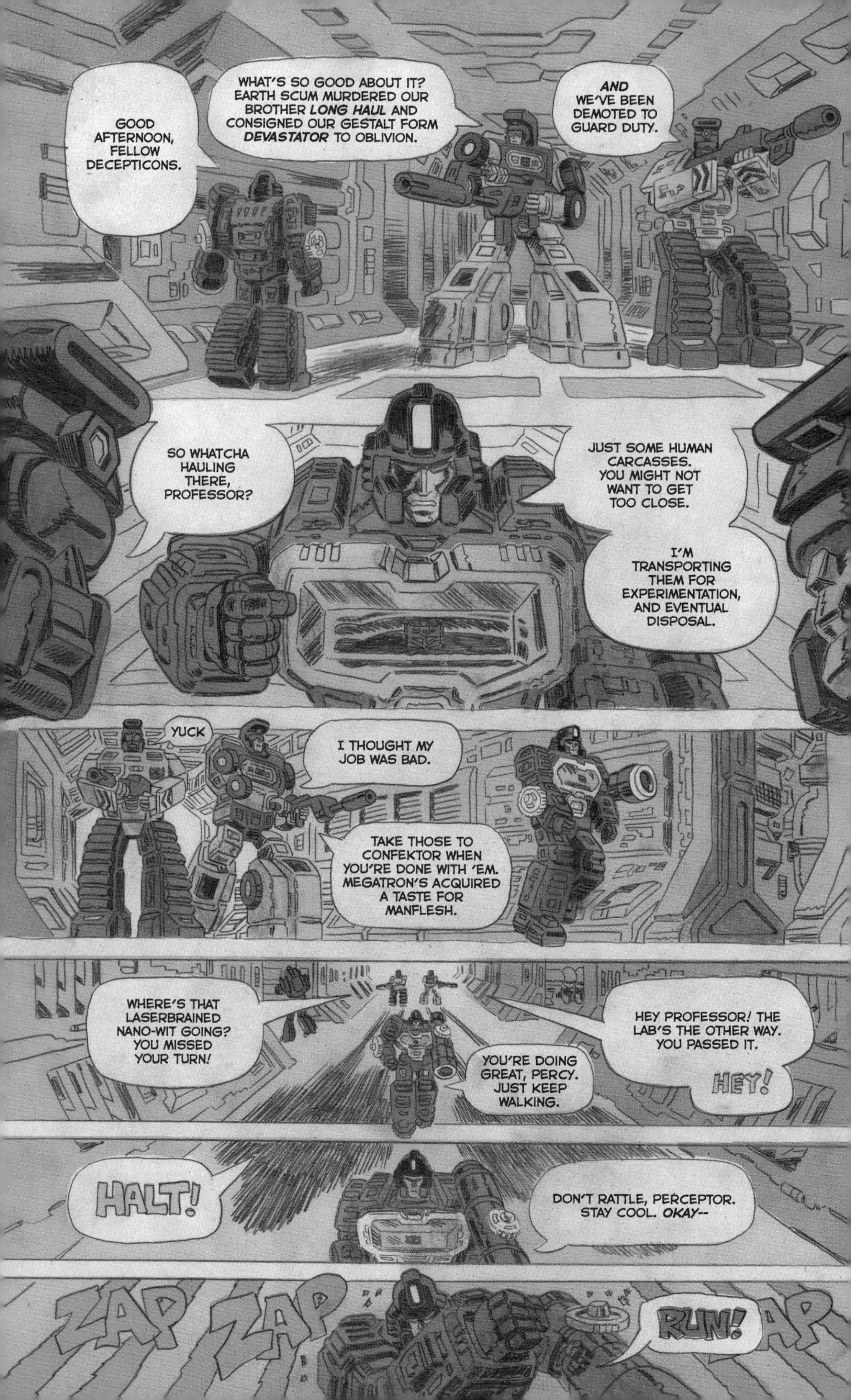
GOOD AFTERNOON, FELLOW DECEPTICONS.
WHAT'S SO GOOD ABOUT IT? EARTH SCUM MURDERED OUR BROTHER *LONG HAUL* AND CONSIGNED OUR GESTALT FORM *DEVASTATOR* TO OBLIVION.
AND WE'VE BEEN DEMOTED TO GUARD DUTY.
SO WHATCHA HAULING THERE, PROFESSOR?
JUST SOME HUMAN CARCASSES. YOU MIGHT NOT WANT TO GET TOO CLOSE.
I'M TRANSPORTING THEM FOR EXPERIMENTATION, AND EVENTUAL DISPOSAL.
YUCK
I THOUGHT MY JOB WAS BAD.
TAKE THOSE TO CONFEKTOR WHEN YOU'RE DONE WITH 'EM. MEGATRON'S ACQUIRED A TASTE FOR MANFLESH.
WHERE'S THAT LASERBRAINED NANO-WIT GOING? YOU MISSED YOUR TURN!
HEY PROFESSOR! THE LAB'S THE OTHER WAY. YOU PASSED IT.
YOU'RE DOING GREAT, PERCY. JUST KEEP WALKING.
HEY!
HALT!
DON'T RATTLE, PERCEPTOR. STAY COOL. *OKAY*--
ZAP ZAP
RUN!
AP

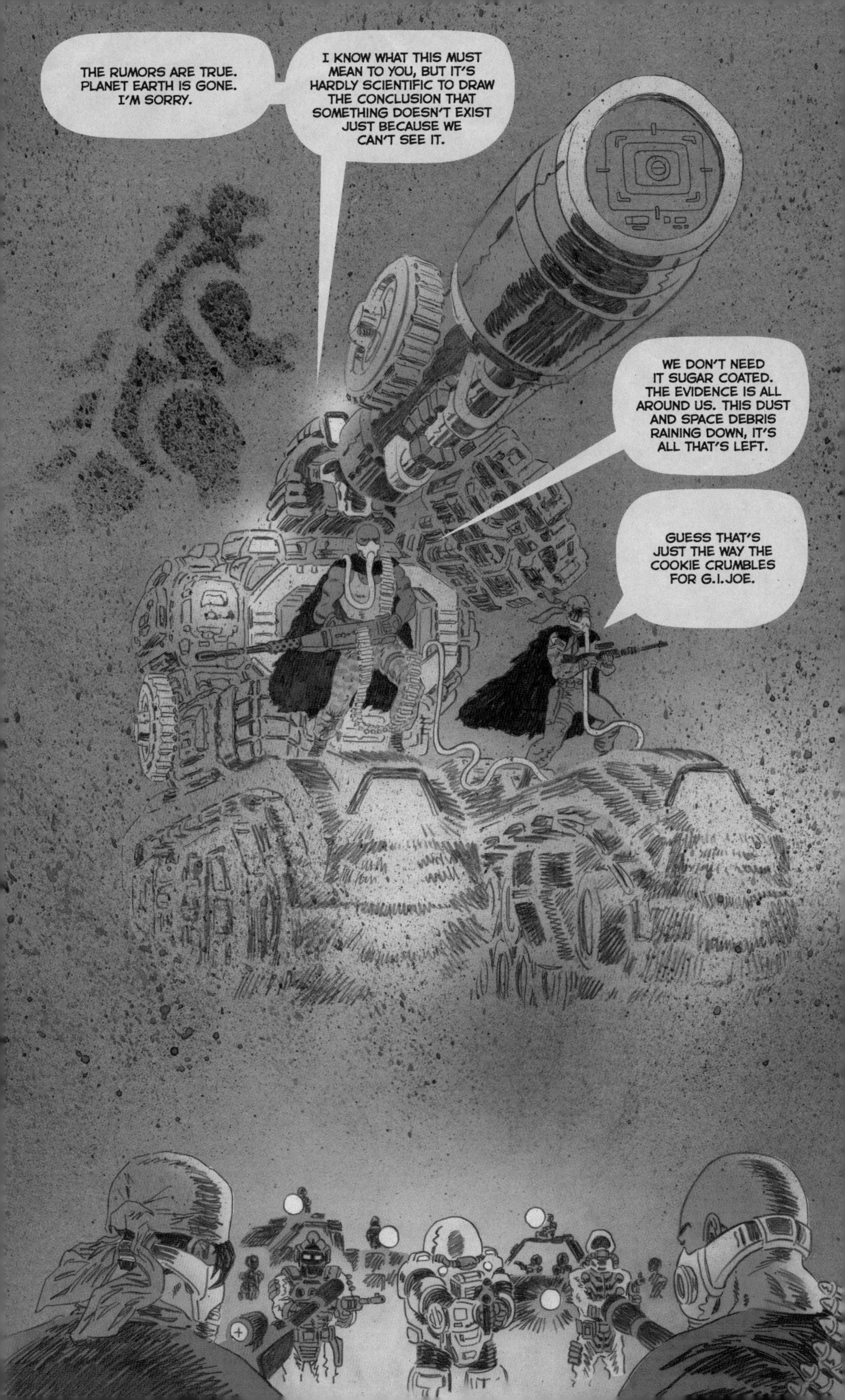
THE RUMORS ARE TRUE. PLANET EARTH IS GONE. I'M SORRY.
I KNOW WHAT THIS MUST MEAN TO YOU, BUT IT'S HARDLY SCIENTIFIC TO DRAW THE CONCLUSION THAT SOMETHING DOESN'T EXIST JUST BECAUSE WE CAN'T SEE IT.
WE DON'T NEED IT SUGAR COATED. THE EVIDENCE IS ALL AROUND US. THIS DUST AND SPACE DEBRIS RAINING DOWN, IT'S ALL THAT'S LEFT.
GUESS THAT'S JUST THE WAY THE COOKIE CRUMBLES FOR G.I.JOE.

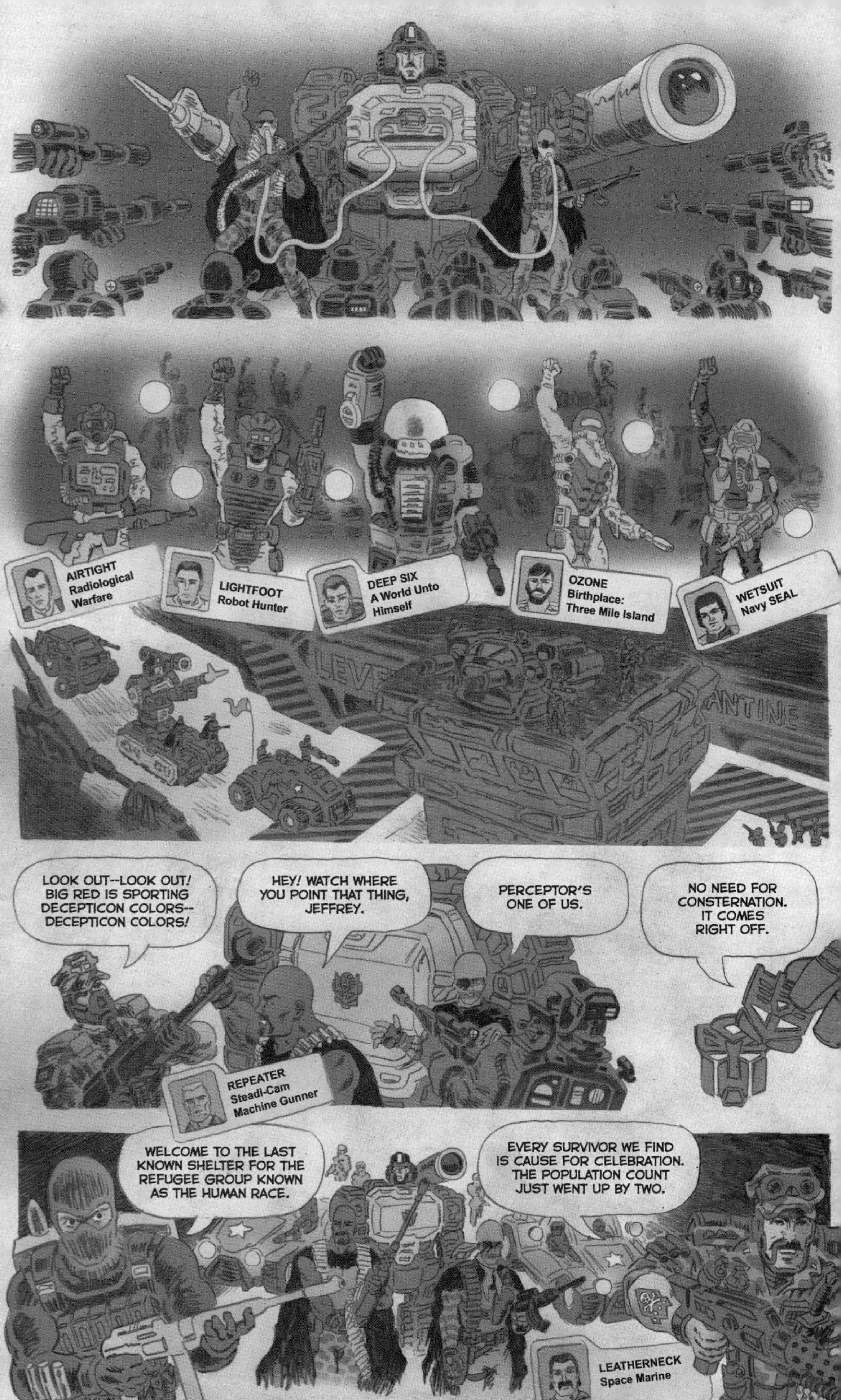

AIRTIGHT
Radiological Warfare
LIGHTFOOT
Robot Hunter
DEEP SIX
A World Unto Himself
OZONE
Birthplace: Three Mile Island
WETSUIT
Navy SEAL
LEVE
ANTINE
LOOK OUT--LOOK OUT! BIG RED IS SPORTING DECEPTICON COLORS--DECEPTICON COLORS!
HEY! WATCH WHERE YOU POINT THAT THING, JEFFREY.
PERCEPTOR'S ONE OF US.
NO NEED FOR CONSTERNATION. IT COMES RIGHT OFF.
REPEATER
Steadi-Cam Machine Gunner
WELCOME TO THE LAST KNOWN SHELTER FOR THE REFUGEE GROUP KNOWN AS THE HUMAN RACE.
EVERY SURVIVOR WE FIND IS CAUSE FOR CELEBRATION. THE POPULATION COUNT JUST WENT UP BY TWO.
LEATHERNECK
Space Marine

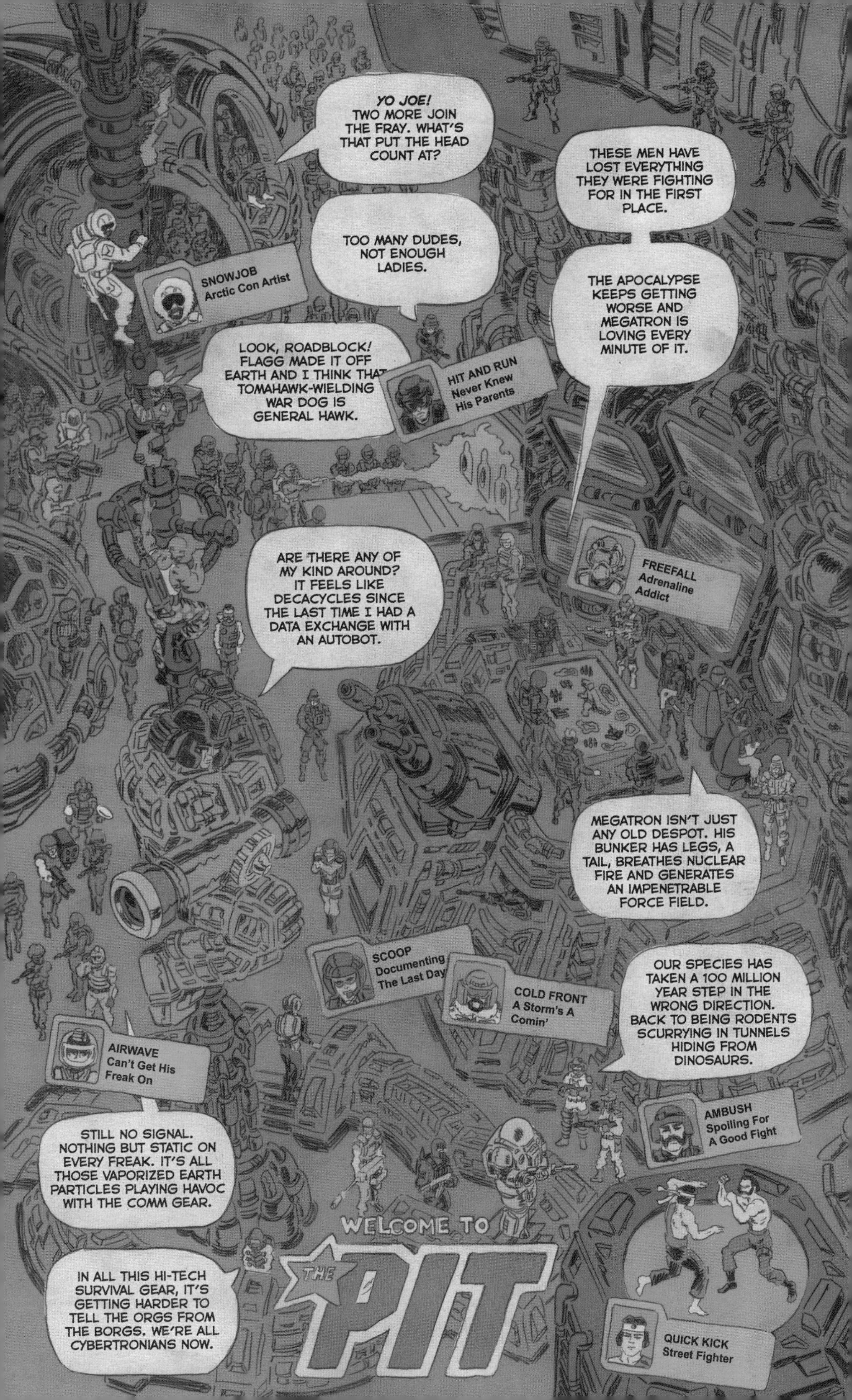

YO JOE! TWO MORE JOIN THE FRAY. WHAT'S THAT PUT THE HEAD COUNT AT?
TOO MANY DUDES, NOT ENOUGH LADIES.
SNOWJOB Arctic Con Artist
THESE MEN HAVE LOST EVERYTHING THEY WERE FIGHTING FOR IN THE FIRST PLACE.
THE APOCALYPSE KEEPS GETTING WORSE AND MEGATRON IS LOVING EVERY MINUTE OF IT.
LOOK, ROADBLOCK! FLAGG MADE IT OFF EARTH AND I THINK THAT TOMAHAWK-WIELDING WAR DOG IS GENERAL HAWK.
HIT AND RUN Never Knew His Parents
ARE THERE ANY OF MY KIND AROUND? IT FEELS LIKE DECACYCLES SINCE THE LAST TIME I HAD A DATA EXCHANGE WITH AN AUTOBOT.
FREEFALL Adrenaline Addict
MEGATRON ISN'T JUST ANY OLD DESPOT. HIS BUNKER HAS LEGS, A TAIL, BREATHES NUCLEAR FIRE AND GENERATES AN IMPENETRABLE FORCE FIELD.
SCOOP Documenting The Last Day
COLD FRONT A Storm's A Comin'
OUR SPECIES HAS TAKEN A 100 MILLION YEAR STEP IN THE WRONG DIRECTION. BACK TO BEING RODENTS SCURRYING IN TUNNELS HIDING FROM DINOSAURS.
AIRWAVE Can't Get His Freak On
AMBUSH Spoiling For A Good Fight
STILL NO SIGNAL. NOTHING BUT STATIC ON EVERY FREAK. IT'S ALL THOSE VAPORIZED EARTH PARTICLES PLAYING HAVOC WITH THE COMM GEAR.
WELCOME TO THE PIT
IN ALL THIS HI-TECH SURVIVAL GEAR, IT'S GETTING HARDER TO TELL THE ORGS FROM THE BORGS. WE'RE ALL CYBERTRONIANS NOW.
QUICK KICK Street Fighter

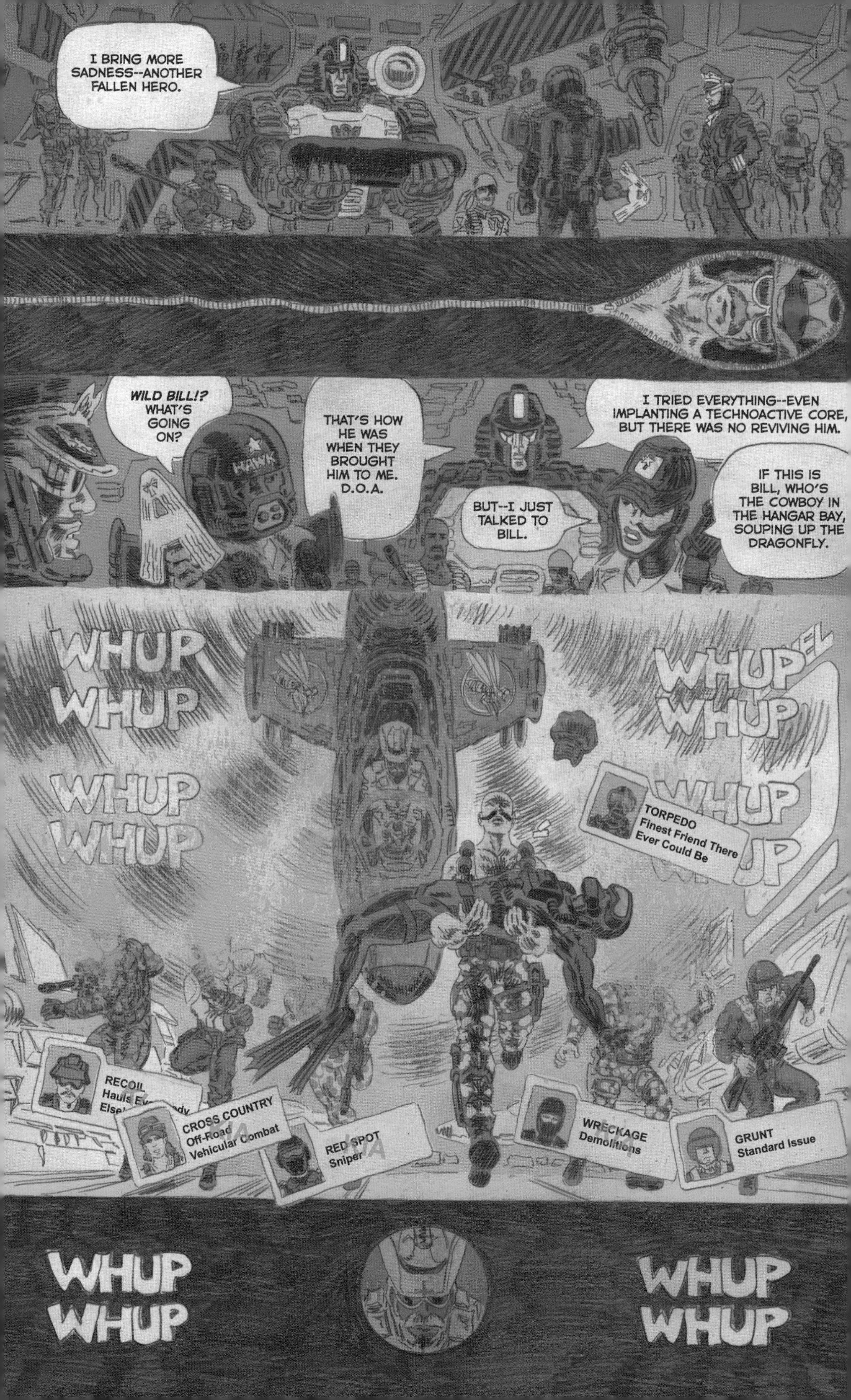
I BRING MORE SADNESS--ANOTHER FALLEN HERO.
WILD BILL!? WHAT'S GOING ON?
THAT'S HOW HE WAS WHEN THEY BROUGHT HIM TO ME. D.O.A.
I TRIED EVERYTHING--EVEN IMPLANTING A TECHNOACTIVE CORE, BUT THERE WAS NO REVIVING HIM.
BUT--I JUST TALKED TO BILL.
IF THIS IS BILL, WHO'S THE COWBOY IN THE HANGAR BAY, SOUPING UP THE DRAGONFLY.
WHUP WHUP
WHUP WHUP
WHUP WHUP
TORPEDO
Finest Friend There Ever Could Be
RECOIL
CROSS COUNTRY
Off-Road Vehicular Combat
RED SPOT
Sniper
WRECKAGE
Demolitions
GRUNT
Standard Issue
WHUP WHUP
WHUP WHUP

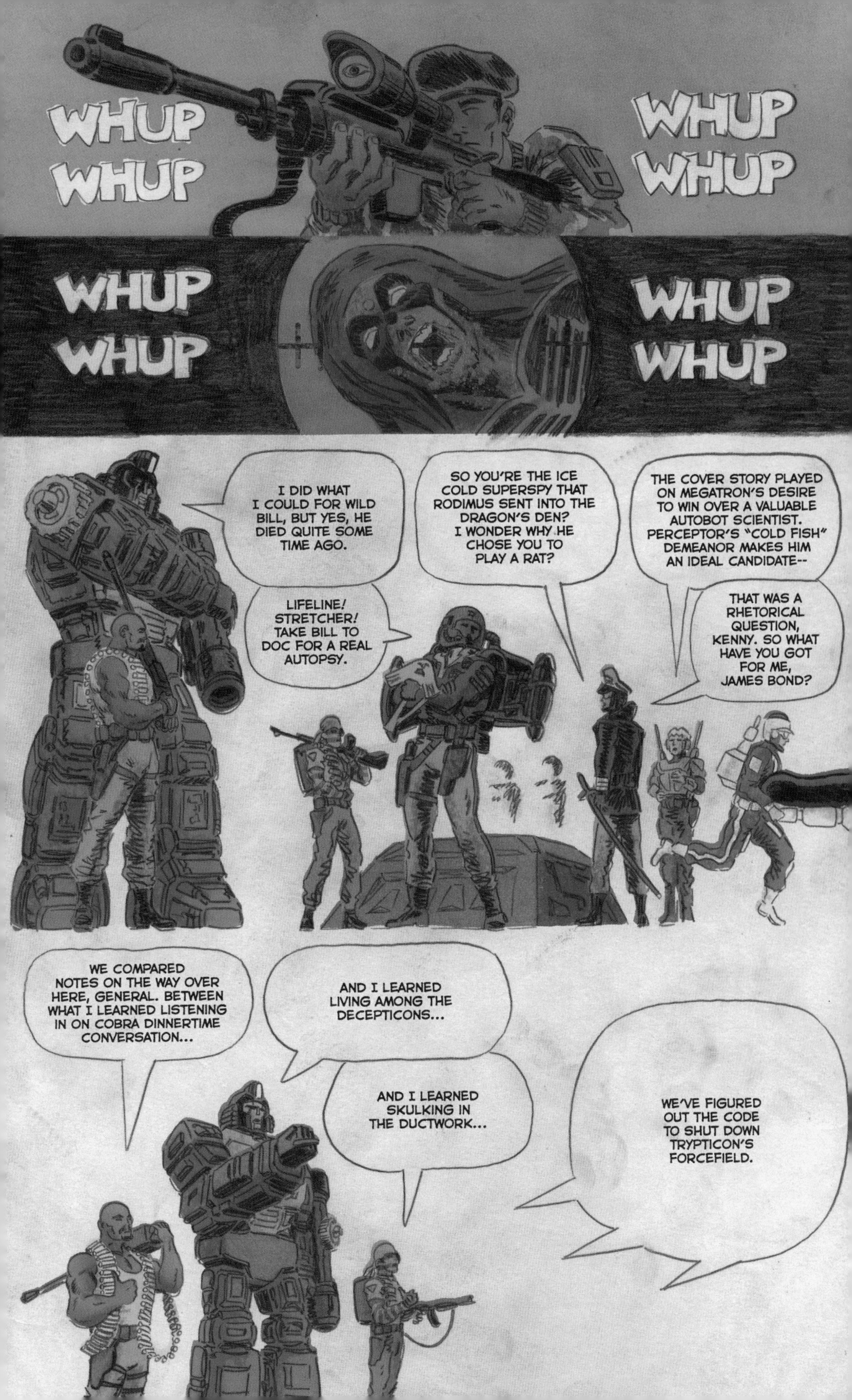

WHUP WHUP
WHUP WHUP
WHUP WHUP
WHUP WHUP
I DID WHAT I COULD FOR WILD BILL, BUT YES, HE DIED QUITE SOME TIME AGO.
LIFELINE! STRETCHER! TAKE BILL TO DOC FOR A REAL AUTOPSY.
SO YOU'RE THE ICE COLD SUPERSPY THAT RODIMUS SENT INTO THE DRAGON'S DEN? I WONDER WHY HE CHOSE YOU TO PLAY A RAT?
THE COVER STORY PLAYED ON MEGATRON'S DESIRE TO WIN OVER A VALUABLE AUTOBOT SCIENTIST. PERCEPTOR'S "COLD FISH" DEMEANOR MAKES HIM AN IDEAL CANDIDATE--
THAT WAS A RHETORICAL QUESTION, KENNY. SO WHAT HAVE YOU GOT FOR ME, JAMES BOND?
WE COMPARED NOTES ON THE WAY OVER HERE, GENERAL. BETWEEN WHAT I LEARNED LISTENING IN ON COBRA DINNERTIME CONVERSATION...
AND I LEARNED LIVING AMONG THE DECEPTICONS...
AND I LEARNED SKULKING IN THE DUCTWORK...
WE'VE FIGURED OUT THE CODE TO SHUT DOWN TRYPTICON'S FORCEFIELD.

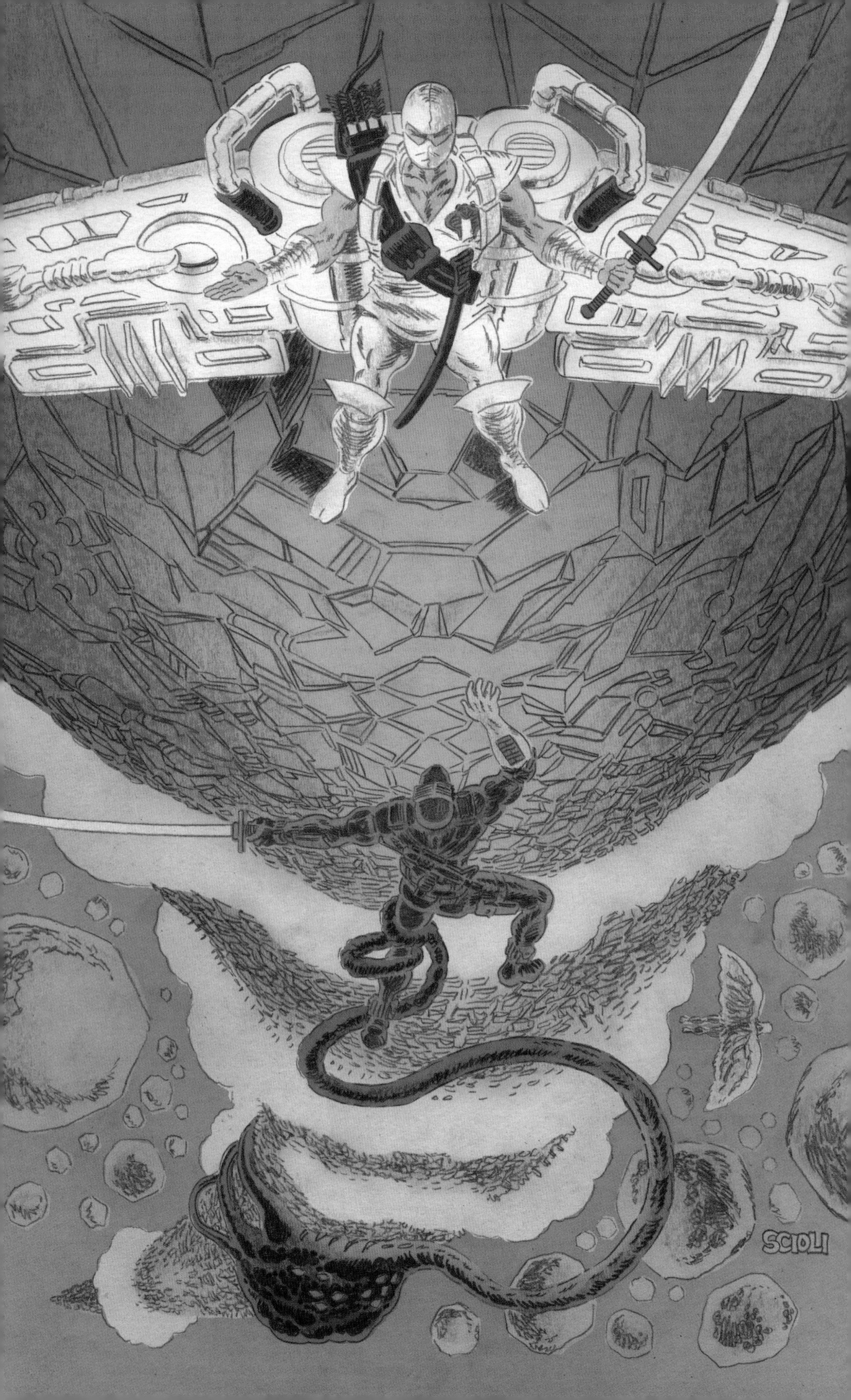
SCIOLI

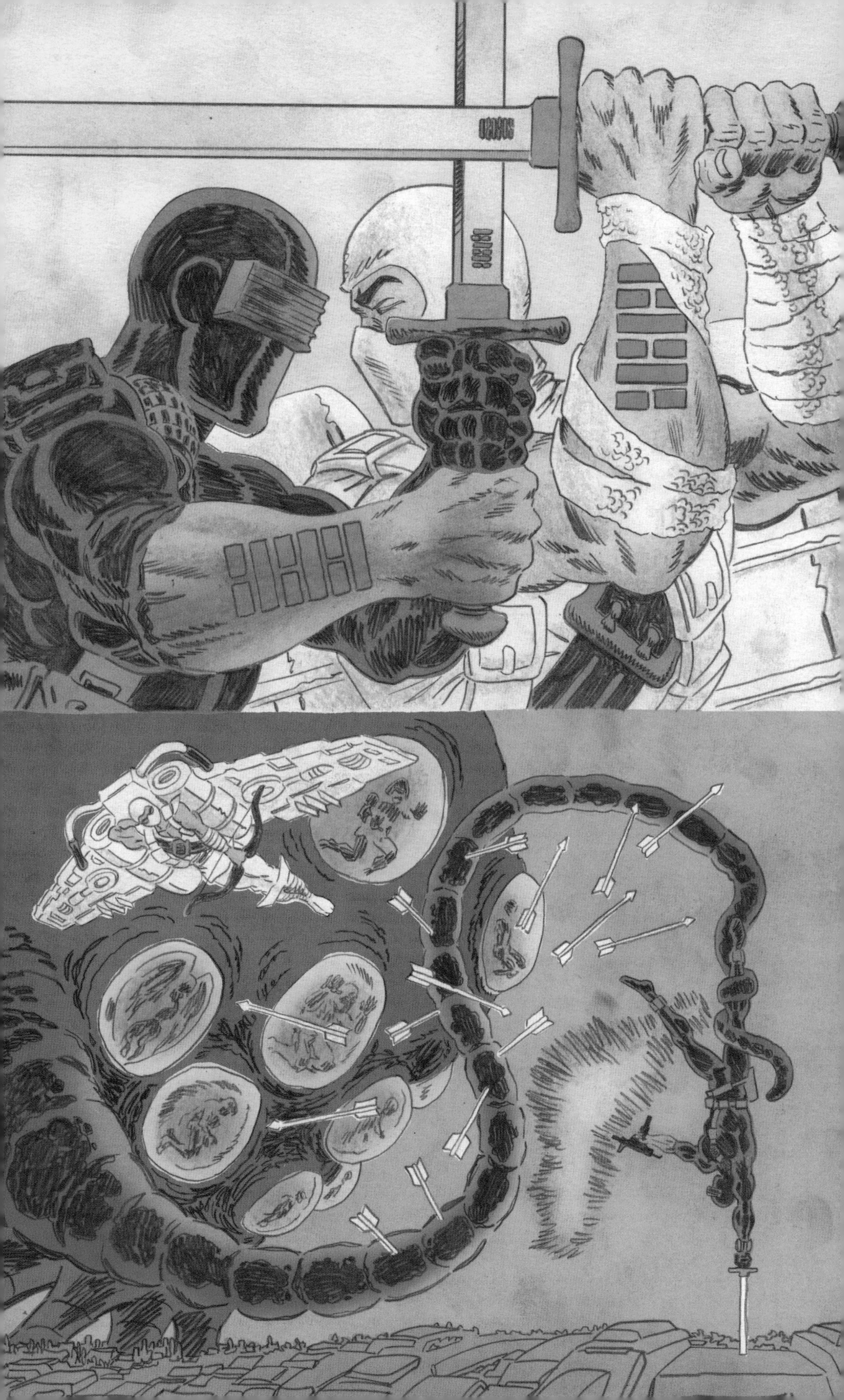

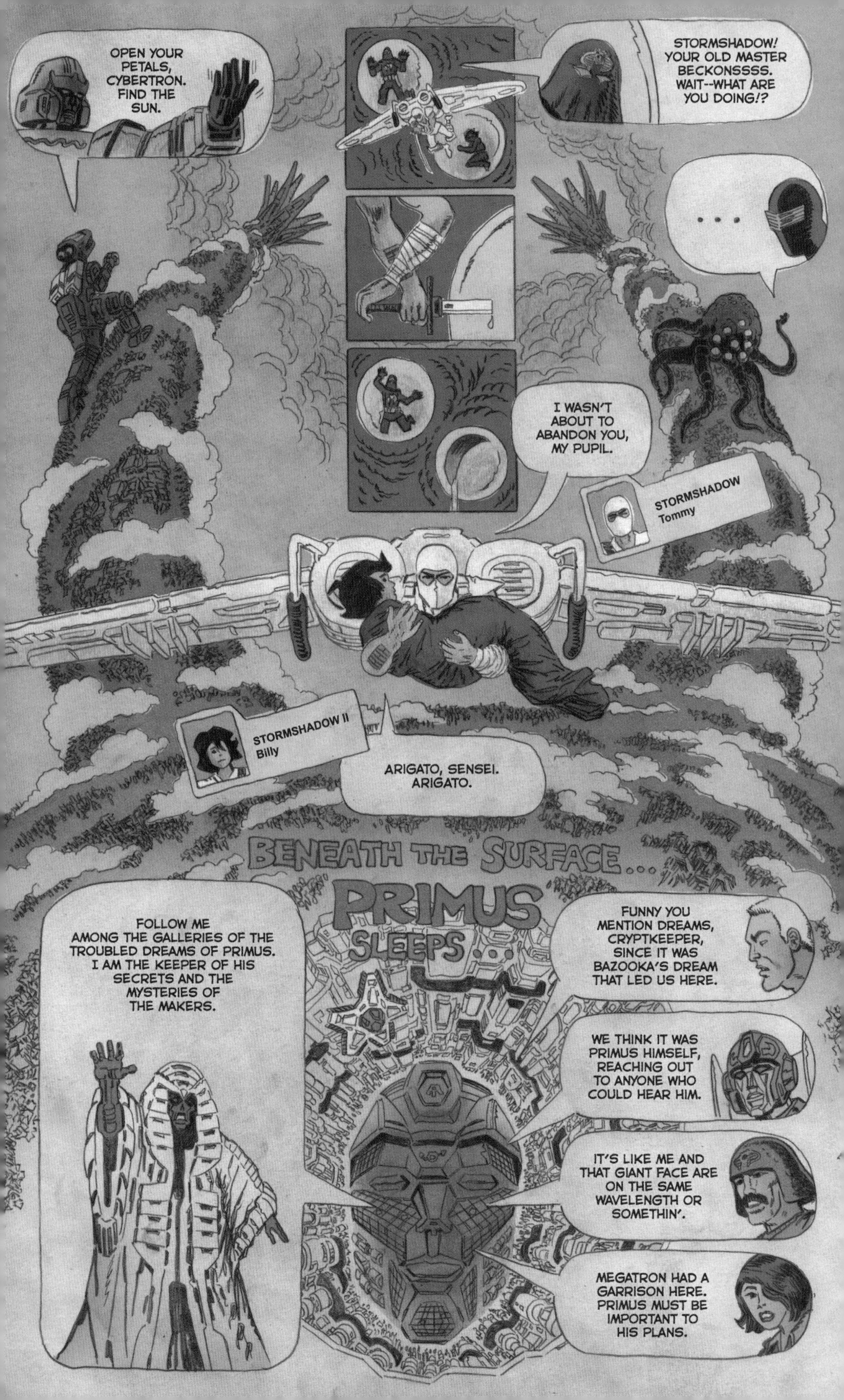
OPEN YOUR PETALS, CYBERTRON. FIND THE SUN.
STORMSHADOW! YOUR OLD MASTER BECKONSSSS. WAIT--WHAT ARE YOU DOING!?
. . .
I WASN'T ABOUT TO ABANDON YOU, MY PUPIL.
STORMSHADOW
Tommy
STORMSHADOW II
Billy
ARIGATO, SENSEI. ARIGATO.
BENEATH THE SURFACE...
PRIMUS SLEEPS...
FOLLOW ME AMONG THE GALLERIES OF THE TROUBLED DREAMS OF PRIMUS. I AM THE KEEPER OF HIS SECRETS AND THE MYSTERIES OF THE MAKERS.
FUNNY YOU MENTION DREAMS, CRYPTKEEPER, SINCE IT WAS BAZOOKA'S DREAM THAT LED US HERE.
WE THINK IT WAS PRIMUS HIMSELF, REACHING OUT TO ANYONE WHO COULD HEAR HIM.
IT'S LIKE ME AND THAT GIANT FACE ARE ON THE SAME WAVELENGTH OR SOMETHIN'.
MEGATRON HAD A GARRISON HERE. PRIMUS MUST BE IMPORTANT TO HIS PLANS.

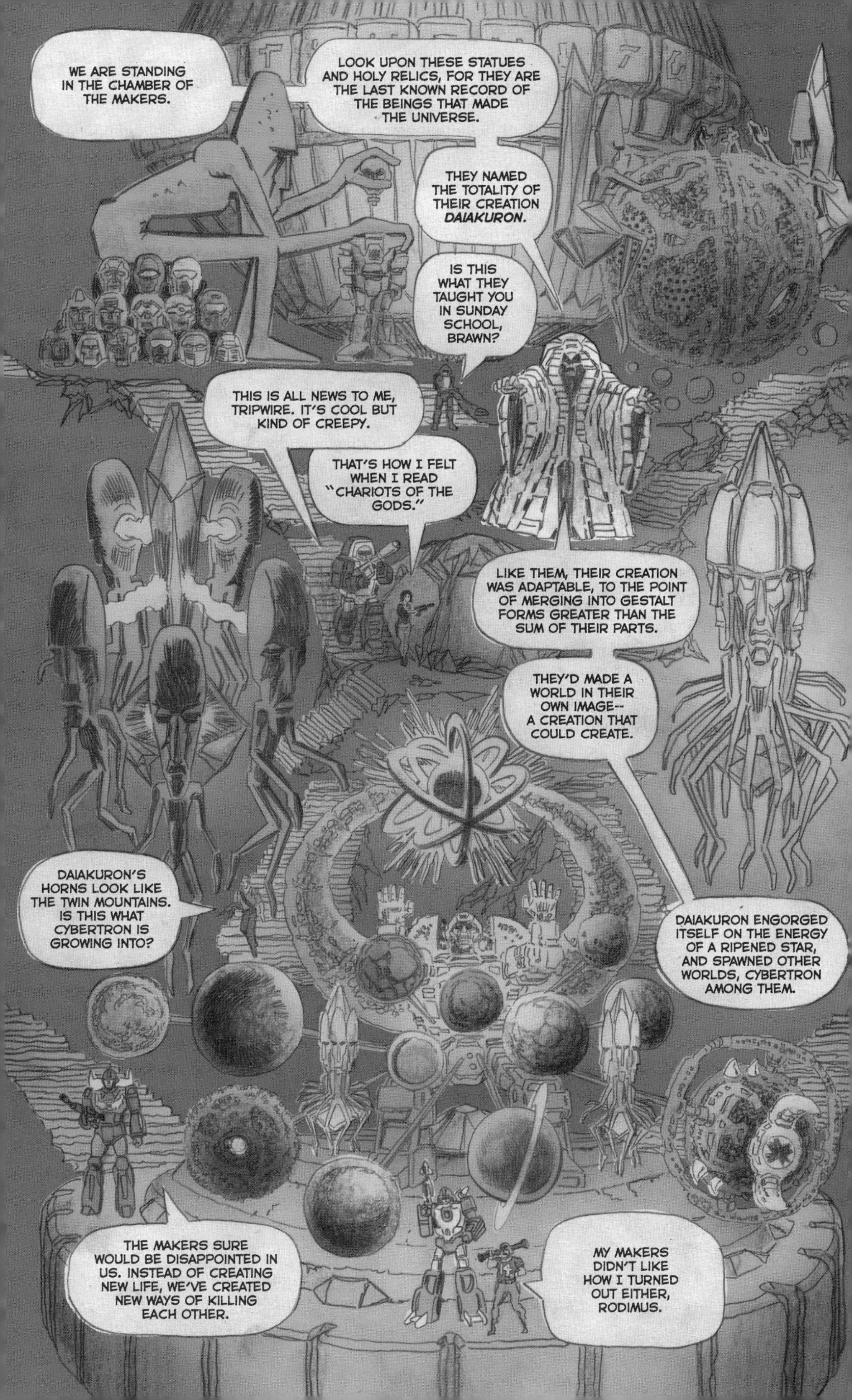
WE ARE STANDING IN THE CHAMBER OF THE MAKERS.
LOOK UPON THESE STATUES AND HOLY RELICS, FOR THEY ARE THE LAST KNOWN RECORD OF THE BEINGS THAT MADE THE UNIVERSE.
THEY NAMED THE TOTALITY OF THEIR CREATION *DAIAKURON*.
IS THIS WHAT THEY TAUGHT YOU IN SUNDAY SCHOOL, BRAWN?
THIS IS ALL NEWS TO ME, TRIPWIRE. IT'S COOL BUT KIND OF CREEPY.
THAT'S HOW I FELT WHEN I READ "CHARIOTS OF THE GODS."
LIKE THEM, THEIR CREATION WAS ADAPTABLE, TO THE POINT OF MERGING INTO GESTALT FORMS GREATER THAN THE SUM OF THEIR PARTS.
THEY'D MADE A WORLD IN THEIR OWN IMAGE-- A CREATION THAT COULD CREATE.
DAIAKURON'S HORNS LOOK LIKE THE TWIN MOUNTAINS. IS THIS WHAT CYBERTRON IS GROWING INTO?
DAIAKURON ENGORGED ITSELF ON THE ENERGY OF A RIPENED STAR, AND SPAWNED OTHER WORLDS, CYBERTRON AMONG THEM.
THE MAKERS SURE WOULD BE DISAPPOINTED IN US. INSTEAD OF CREATING NEW LIFE, WE'VE CREATED NEW WAYS OF KILLING EACH OTHER.
MY MAKERS DIDN'T LIKE HOW I TURNED OUT EITHER, RODIMUS.

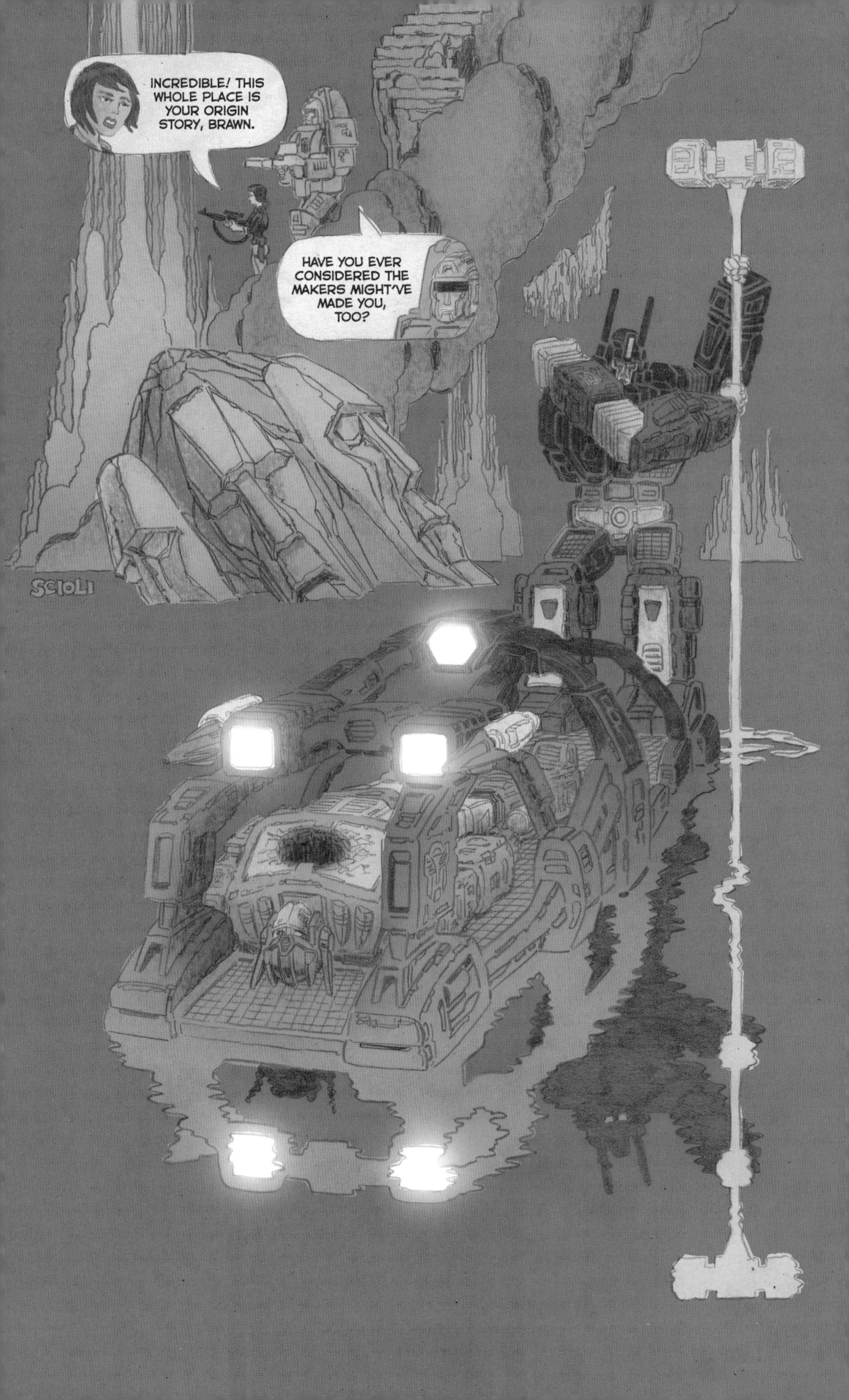
INCREDIBLE! THIS WHOLE PLACE IS YOUR ORIGIN STORY, BRAWN.
HAVE YOU EVER CONSIDERED THE MAKERS MIGHT'VE MADE YOU, TOO?
SCIOLI

ARTWORK BY **ULISES FARINAS**

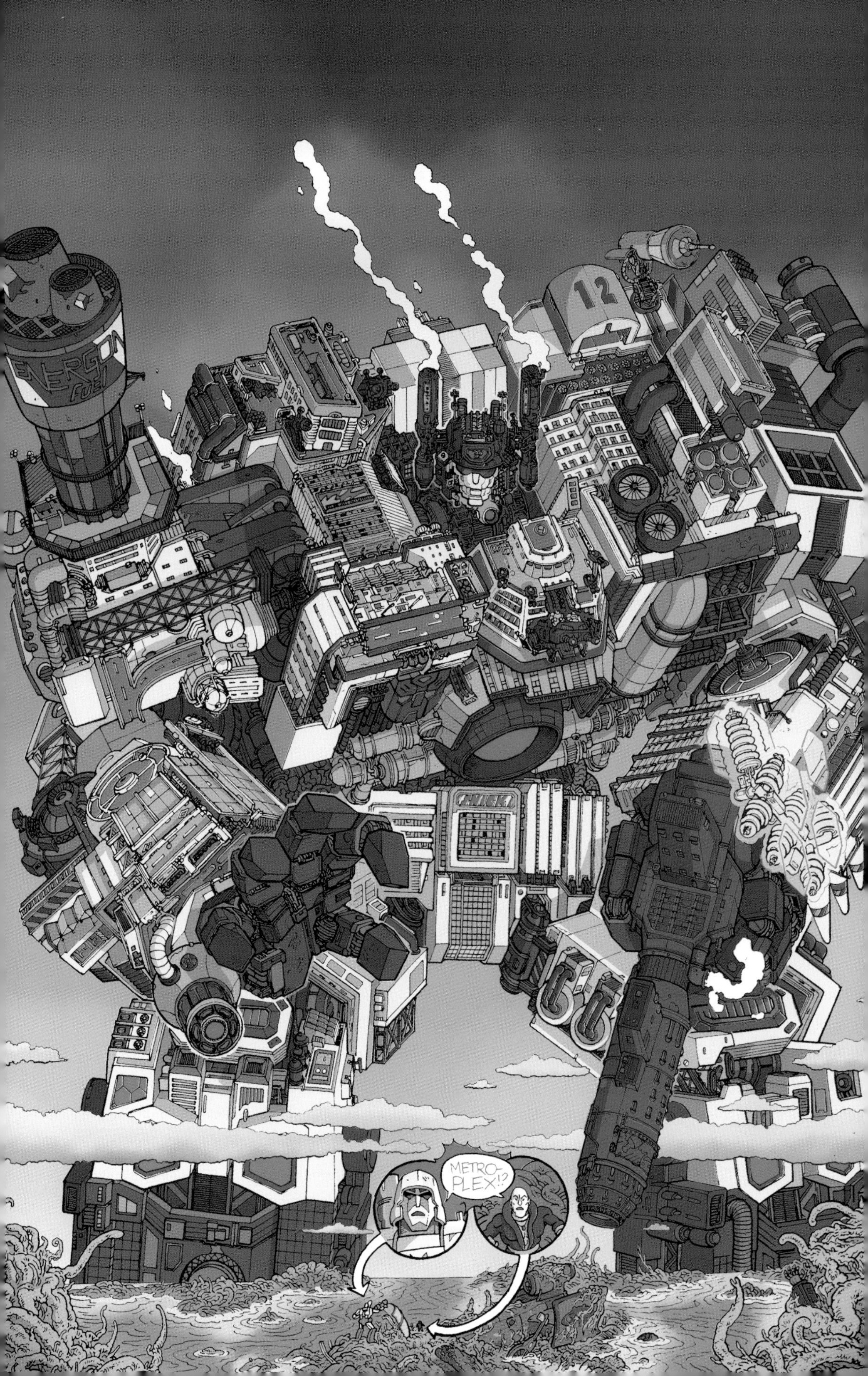
ENERGON
fuel
12
METRO-PLEX!?

CHAPTER 11

ARTWORK BY TOM SCIOLI

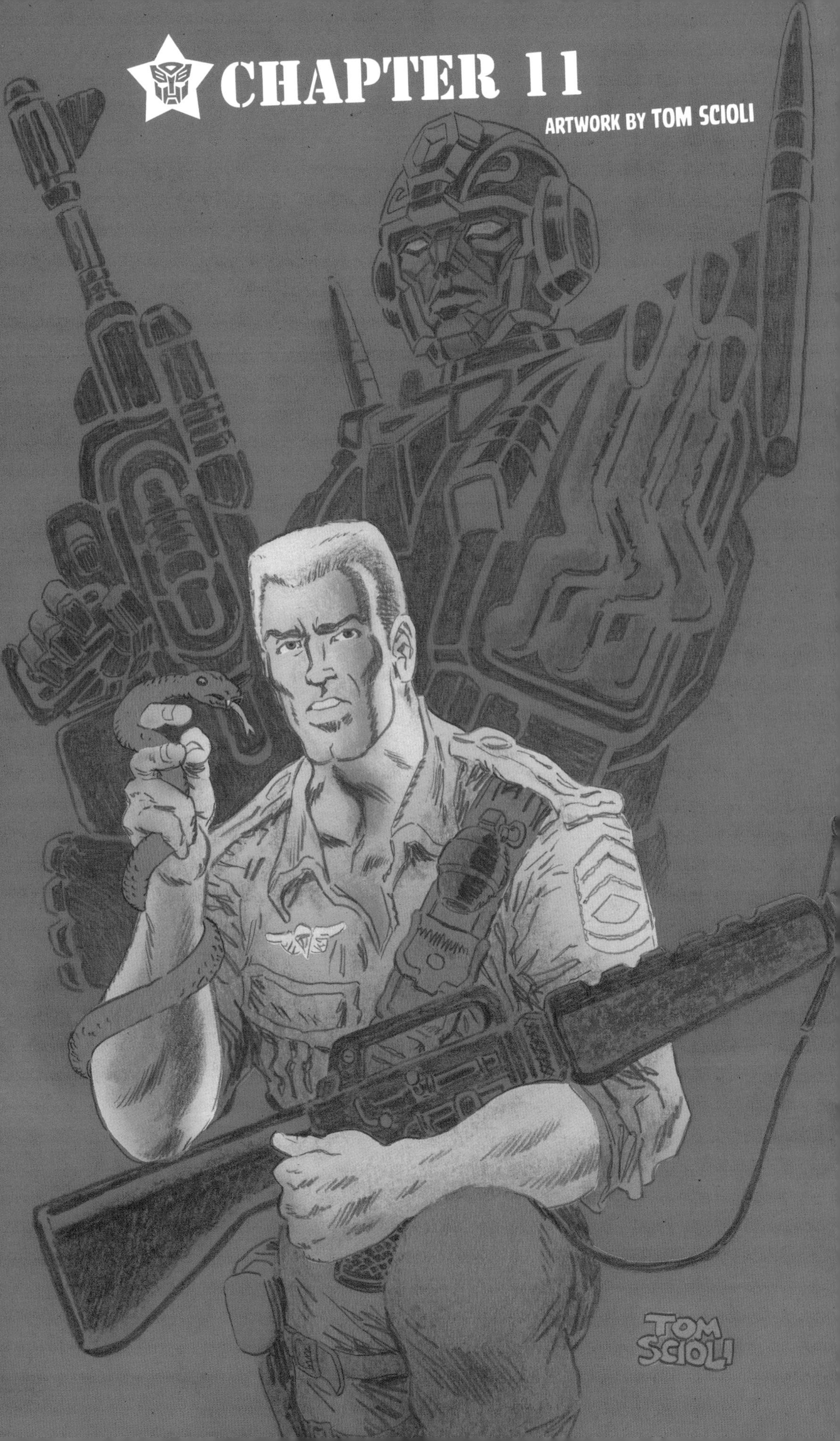
TOM SCIOLI

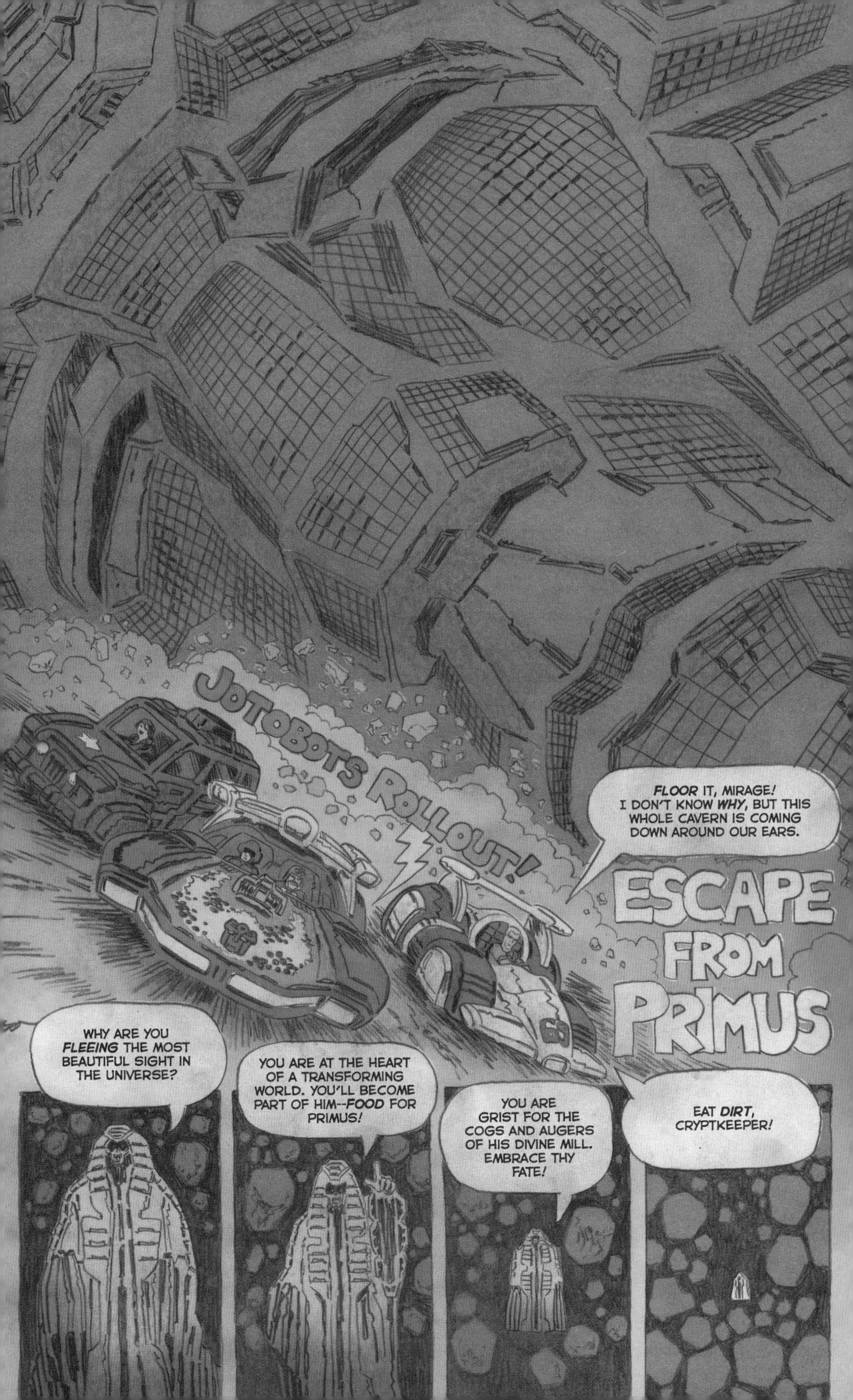
JOTOBOTS ROLLOUT!
FLOOR IT, MIRAGE! I DON'T KNOW WHY, BUT THIS WHOLE CAVERN IS COMING DOWN AROUND OUR EARS.
ESCAPE FROM PRIMUS
WHY ARE YOU FLEEING THE MOST BEAUTIFUL SIGHT IN THE UNIVERSE?
YOU ARE AT THE HEART OF A TRANSFORMING WORLD. YOU'LL BECOME PART OF HIM--FOOD FOR PRIMUS!
YOU ARE GRIST FOR THE COGS AND AUGERS OF HIS DIVINE MILL. EMBRACE THY FATE!
EAT DIRT, CRYPTKEEPER!

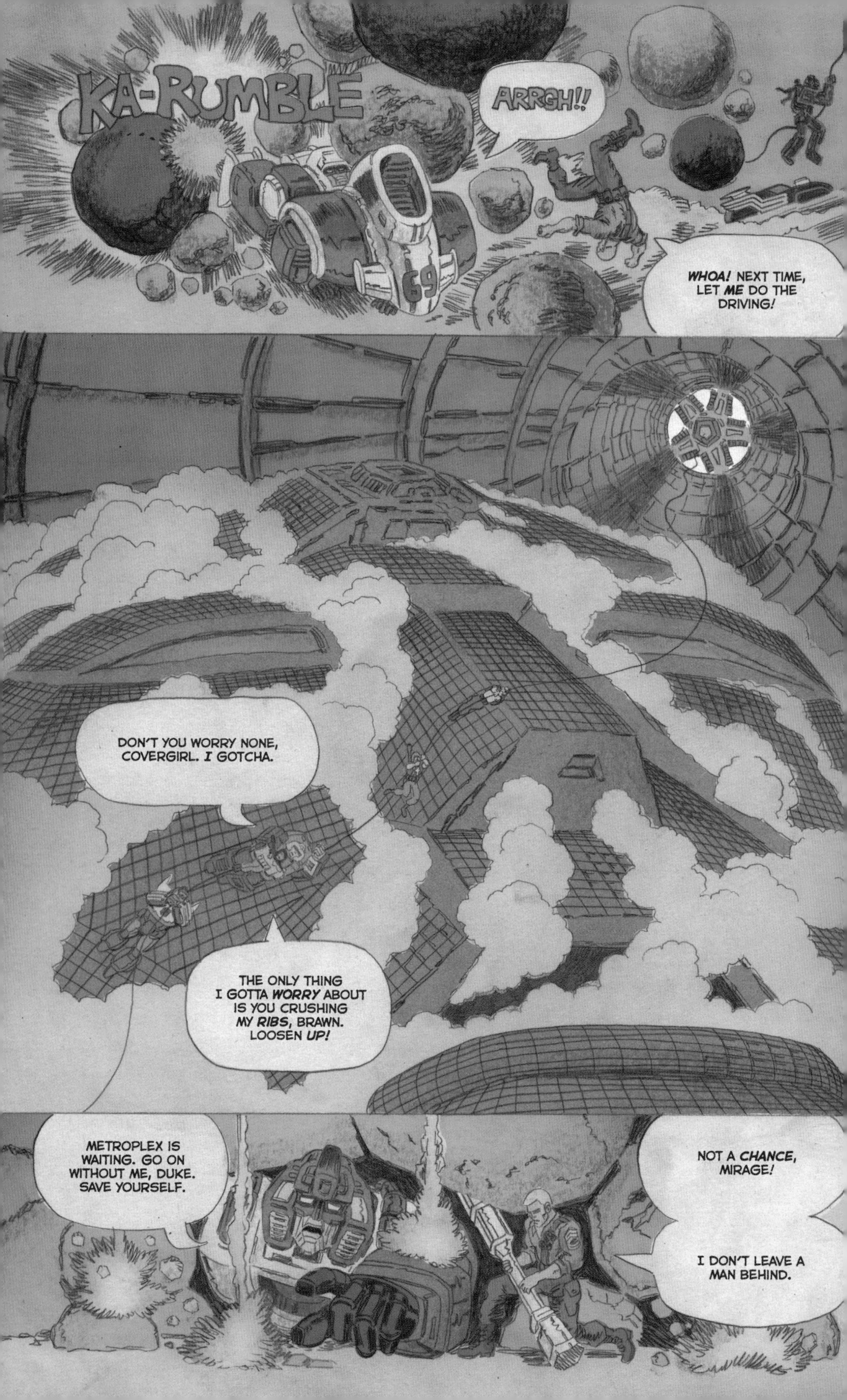
KA-RUMBLE
ARRGH!!
WHOA! NEXT TIME, LET ME DO THE DRIVING!
DON'T YOU WORRY NONE, COVERGIRL. I GOTCHA.
THE ONLY THING I GOTTA WORRY ABOUT IS YOU CRUSHING MY RIBS, BRAWN. LOOSEN UP!
METROPLEX IS WAITING. GO ON WITHOUT ME, DUKE. SAVE YOURSELF.
NOT A CHANCE, MIRAGE!
I DON'T LEAVE A MAN BEHIND.

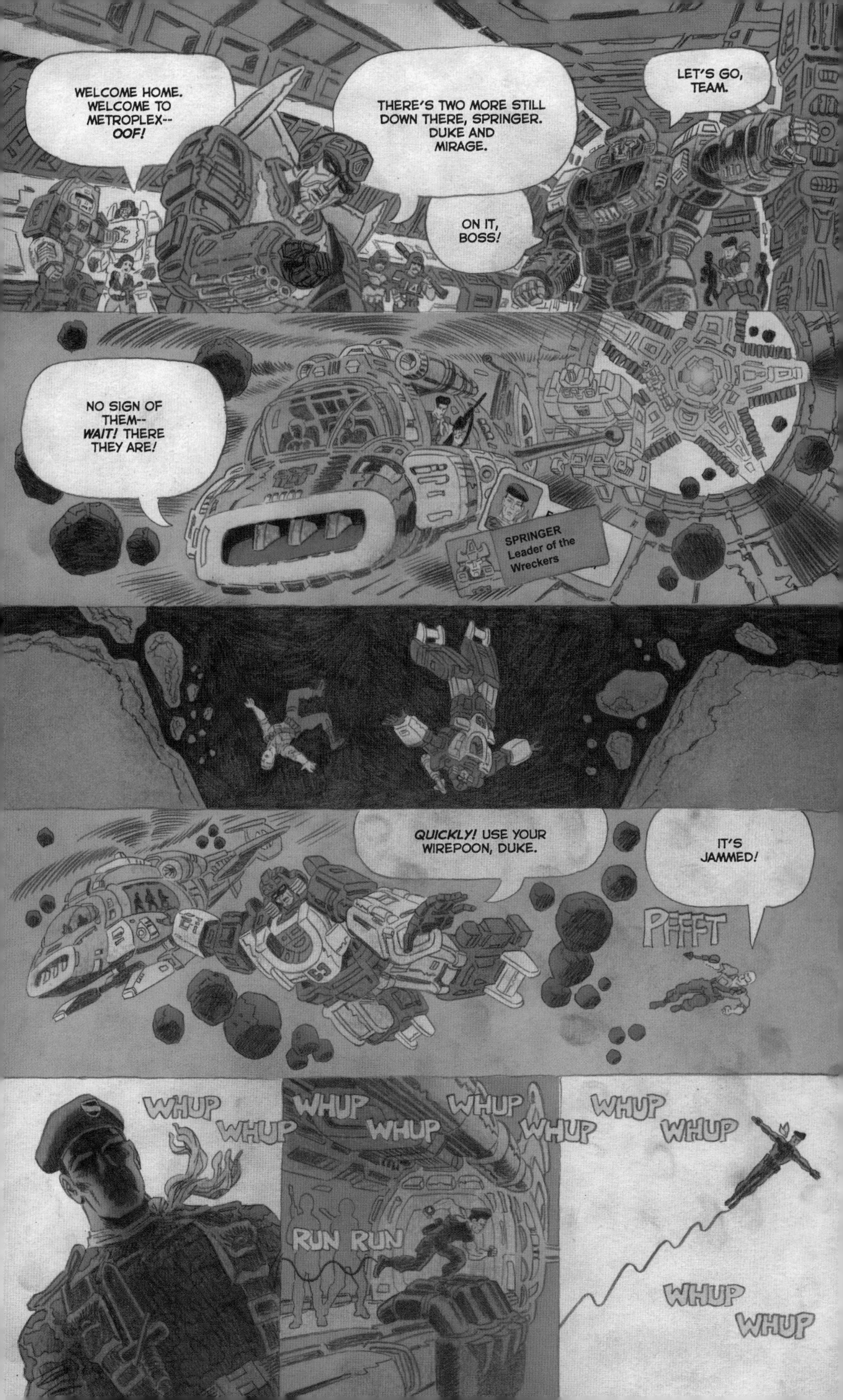
WELCOME HOME. WELCOME TO METROPLEX-- *OOF!*
THERE'S TWO MORE STILL DOWN THERE, SPRINGER. DUKE AND MIRAGE.
ON IT, BOSS!
LET'S GO, TEAM.
NO SIGN OF THEM-- *WAIT!* THERE THEY ARE!
SPRINGER Leader of the Wreckers
QUICKLY! USE YOUR WIREPOON, DUKE.
IT'S JAMMED!
PFFFT
WHUP WHUP
WHUP WHUP
WHUP WHUP
WHUP WHUP
RUN RUN
WHUP WHUP

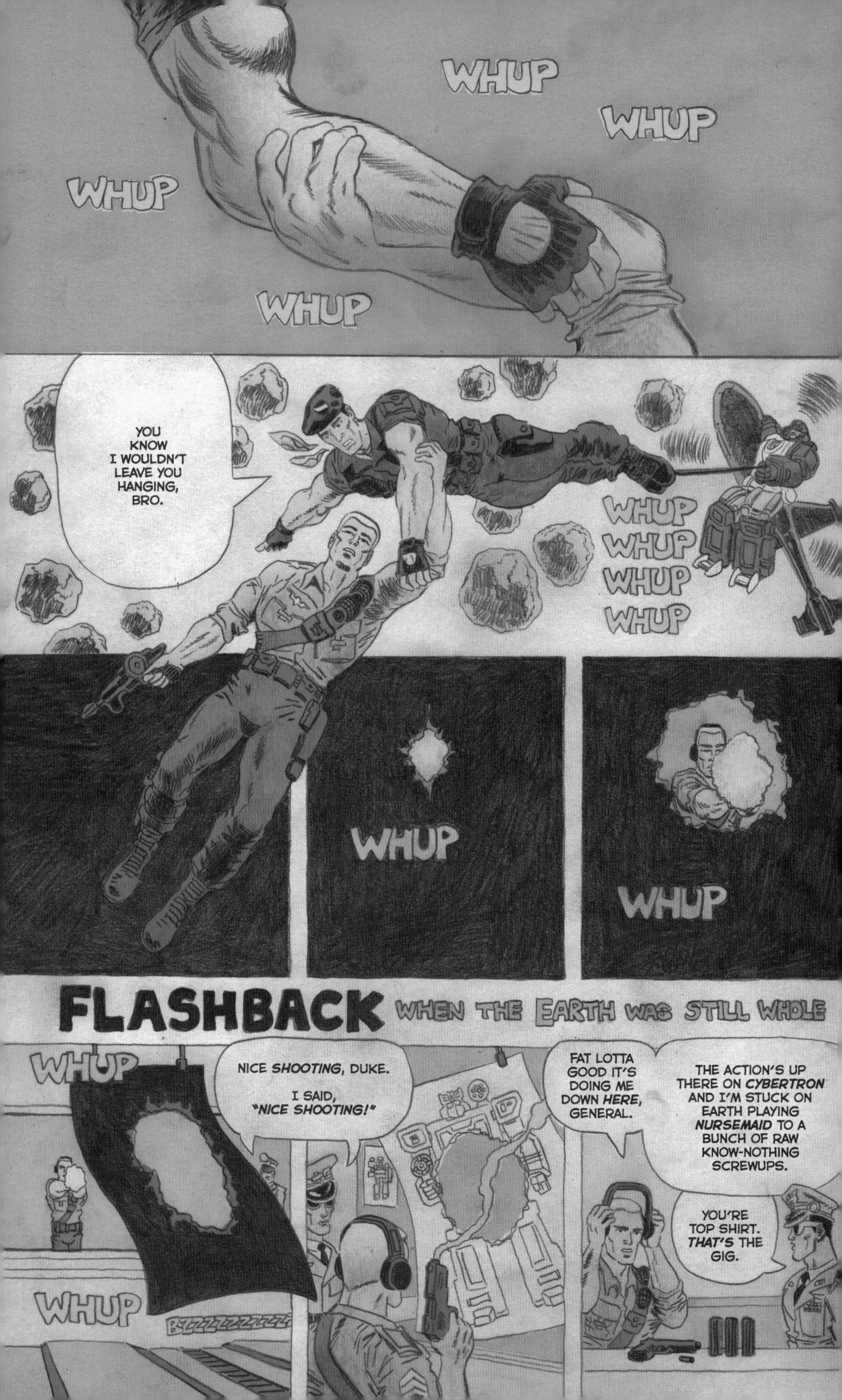
WHUP
WHUP
WHUP
WHUP
YOU KNOW I WOULDN'T LEAVE YOU HANGING, BRO.
WHUP
WHUP
WHUP
WHUP
WHUP
WHUP
FLASHBACK
WHEN THE EARTH WAS STILL WHOLE
WHUP
NICE SHOOTING, DUKE.
I SAID, "NICE SHOOTING!"
WHUP
BZZZZZZZZZZ
FAT LOTTA GOOD IT'S DOING ME DOWN HERE, GENERAL.
THE ACTION'S UP THERE ON CYBERTRON AND I'M STUCK ON EARTH PLAYING NURSEMAID TO A BUNCH OF RAW KNOW-NOTHING SCREWUPS.
YOU'RE TOP SHIRT. THAT'S THE GIG.

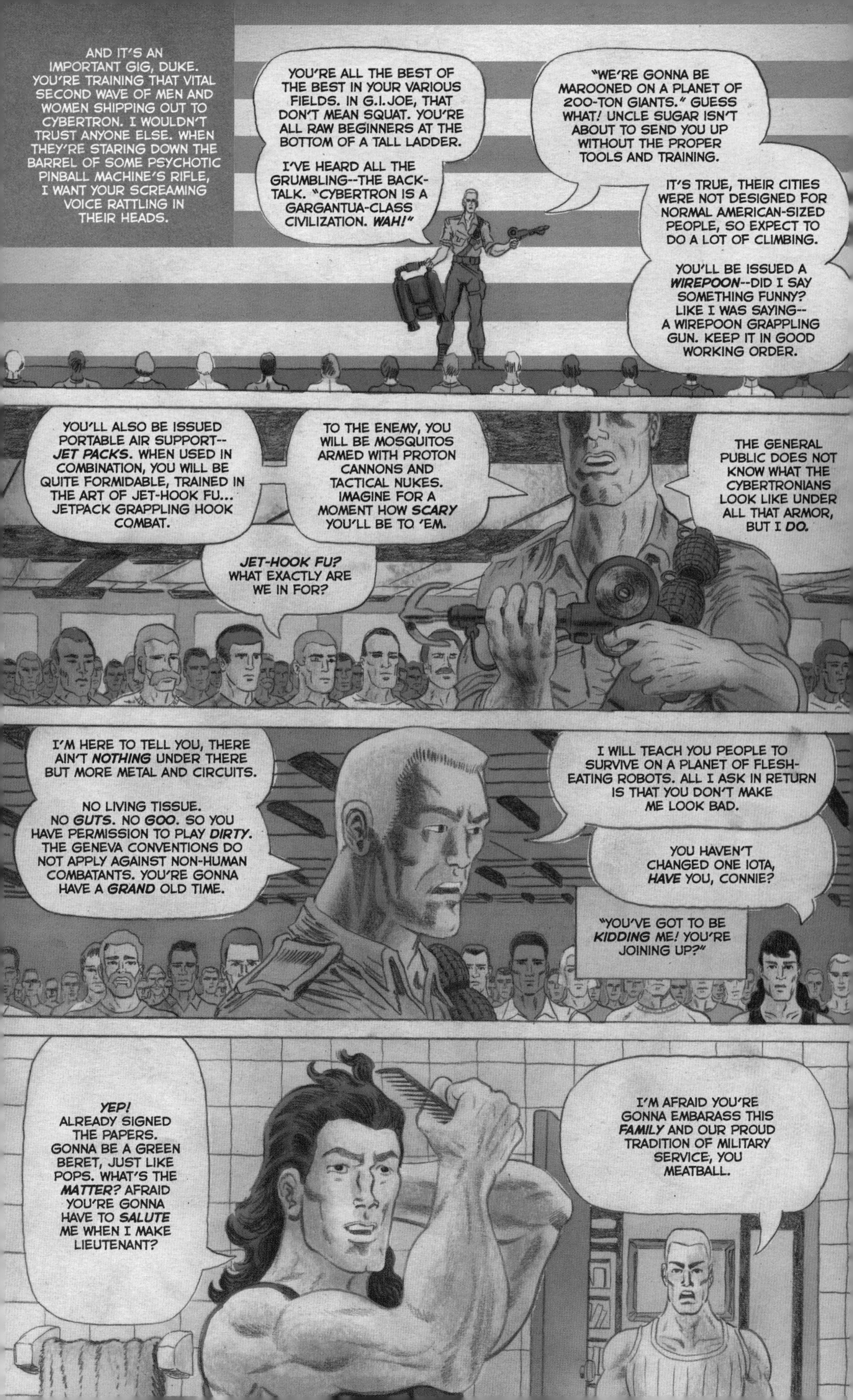
AND IT'S AN IMPORTANT GIG, DUKE. YOU'RE TRAINING THAT VITAL SECOND WAVE OF MEN AND WOMEN SHIPPING OUT TO CYBERTRON. I WOULDN'T TRUST ANYONE ELSE. WHEN THEY'RE STARING DOWN THE BARREL OF SOME PSYCHOTIC PINBALL MACHINE'S RIFLE, I WANT YOUR SCREAMING VOICE RATTLING IN THEIR HEADS.
YOU'RE ALL THE BEST OF THE BEST IN YOUR VARIOUS FIELDS. IN G.I. JOE, THAT DON'T MEAN SQUAT. YOU'RE ALL RAW BEGINNERS AT THE BOTTOM OF A TALL LADDER.
I'VE HEARD ALL THE GRUMBLING--THE BACK-TALK. "CYBERTRON IS A GARGANTUA-CLASS CIVILIZATION. *WAH!*"
"WE'RE GONNA BE MAROONED ON A PLANET OF 200-TON GIANTS." GUESS WHAT! UNCLE SUGAR ISN'T ABOUT TO SEND YOU UP WITHOUT THE PROPER TOOLS AND TRAINING.
IT'S TRUE, THEIR CITIES WERE NOT DESIGNED FOR NORMAL AMERICAN-SIZED PEOPLE, SO EXPECT TO DO A LOT OF CLIMBING.
YOU'LL BE ISSUED A *WIREPOON*--DID I SAY SOMETHING FUNNY? LIKE I WAS SAYING-- A WIREPOON GRAPPLING GUN. KEEP IT IN GOOD WORKING ORDER.
YOU'LL ALSO BE ISSUED PORTABLE AIR SUPPORT-- *JET PACKS*. WHEN USED IN COMBINATION, YOU WILL BE QUITE FORMIDABLE, TRAINED IN THE ART OF JET-HOOK FU... JETPACK GRAPPLING HOOK COMBAT.
TO THE ENEMY, YOU WILL BE MOSQUITOS ARMED WITH PROTON CANNONS AND TACTICAL NUKES. IMAGINE FOR A MOMENT HOW *SCARY* YOU'LL BE TO 'EM.
JET-HOOK FU? WHAT EXACTLY ARE WE IN FOR?
THE GENERAL PUBLIC DOES NOT KNOW WHAT THE CYBERTRONIANS LOOK LIKE UNDER ALL THAT ARMOR, BUT I *DO.*
I'M HERE TO TELL YOU, THERE AIN'T *NOTHING* UNDER THERE BUT MORE METAL AND CIRCUITS.
NO LIVING TISSUE. NO *GUTS*. NO *GOO*. SO YOU HAVE PERMISSION TO PLAY *DIRTY*. THE GENEVA CONVENTIONS DO NOT APPLY AGAINST NON-HUMAN COMBATANTS. YOU'RE GONNA HAVE A *GRAND* OLD TIME.
I WILL TEACH YOU PEOPLE TO SURVIVE ON A PLANET OF FLESH-EATING ROBOTS. ALL I ASK IN RETURN IS THAT YOU DON'T MAKE ME LOOK BAD.
YOU HAVEN'T CHANGED ONE IOTA, *HAVE* YOU, CONNIE?
"YOU'VE GOT TO BE *KIDDING ME!* YOU'RE JOINING UP?"
YEP! ALREADY SIGNED THE PAPERS. GONNA BE A GREEN BERET, JUST LIKE POPS. WHAT'S THE *MATTER?* AFRAID YOU'RE GONNA HAVE TO *SALUTE* ME WHEN I MAKE LIEUTENANT?
I'M AFRAID YOU'RE GONNA EMBARASS THIS *FAMILY* AND OUR PROUD TRADITION OF MILITARY SERVICE, YOU MEATBALL.

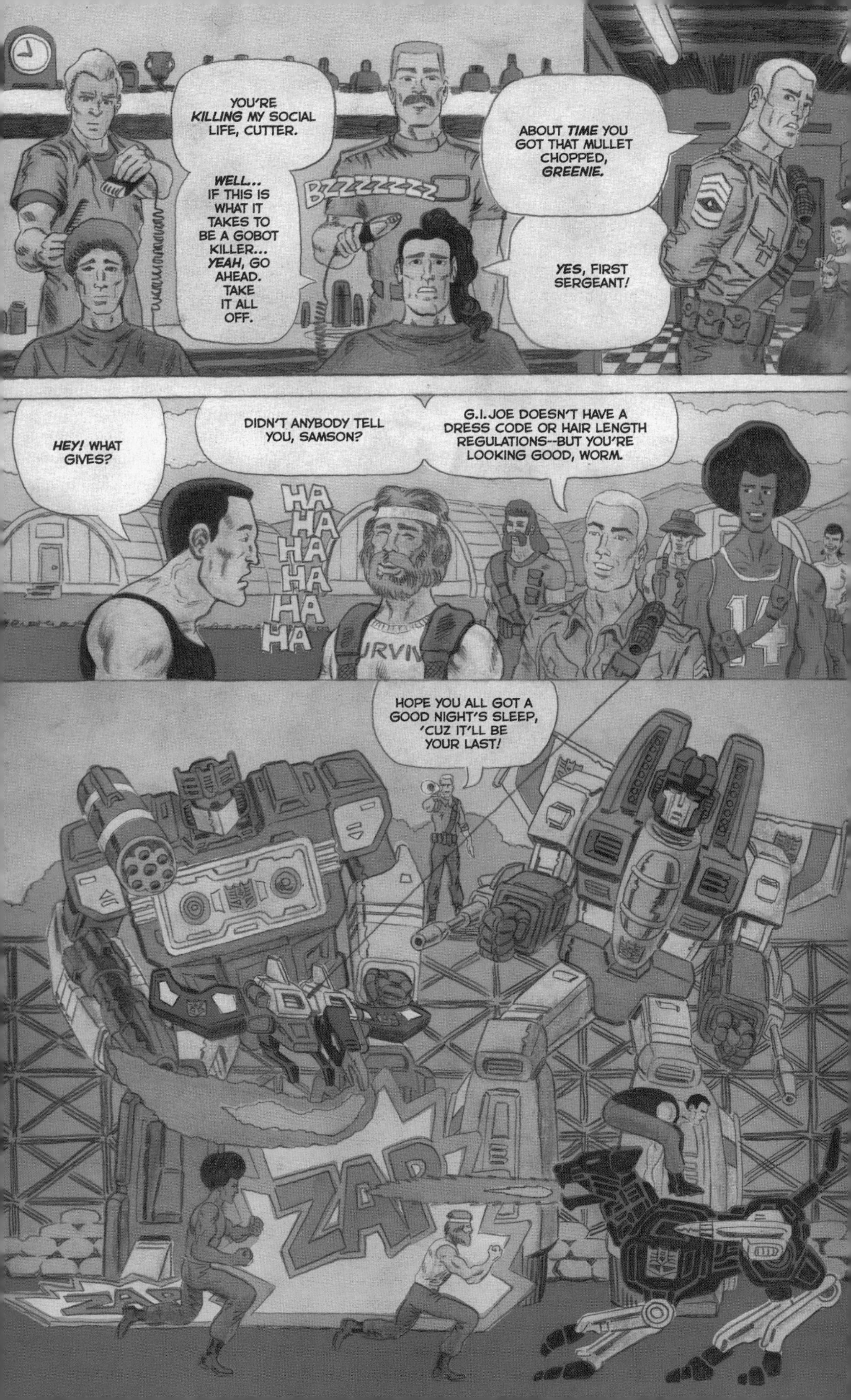

YOU'RE KILLING MY SOCIAL LIFE, CUTTER.
WELL... IF THIS IS WHAT IT TAKES TO BE A GOBOT KILLER... YEAH, GO AHEAD. TAKE IT ALL OFF.
BZZZZZZZ
ABOUT TIME YOU GOT THAT MULLET CHOPPED, GREENIE.
YES, FIRST SERGEANT!
HEY! WHAT GIVES?
DIDN'T ANYBODY TELL YOU, SAMSON?
G.I.JOE DOESN'T HAVE A DRESS CODE OR HAIR LENGTH REGULATIONS--BUT YOU'RE LOOKING GOOD, WORM.
HA HA HA HA HA HA
HOPE YOU ALL GOT A GOOD NIGHT'S SLEEP, 'CUZ IT'LL BE YOUR LAST!
ZAP
ZAP

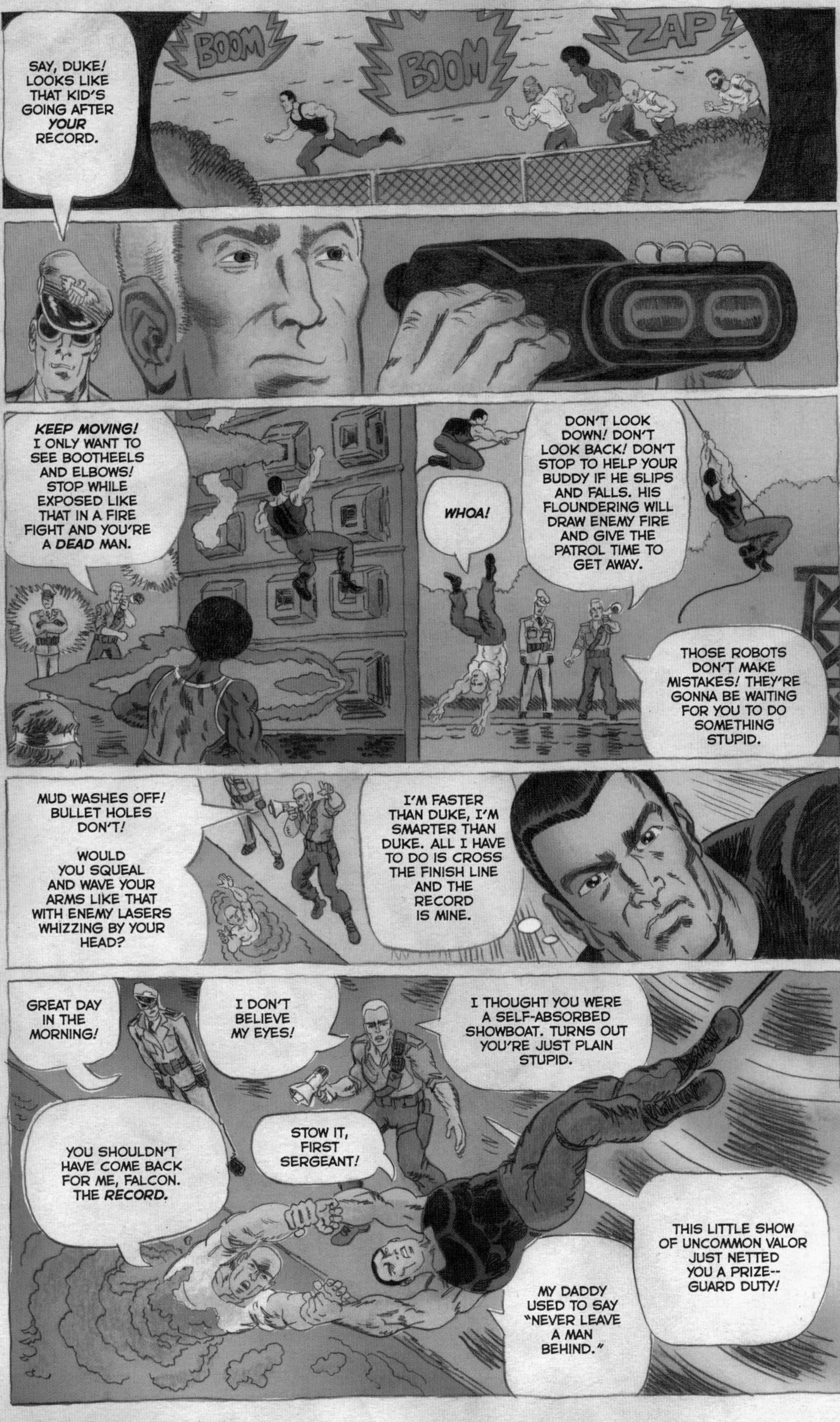

BOOM
BOOM
ZAP
SAY, DUKE! LOOKS LIKE THAT KID'S GOING AFTER YOUR RECORD.
KEEP MOVING! I ONLY WANT TO SEE BOOTHEELS AND ELBOWS! STOP WHILE EXPOSED LIKE THAT IN A FIRE FIGHT AND YOU'RE A DEAD MAN.
WHOA!
DON'T LOOK DOWN! DON'T LOOK BACK! DON'T STOP TO HELP YOUR BUDDY IF HE SLIPS AND FALLS. HIS FLOUNDERING WILL DRAW ENEMY FIRE AND GIVE THE PATROL TIME TO GET AWAY.
THOSE ROBOTS DON'T MAKE MISTAKES! THEY'RE GONNA BE WAITING FOR YOU TO DO SOMETHING STUPID.
MUD WASHES OFF! BULLET HOLES DON'T!
WOULD YOU SQUEAL AND WAVE YOUR ARMS LIKE THAT WITH ENEMY LASERS WHIZZING BY YOUR HEAD?
I'M FASTER THAN DUKE, I'M SMARTER THAN DUKE. ALL I HAVE TO DO IS CROSS THE FINISH LINE AND THE RECORD IS MINE.
GREAT DAY IN THE MORNING!
I DON'T BELIEVE MY EYES!
I THOUGHT YOU WERE A SELF-ABSORBED SHOWBOAT. TURNS OUT YOU'RE JUST PLAIN STUPID.
YOU SHOULDN'T HAVE COME BACK FOR ME, FALCON. THE RECORD.
STOW IT, FIRST SERGEANT!
MY DADDY USED TO SAY "NEVER LEAVE A MAN BEHIND."
THIS LITTLE SHOW OF UNCOMMON VALOR JUST NETTED YOU A PRIZE-- GUARD DUTY!

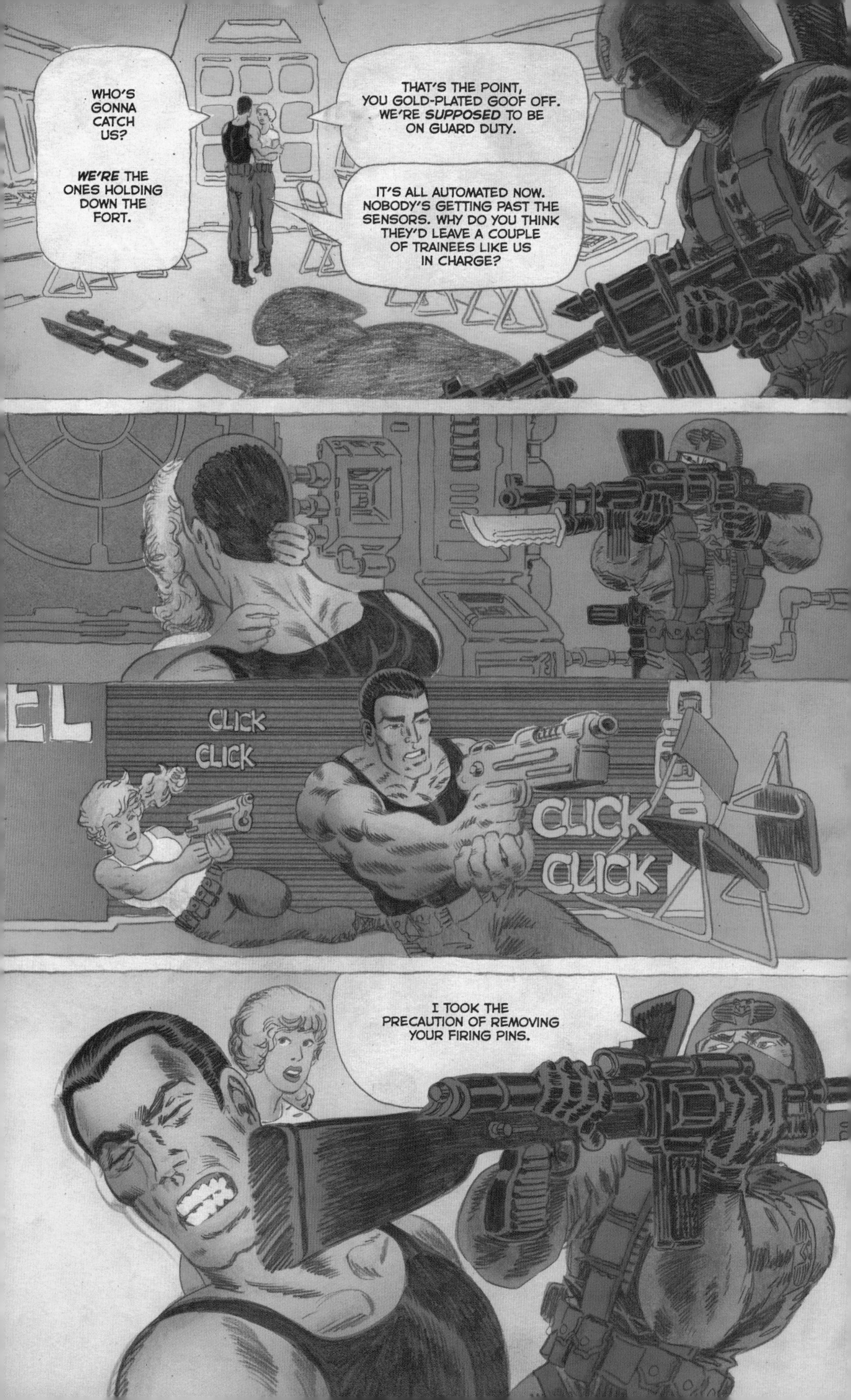
WHO'S GONNA CATCH US?
THAT'S THE POINT, YOU GOLD-PLATED GOOF OFF. WE'RE *SUPPOSED* TO BE ON GUARD DUTY.
WE'RE THE ONES HOLDING DOWN THE FORT.
IT'S ALL AUTOMATED NOW. NOBODY'S GETTING PAST THE SENSORS. WHY DO YOU THINK THEY'D LEAVE A COUPLE OF TRAINEES LIKE US IN CHARGE?
CLICK
CLICK
CLICK
CLICK
I TOOK THE PRECAUTION OF REMOVING YOUR FIRING PINS.

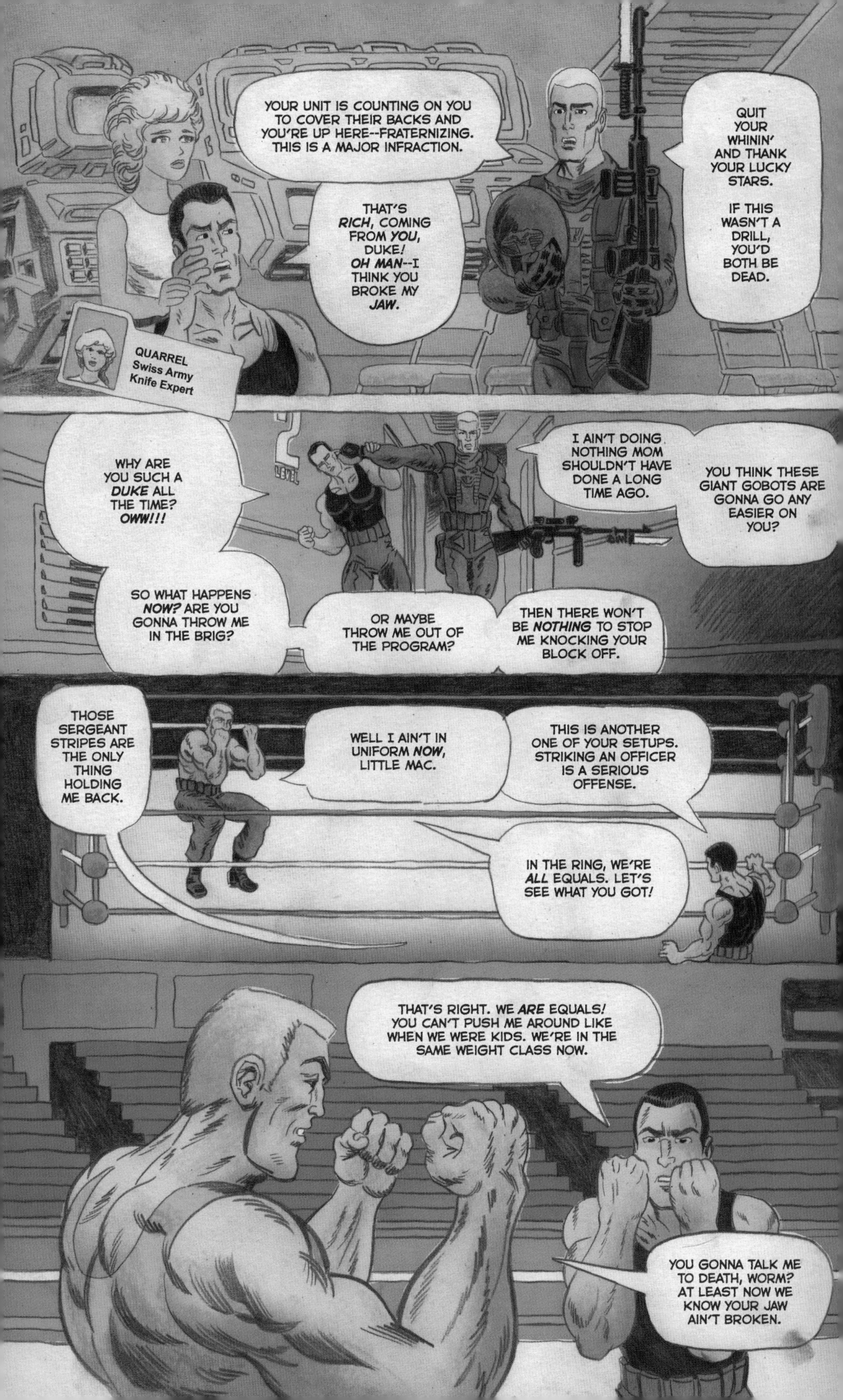
YOUR UNIT IS COUNTING ON YOU TO COVER THEIR BACKS AND YOU'RE UP HERE--FRATERNIZING. THIS IS A MAJOR INFRACTION.
THAT'S *RICH*, COMING FROM *YOU*, DUKE! *OH MAN*--I THINK YOU BROKE MY *JAW*.
QUIT YOUR WHININ' AND THANK YOUR LUCKY STARS.
IF THIS WASN'T A DRILL, YOU'D BOTH BE DEAD.
QUARREL Swiss Army Knife Expert
WHY ARE YOU SUCH A *DUKE* ALL THE TIME? *OWW!!!*
I AIN'T DOING NOTHING MOM SHOULDN'T HAVE DONE A LONG TIME AGO.
YOU THINK THESE GIANT GOBOTS ARE GONNA GO ANY EASIER ON YOU?
SO WHAT HAPPENS *NOW?* ARE YOU GONNA THROW ME IN THE BRIG?
OR MAYBE THROW ME OUT OF THE PROGRAM?
THEN THERE WON'T BE *NOTHING* TO STOP ME KNOCKING YOUR BLOCK OFF.
THOSE SERGEANT STRIPES ARE THE ONLY THING HOLDING ME BACK.
WELL I AIN'T IN UNIFORM *NOW*, LITTLE MAC.
THIS IS ANOTHER ONE OF YOUR SETUPS. STRIKING AN OFFICER IS A SERIOUS OFFENSE.
IN THE RING, WE'RE *ALL* EQUALS. LET'S SEE WHAT YOU GOT!
THAT'S RIGHT. WE *ARE* EQUALS! YOU CAN'T PUSH ME AROUND LIKE WHEN WE WERE KIDS. WE'RE IN THE SAME WEIGHT CLASS NOW.
YOU GONNA TALK ME TO DEATH, WORM? AT LEAST NOW WE KNOW YOUR JAW AIN'T BROKEN.

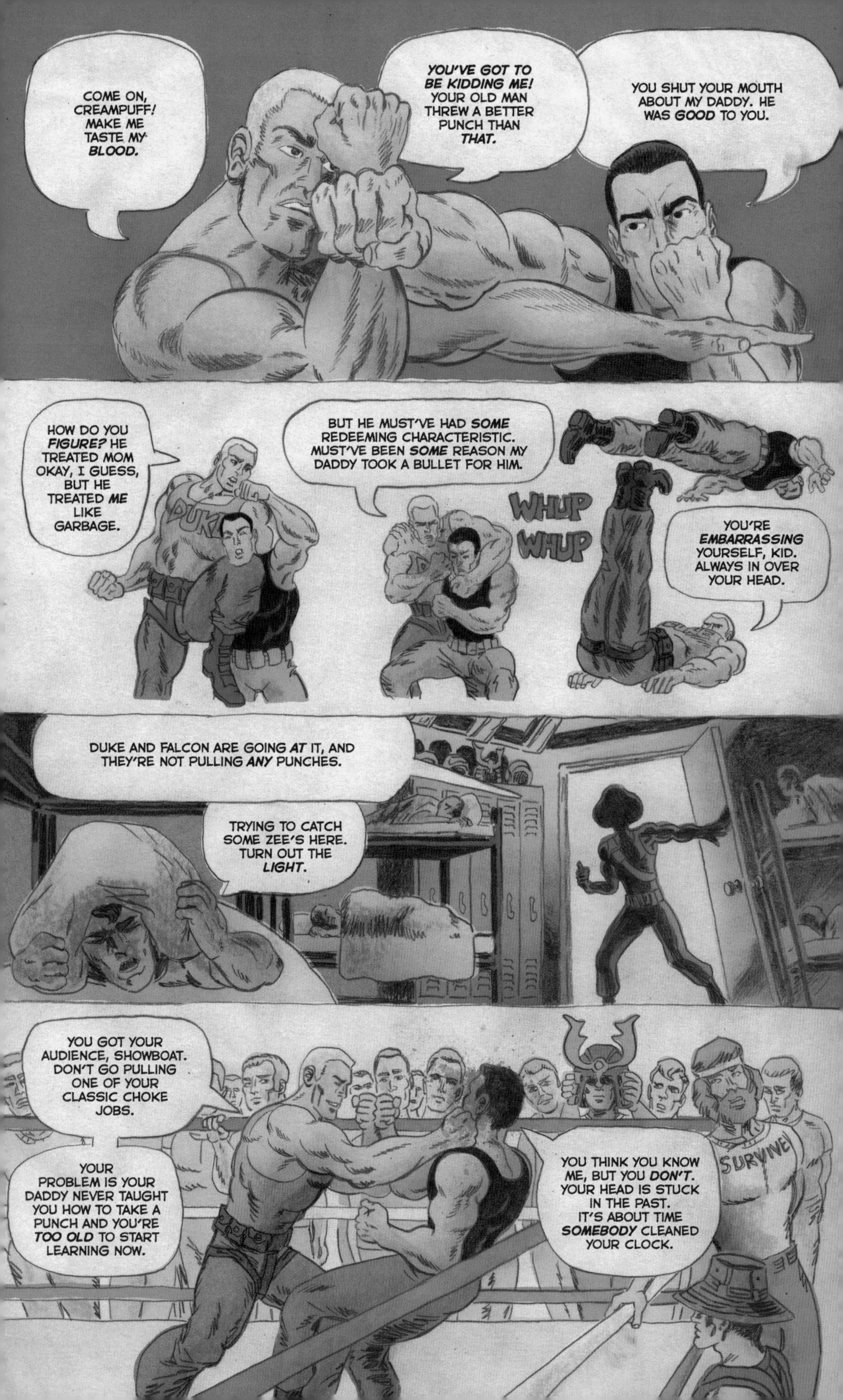
COME ON, CREAMPUFF! MAKE ME TASTE MY BLOOD.
YOU'VE GOT TO BE KIDDING ME! YOUR OLD MAN THREW A BETTER PUNCH THAN THAT.
YOU SHUT YOUR MOUTH ABOUT MY DADDY. HE WAS GOOD TO YOU.
HOW DO YOU FIGURE? HE TREATED MOM OKAY, I GUESS, BUT HE TREATED ME LIKE GARBAGE.
DUKE
BUT HE MUST'VE HAD SOME REDEEMING CHARACTERISTIC. MUST'VE BEEN SOME REASON MY DADDY TOOK A BULLET FOR HIM.
WHUP
WHUP
YOU'RE EMBARRASSING YOURSELF, KID. ALWAYS IN OVER YOUR HEAD.
DUKE AND FALCON ARE GOING AT IT, AND THEY'RE NOT PULLING ANY PUNCHES.
TRYING TO CATCH SOME ZEE'S HERE. TURN OUT THE LIGHT.
YOU GOT YOUR AUDIENCE, SHOWBOAT. DON'T GO PULLING ONE OF YOUR CLASSIC CHOKE JOBS.
YOUR PROBLEM IS YOUR DADDY NEVER TAUGHT YOU HOW TO TAKE A PUNCH AND YOU'RE TOO OLD TO START LEARNING NOW.
SURVIVE
YOU THINK YOU KNOW ME, BUT YOU DON'T. YOUR HEAD IS STUCK IN THE PAST. IT'S ABOUT TIME SOMEBODY CLEANED YOUR CLOCK.

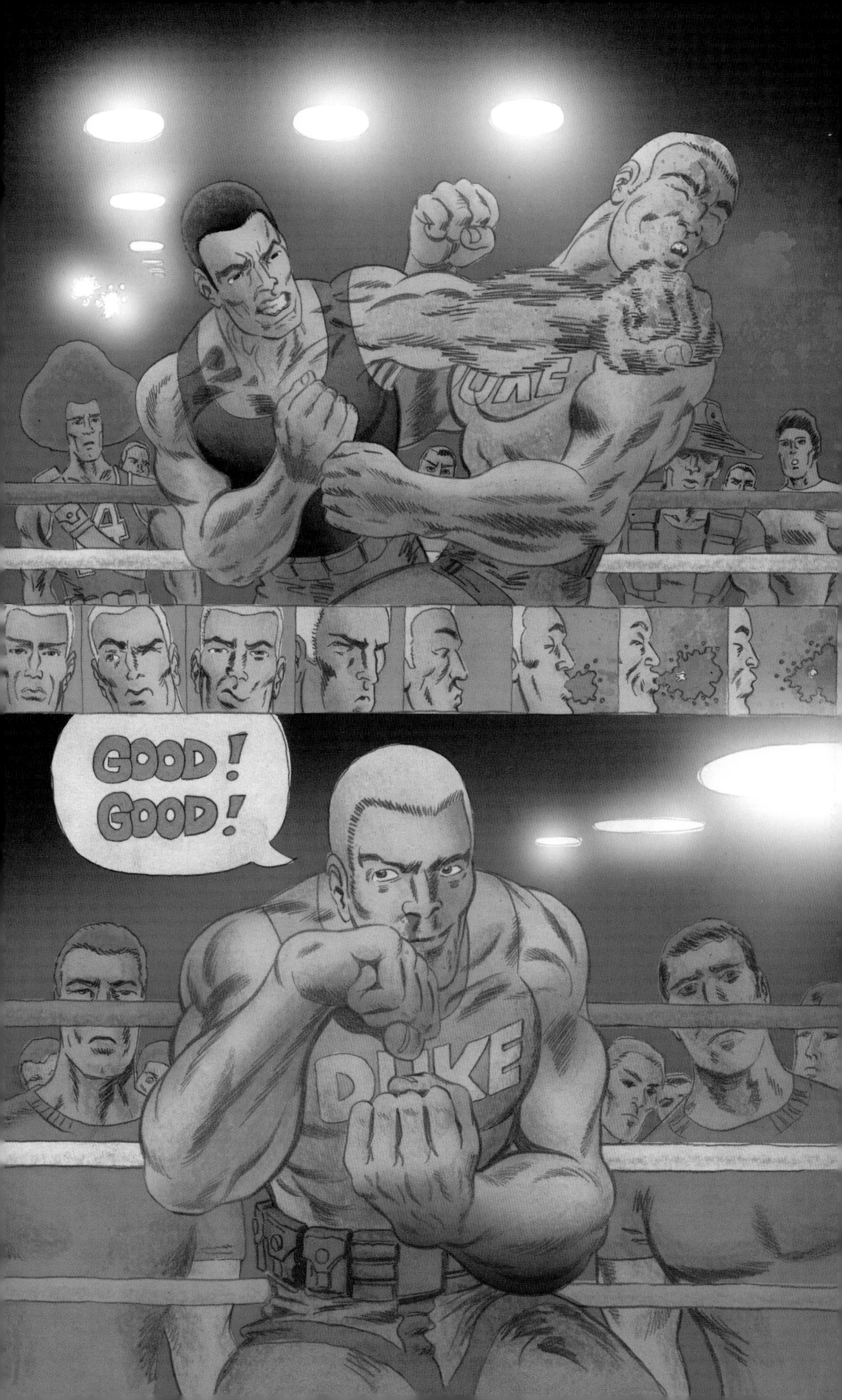
GOOD! GOOD!

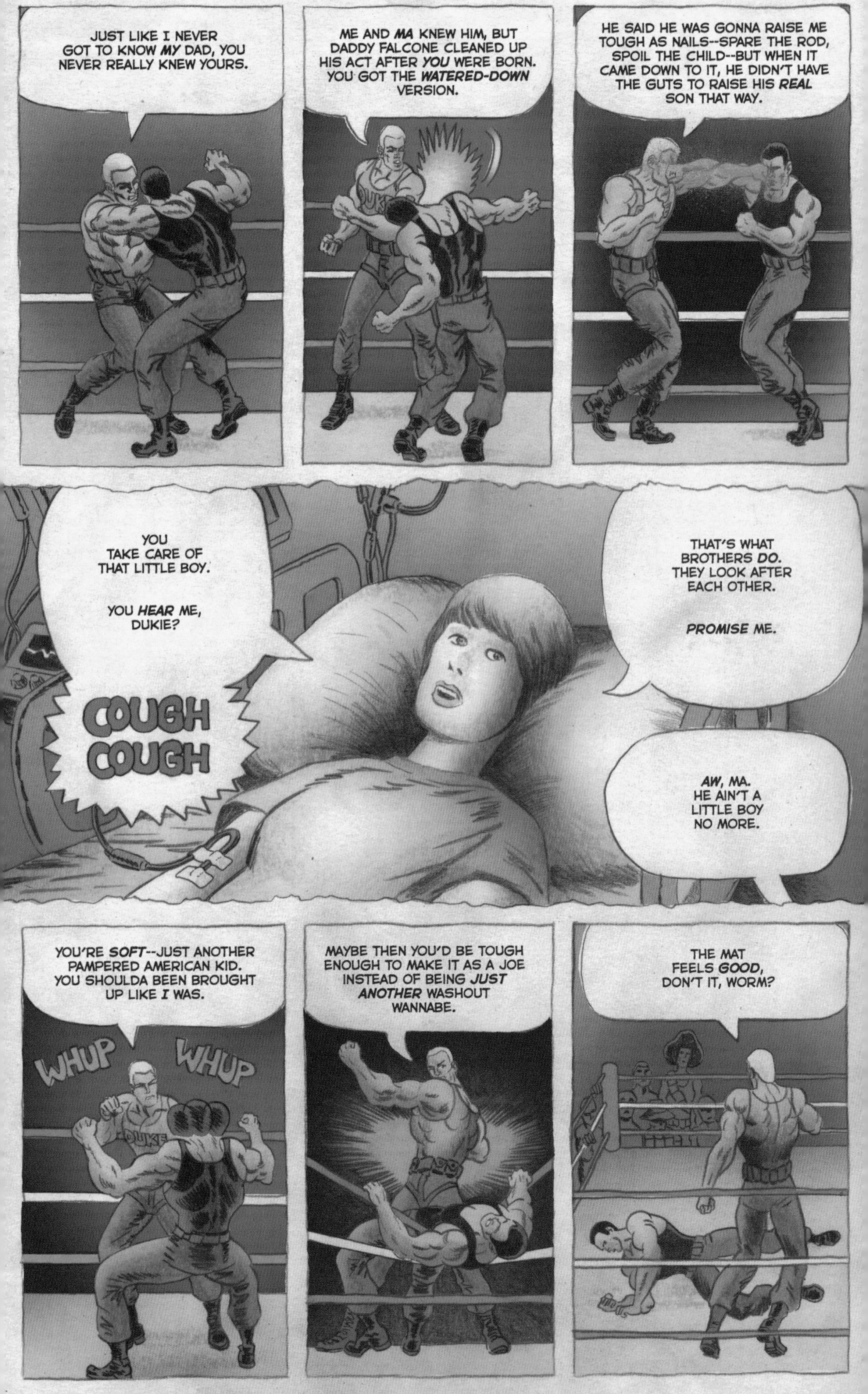

JUST LIKE I NEVER GOT TO KNOW MY DAD, YOU NEVER REALLY KNEW YOURS.
ME AND MA KNEW HIM, BUT DADDY FALCONE CLEANED UP HIS ACT AFTER YOU WERE BORN. YOU GOT THE WATERED-DOWN VERSION.
DUKE
HE SAID HE WAS GONNA RAISE ME TOUGH AS NAILS--SPARE THE ROD, SPOIL THE CHILD--BUT WHEN IT CAME DOWN TO IT, HE DIDN'T HAVE THE GUTS TO RAISE HIS REAL SON THAT WAY.
YOU TAKE CARE OF THAT LITTLE BOY.
YOU HEAR ME, DUKIE?
COUGH COUGH
THAT'S WHAT BROTHERS DO. THEY LOOK AFTER EACH OTHER.
PROMISE ME.
AW, MA. HE AIN'T A LITTLE BOY NO MORE.
YOU'RE SOFT--JUST ANOTHER PAMPERED AMERICAN KID. YOU SHOULDA BEEN BROUGHT UP LIKE I WAS.
WHUP
WHUP
DUKE
MAYBE THEN YOU'D BE TOUGH ENOUGH TO MAKE IT AS A JOE INSTEAD OF BEING JUST ANOTHER WASHOUT WANNABE.
THE MAT FEELS GOOD, DON'T IT, WORM?

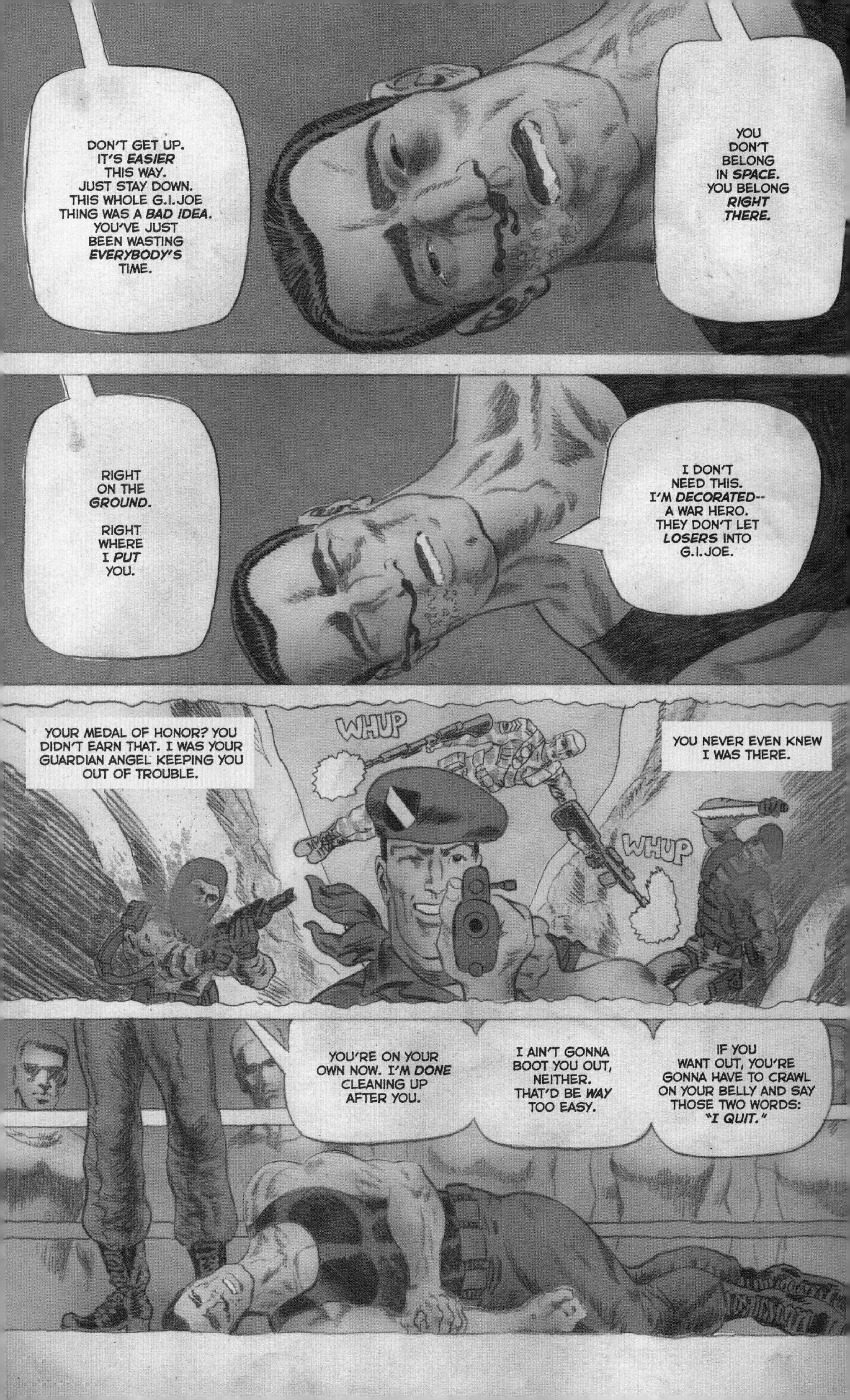
DON'T GET UP. IT'S EASIER THIS WAY. JUST STAY DOWN. THIS WHOLE G.I. JOE THING WAS A BAD IDEA. YOU'VE JUST BEEN WASTING EVERYBODY'S TIME.
YOU DON'T BELONG IN SPACE. YOU BELONG RIGHT THERE.
RIGHT ON THE GROUND.
RIGHT WHERE I PUT YOU.
I DON'T NEED THIS. I'M DECORATED-- A WAR HERO. THEY DON'T LET LOSERS INTO G.I. JOE.
YOUR MEDAL OF HONOR? YOU DIDN'T EARN THAT. I WAS YOUR GUARDIAN ANGEL KEEPING YOU OUT OF TROUBLE.
WHUP
WHUP
YOU NEVER EVEN KNEW I WAS THERE.
YOU'RE ON YOUR OWN NOW. I'M DONE CLEANING UP AFTER YOU.
I AIN'T GONNA BOOT YOU OUT, NEITHER. THAT'D BE WAY TOO EASY.
IF YOU WANT OUT, YOU'RE GONNA HAVE TO CRAWL ON YOUR BELLY AND SAY THOSE TWO WORDS: "I QUIT."

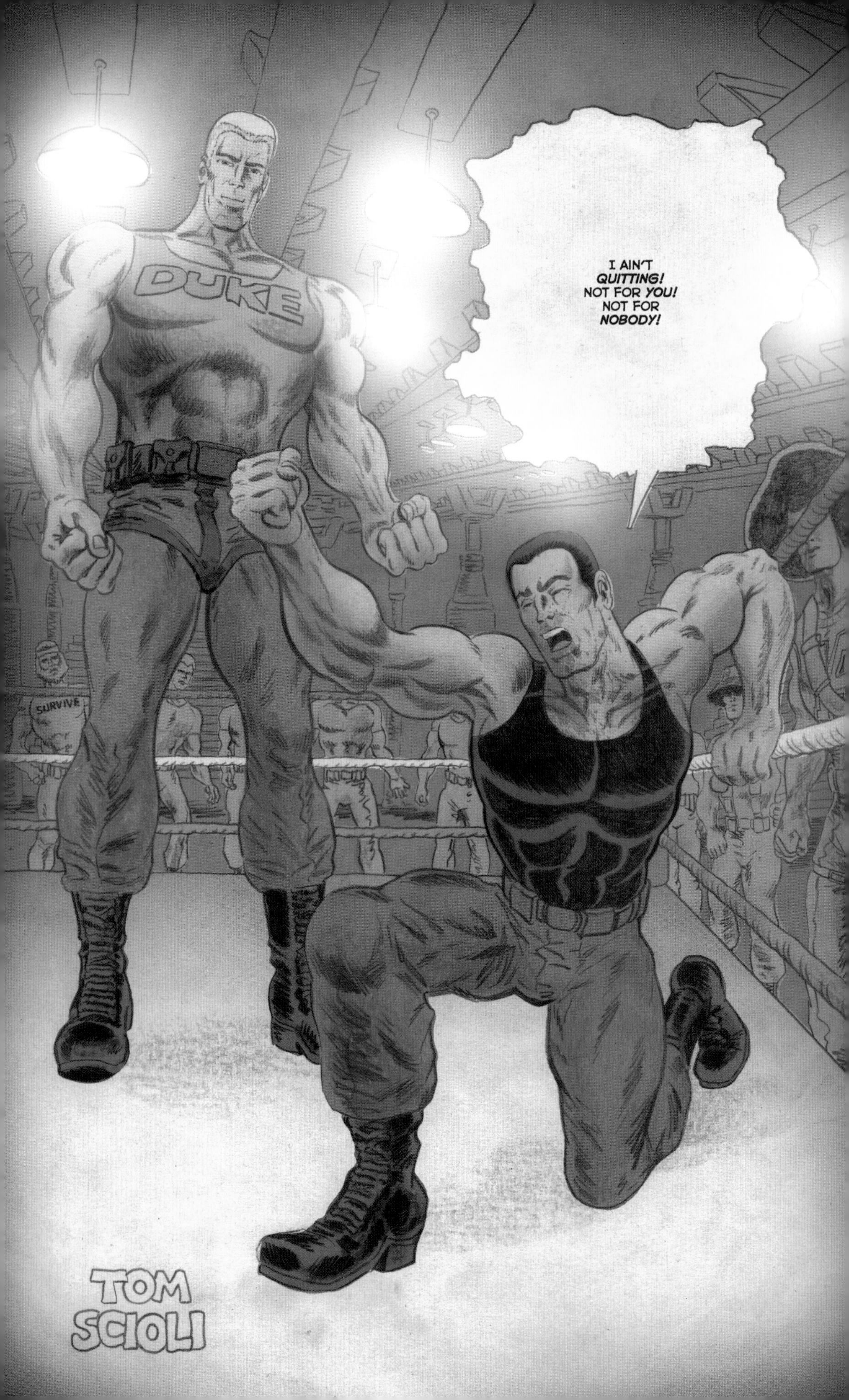
DUKE
SURVIVE
I AIN'T *QUITTING!* NOT FOR *YOU!* NOT FOR *NOBODY!*
TOM SCIOLI

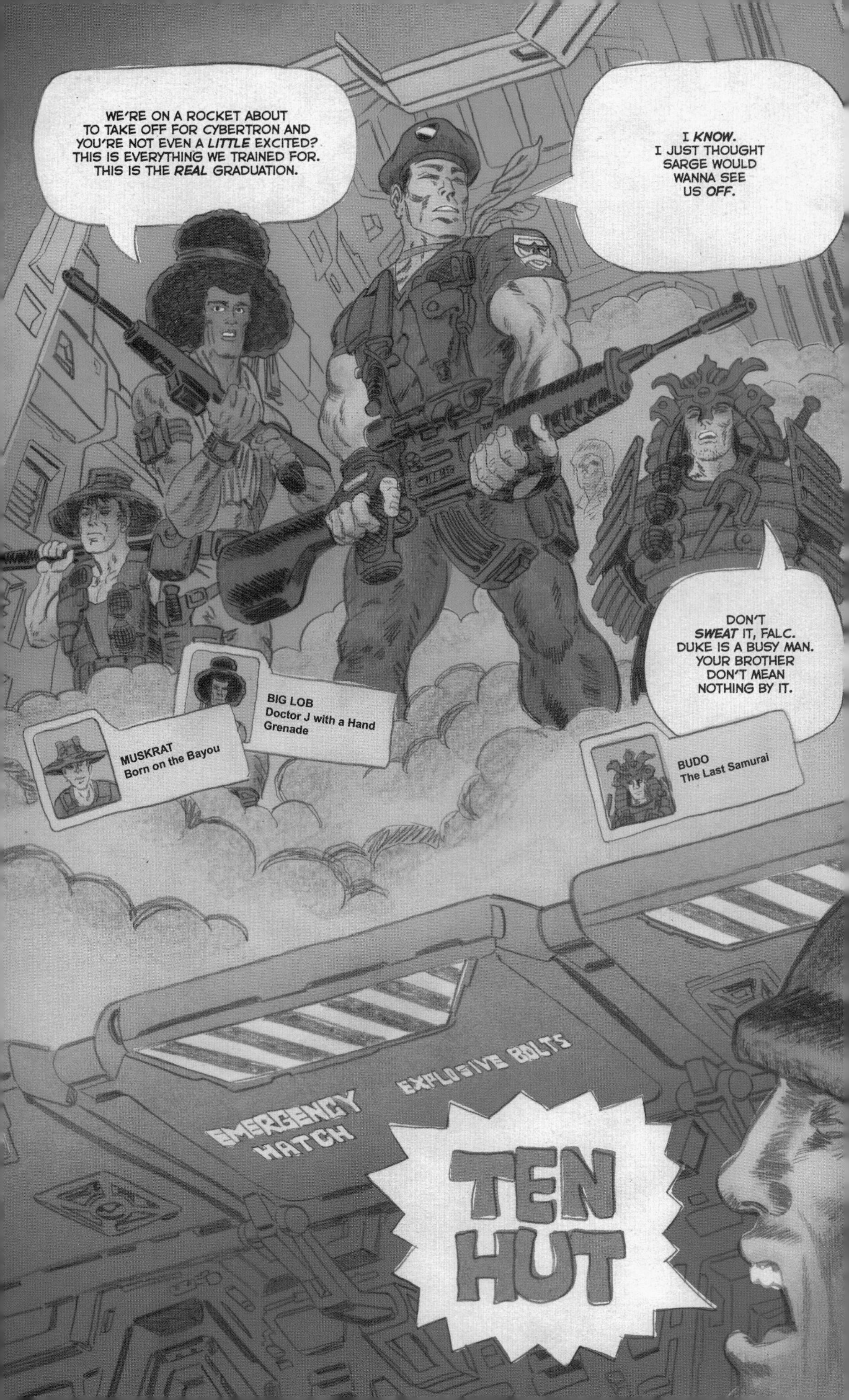
WE'RE ON A ROCKET ABOUT TO TAKE OFF FOR CYBERTRON AND YOU'RE NOT EVEN A LITTLE EXCITED? THIS IS EVERYTHING WE TRAINED FOR. THIS IS THE REAL GRADUATION.
I KNOW. I JUST THOUGHT SARGE WOULD WANNA SEE US OFF.
DON'T SWEAT IT, FALC. DUKE IS A BUSY MAN. YOUR BROTHER DON'T MEAN NOTHING BY IT.
BIG LOB
Doctor J with a Hand Grenade
MUSKRAT
Born on the Bayou
BUDO
The Last Samurai
EXPLOSIVE BOLTS
EMERGENCY HATCH
TEN HUT

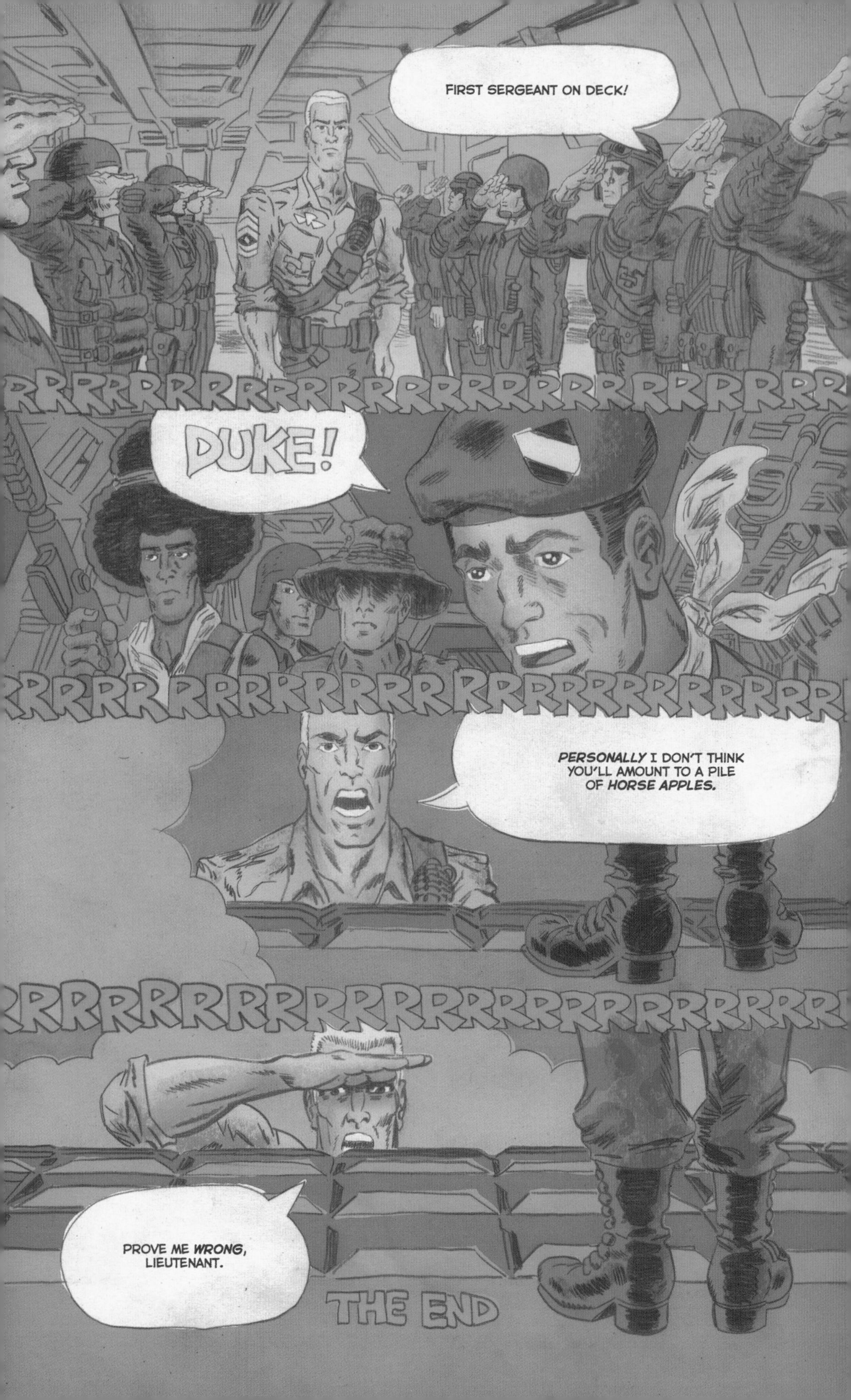
FIRST SERGEANT ON DECK!
RRRRRRRRRRRRRRRRRRRRR
DUKE!
RRRRRRRRRRRRRRRRRRRRRRR
PERSONALLY I DON'T THINK YOU'LL AMOUNT TO A PILE OF HORSE APPLES.
RRRRRRRRRRRRRRRRRRRRRRR
PROVE ME WRONG, LIEUTENANT.
THE END

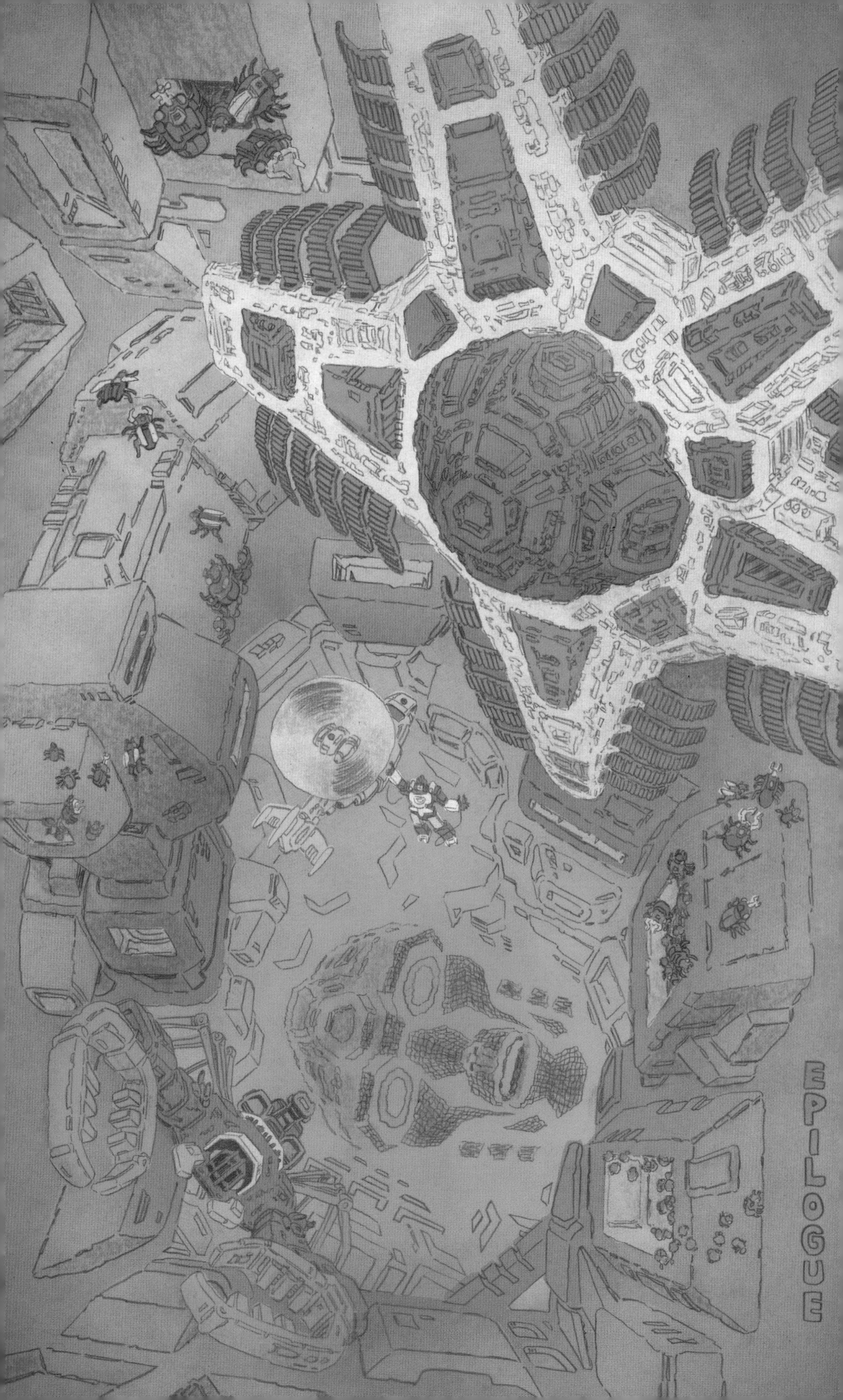
EPILOGUE

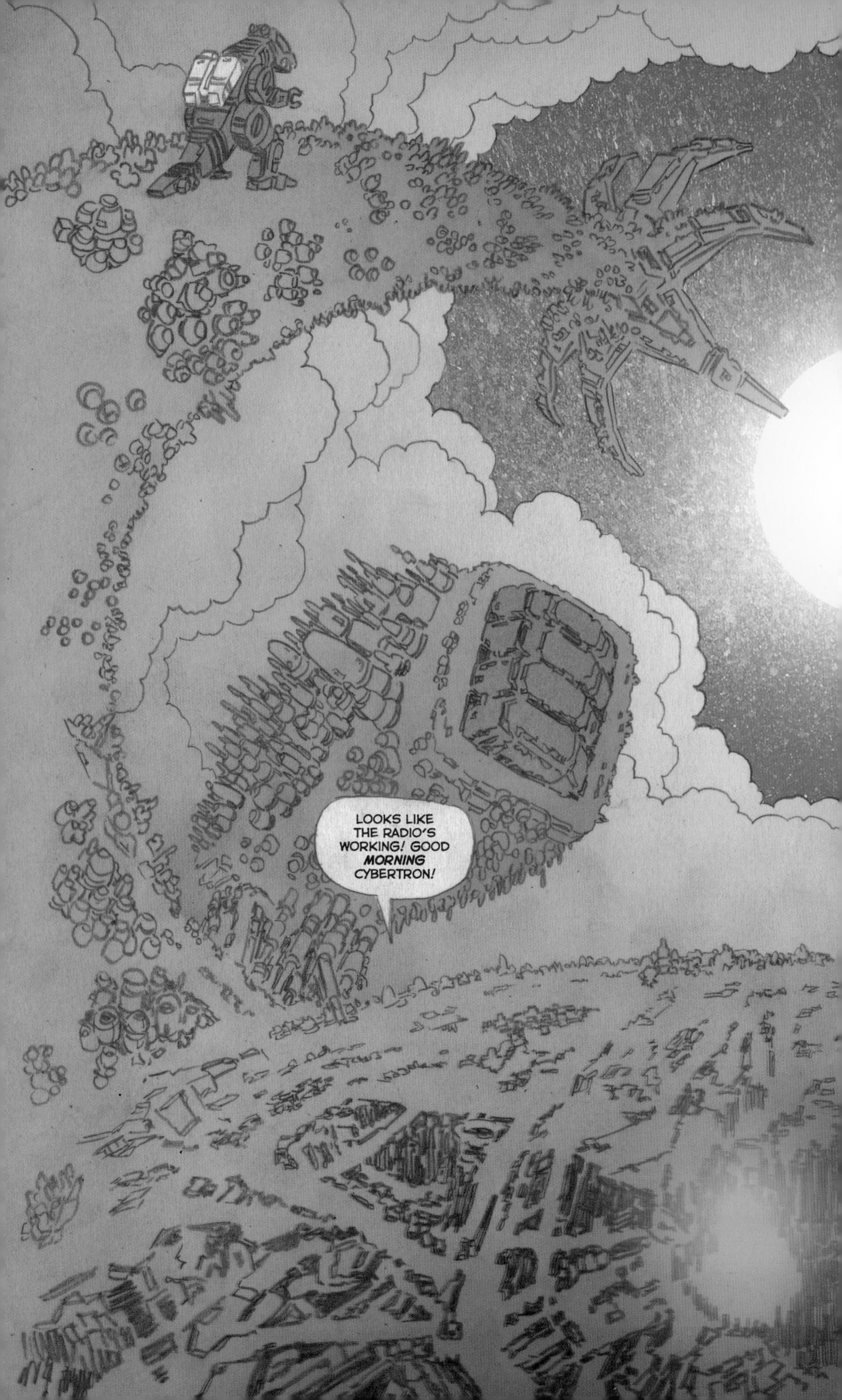
LOOKS LIKE THE RADIO'S WORKING! GOOD *MORNING* CYBERTRON!

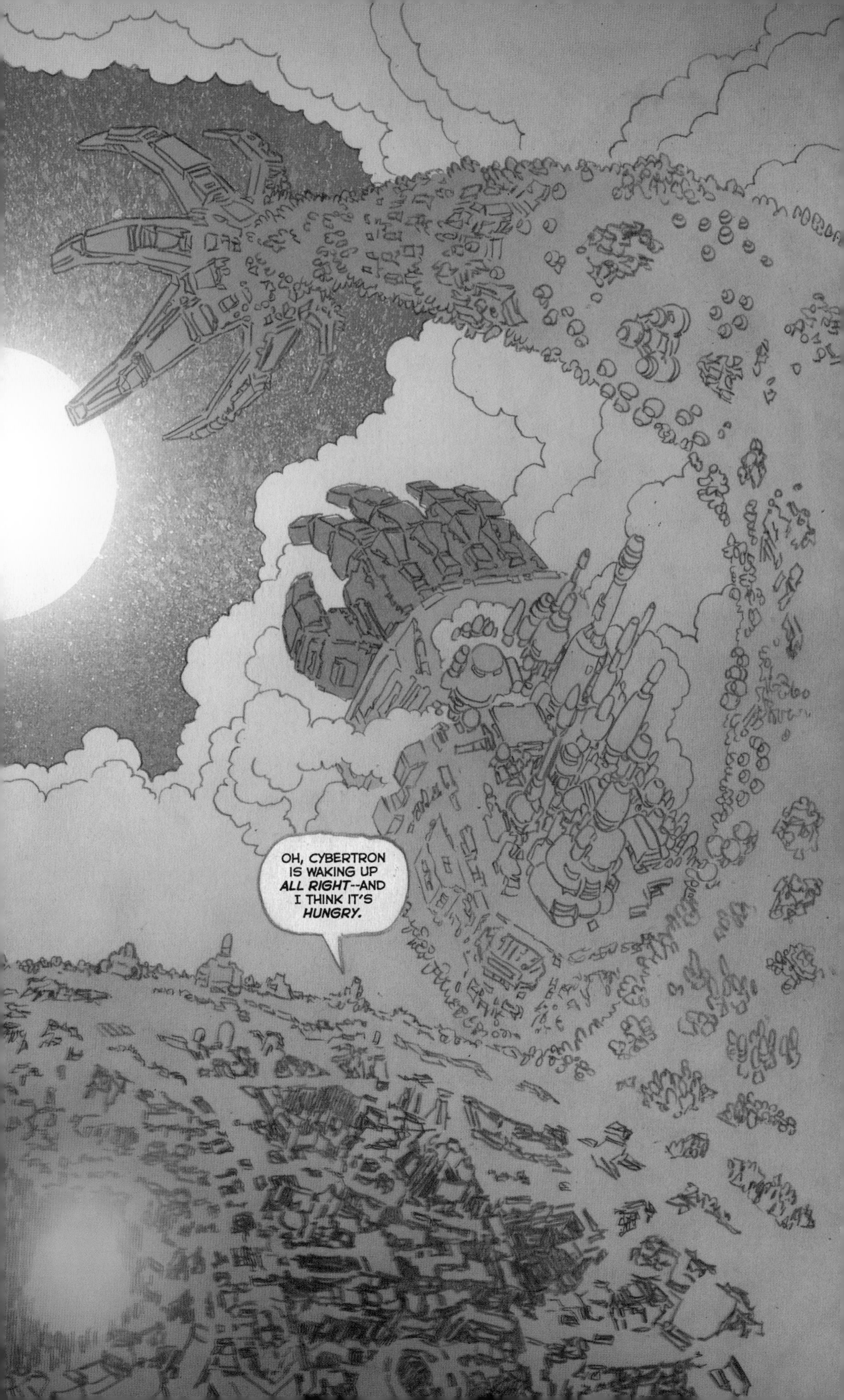
OH, CYBERTRON IS WAKING UP ALL RIGHT--AND I THINK IT'S HUNGRY.

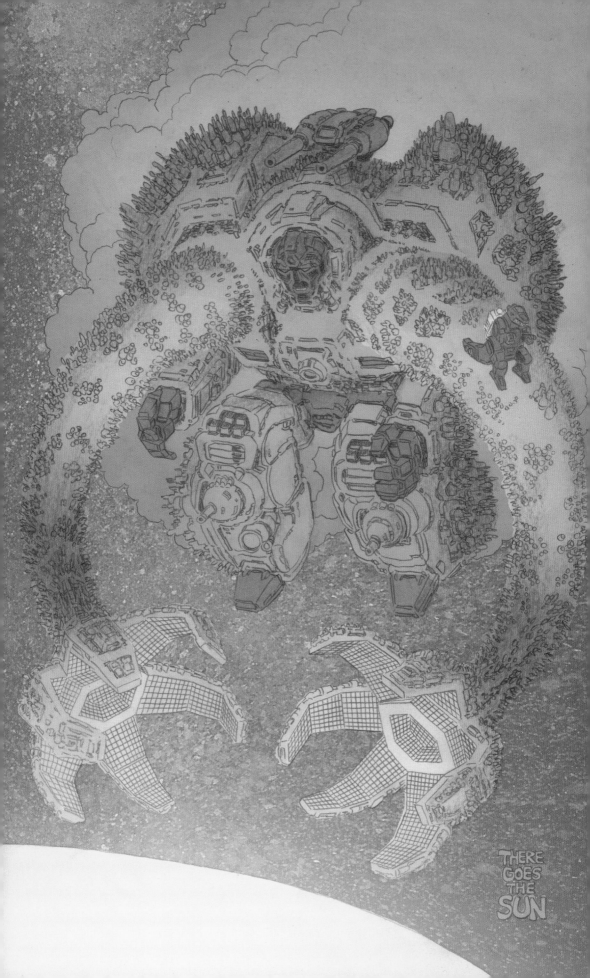

THERE
GOES
THE
SUN

ARTWORK BY **TOM NEELY**
COLORS BY **MARC J. PALM**

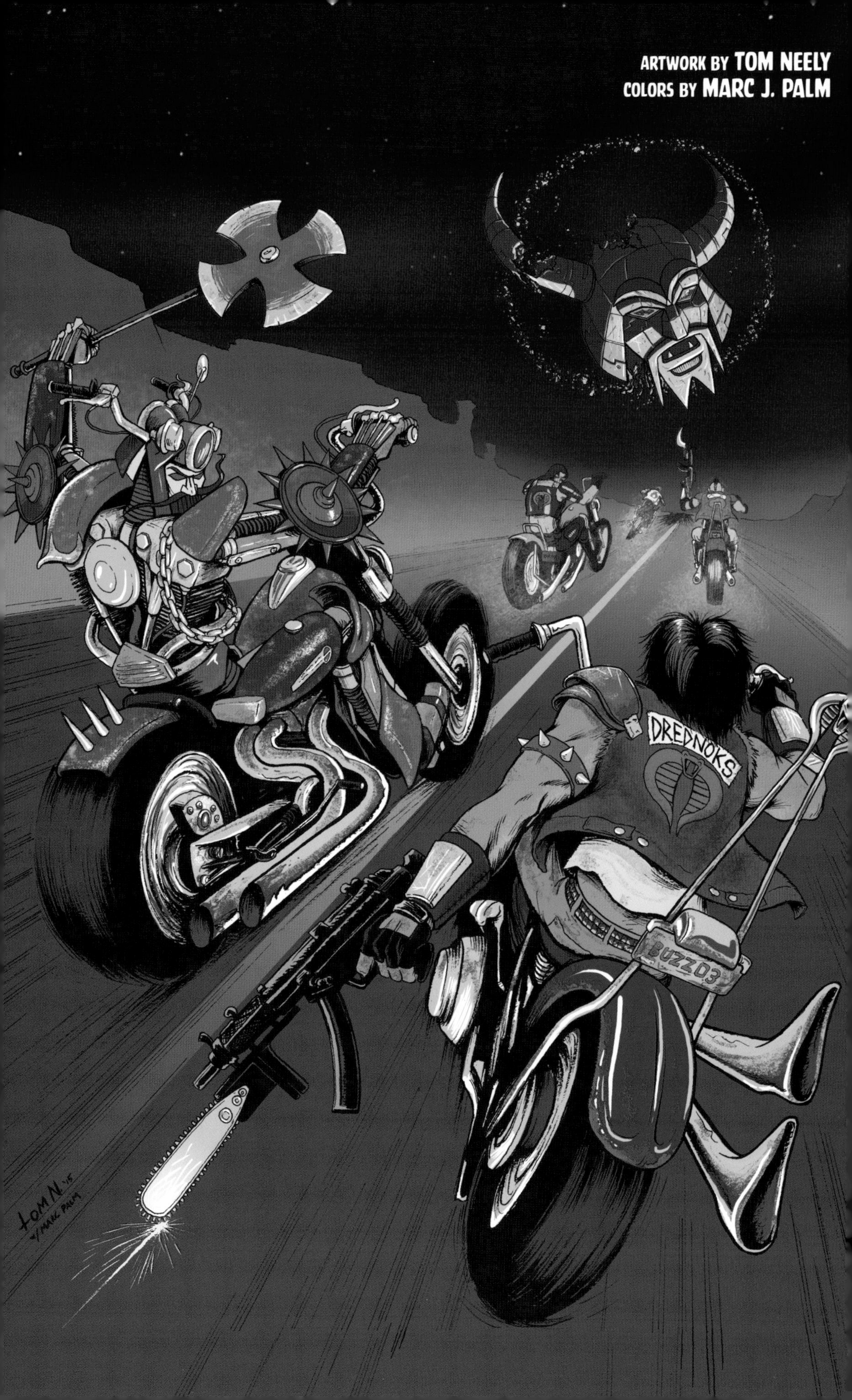
DREDNOKS
BUZZ03
tom N. '15
w/ MARC PALM

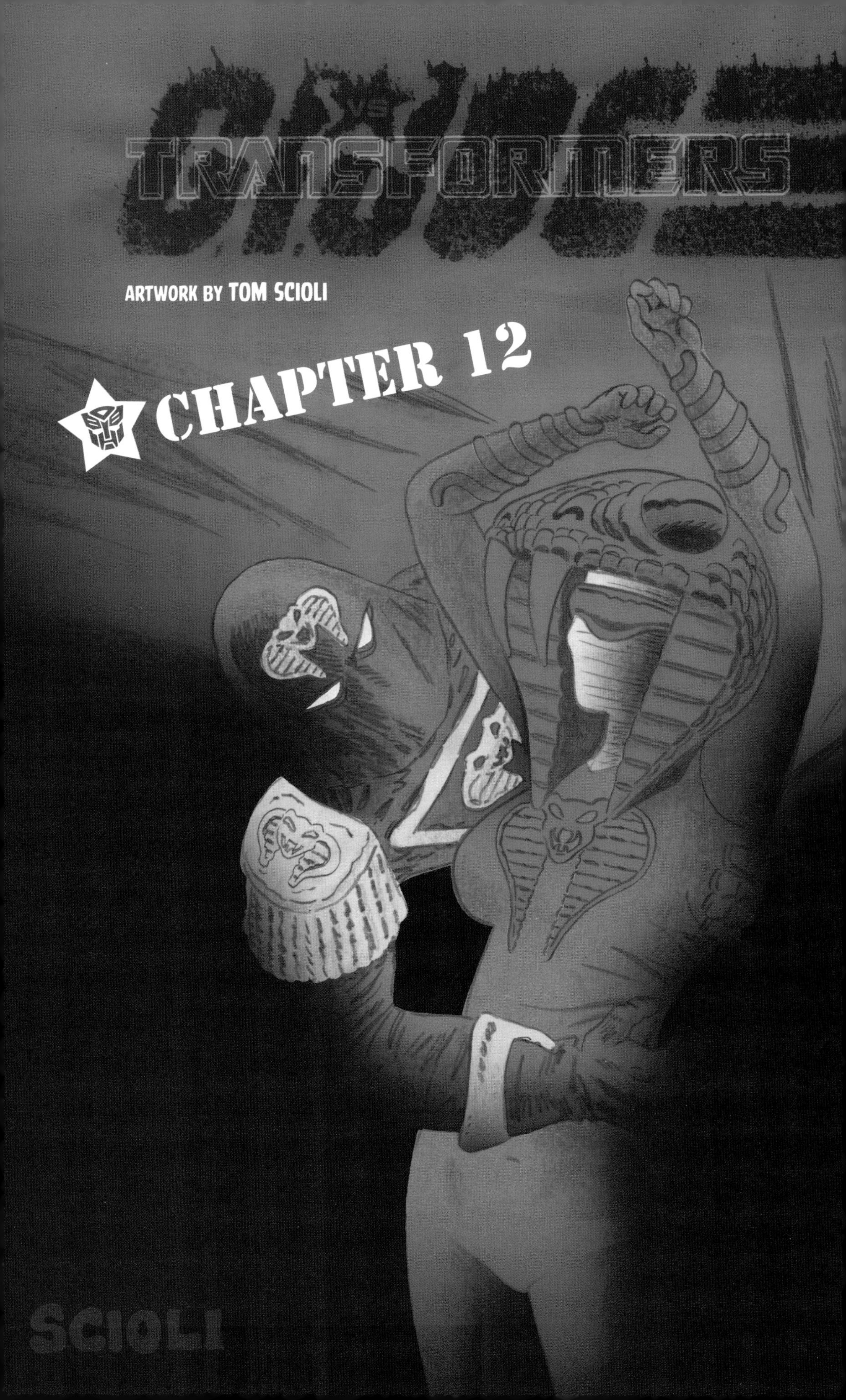
G.I. JOE
VS
TRANSFORMERS
ARTWORK BY TOM SCIOLI
CHAPTER 12
SCIOLI

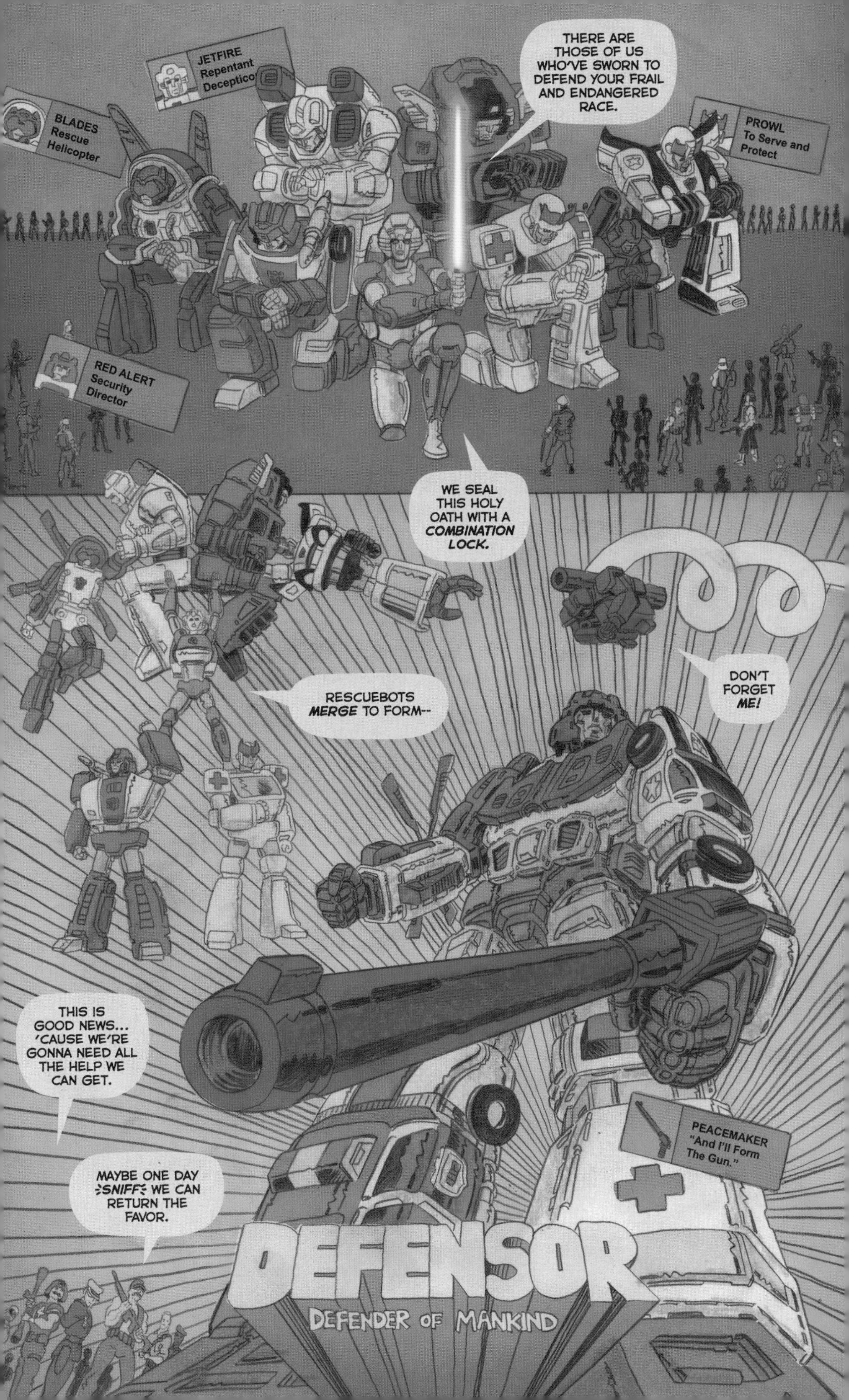
JETFIRE
Repentant Decepticon
BLADES
Rescue Helicopter
THERE ARE THOSE OF US WHO'VE SWORN TO DEFEND YOUR FRAIL AND ENDANGERED RACE.
PROWL
To Serve and Protect
RED ALERT
Security Director
WE SEAL THIS HOLY OATH WITH A *COMBINATION LOCK.*
RESCUEBOTS *MERGE* TO FORM--
DON'T FORGET *ME!*
THIS IS GOOD NEWS... 'CAUSE WE'RE GONNA NEED ALL THE HELP WE CAN GET.
MAYBE ONE DAY *SNIFF* WE CAN RETURN THE FAVOR.
PEACEMAKER
"And I'll Form The Gun."
DEFENSOR
DEFENDER OF MANKIND

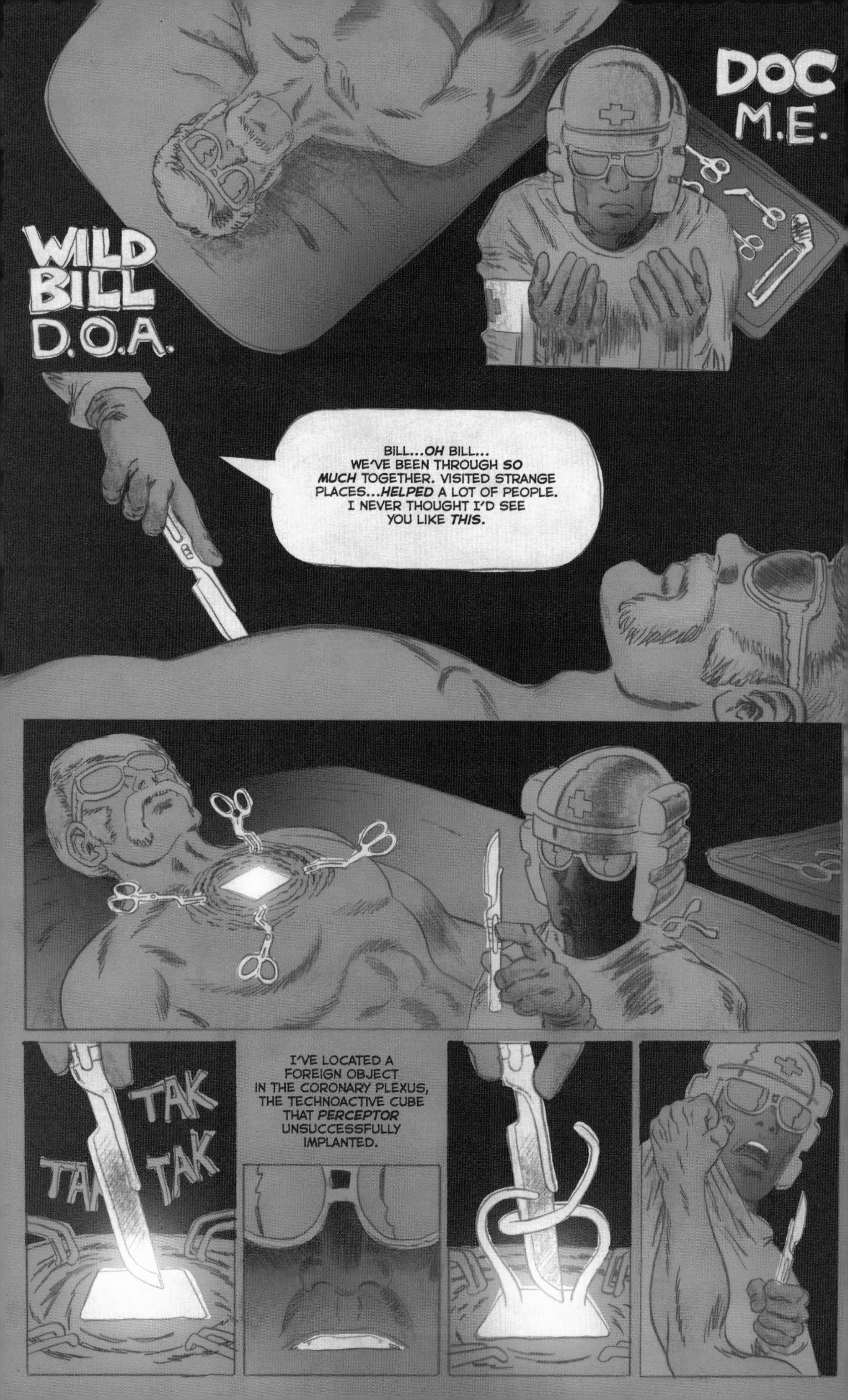
DOC M.E.
WILD BILL D.O.A.
BILL...OH BILL... WE'VE BEEN THROUGH SO MUCH TOGETHER. VISITED STRANGE PLACES...HELPED A LOT OF PEOPLE. I NEVER THOUGHT I'D SEE YOU LIKE THIS.
TAK TAK TAK
I'VE LOCATED A FOREIGN OBJECT IN THE CORONARY PLEXUS, THE TECHNOACTIVE CUBE THAT PERCEPTOR UNSUCCESSFULLY IMPLANTED.

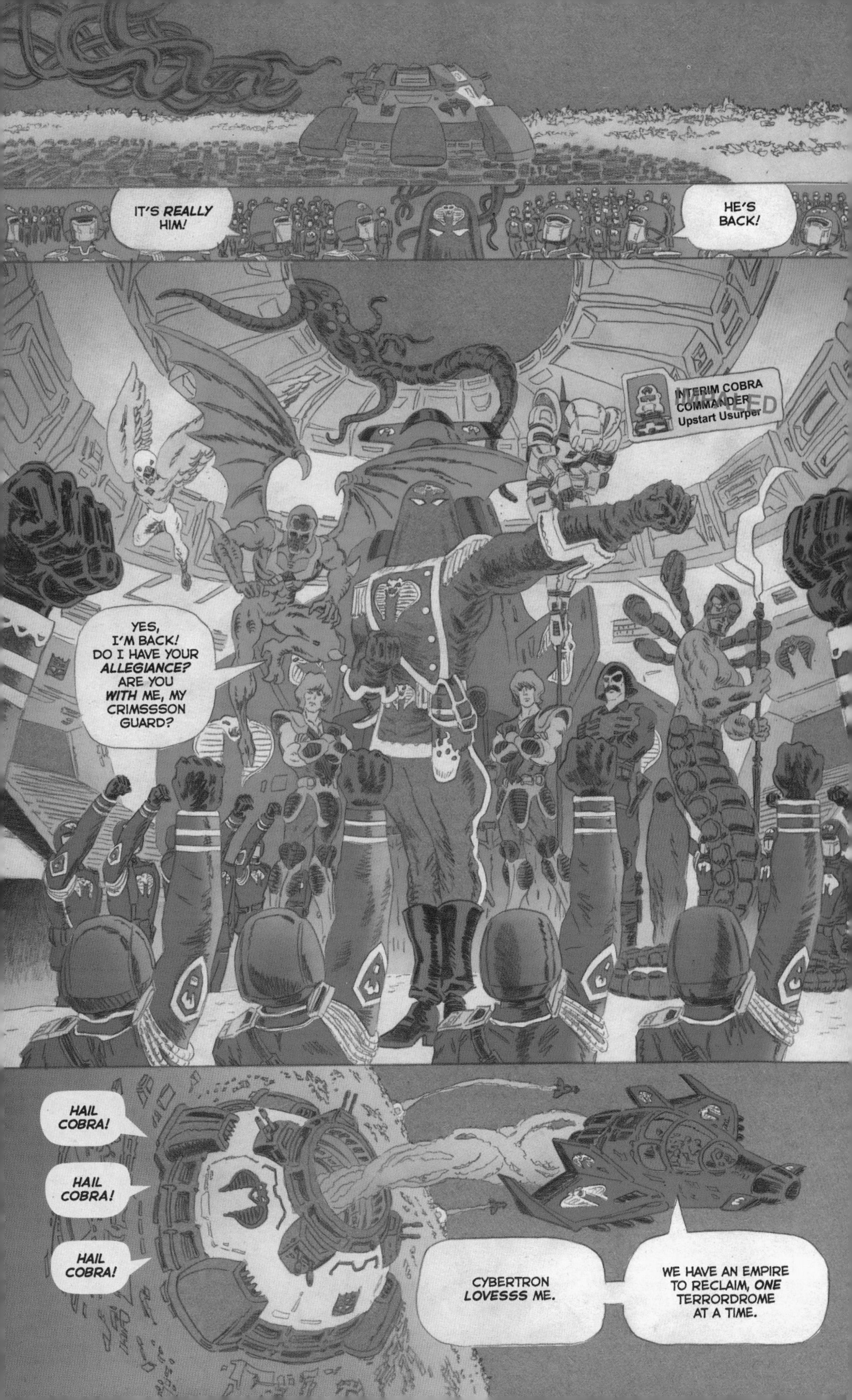
IT'S *REALLY* HIM!
HE'S BACK!
INTERIM COBRA COMMANDER
Upstart Usurper
YES, I'M BACK! DO I HAVE YOUR *ALLEGIANCE?* ARE YOU *WITH ME,* MY CRIMSSSON GUARD?
HAIL COBRA!
HAIL COBRA!
HAIL COBRA!
CYBERTRON *LOVESSS* ME.
WE HAVE AN EMPIRE TO RECLAIM, *ONE* TERRORDROME AT A TIME.

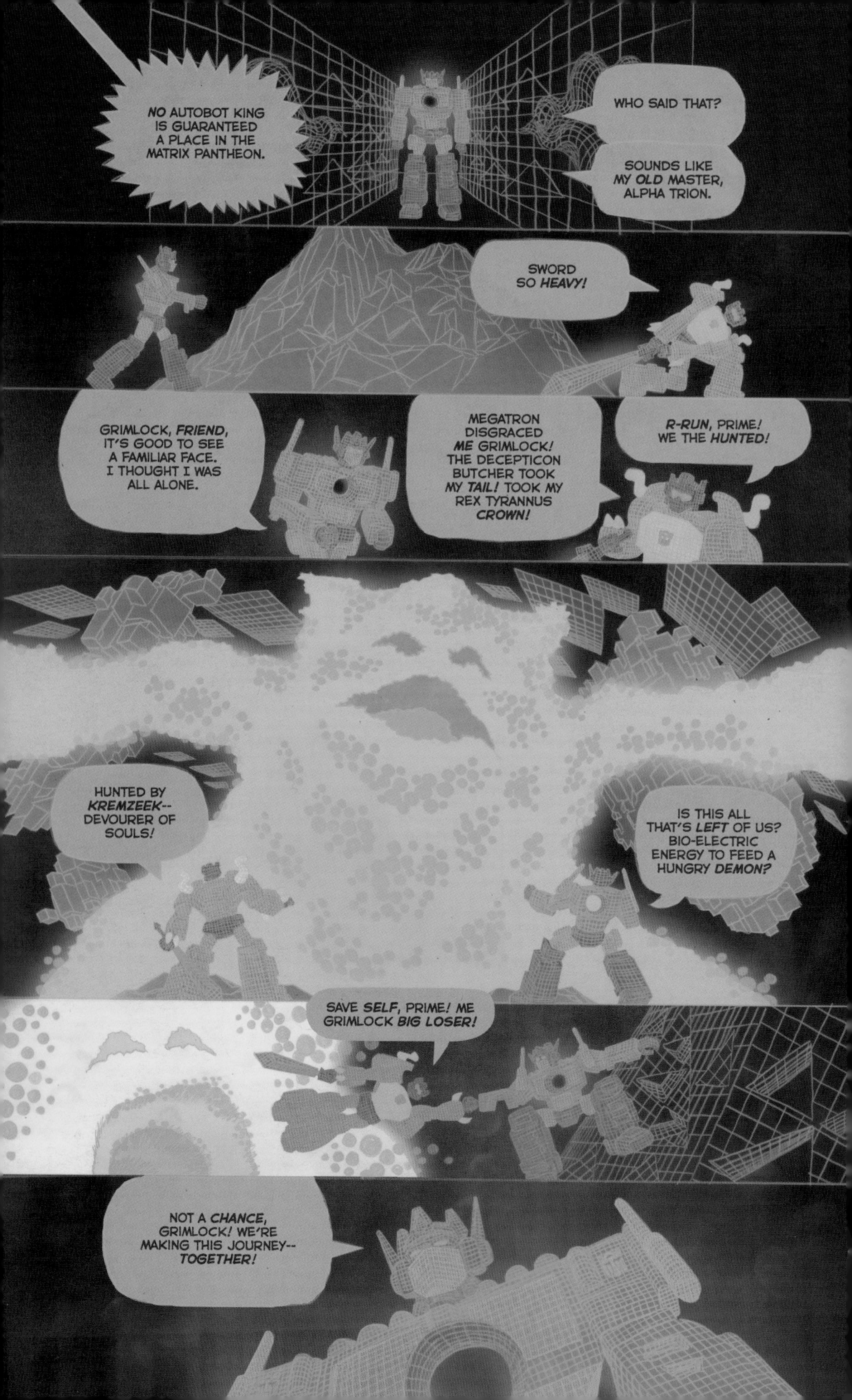
NO AUTOBOT KING IS GUARANTEED A PLACE IN THE MATRIX PANTHEON.
WHO SAID THAT?
SOUNDS LIKE MY OLD MASTER, ALPHA TRION.
SWORD SO HEAVY!
GRIMLOCK, FRIEND, IT'S GOOD TO SEE A FAMILIAR FACE. I THOUGHT I WAS ALL ALONE.
MEGATRON DISGRACED ME GRIMLOCK! THE DECEPTICON BUTCHER TOOK MY TAIL! TOOK MY REX TYRANNUS CROWN!
R-RUN, PRIME! WE THE HUNTED!
HUNTED BY KREMZEEK-- DEVOURER OF SOULS!
IS THIS ALL THAT'S LEFT OF US? BIO-ELECTRIC ENERGY TO FEED A HUNGRY DEMON?
SAVE SELF, PRIME! ME GRIMLOCK BIG LOSER!
NOT A CHANCE, GRIMLOCK! WE'RE MAKING THIS JOURNEY-- TOGETHER!

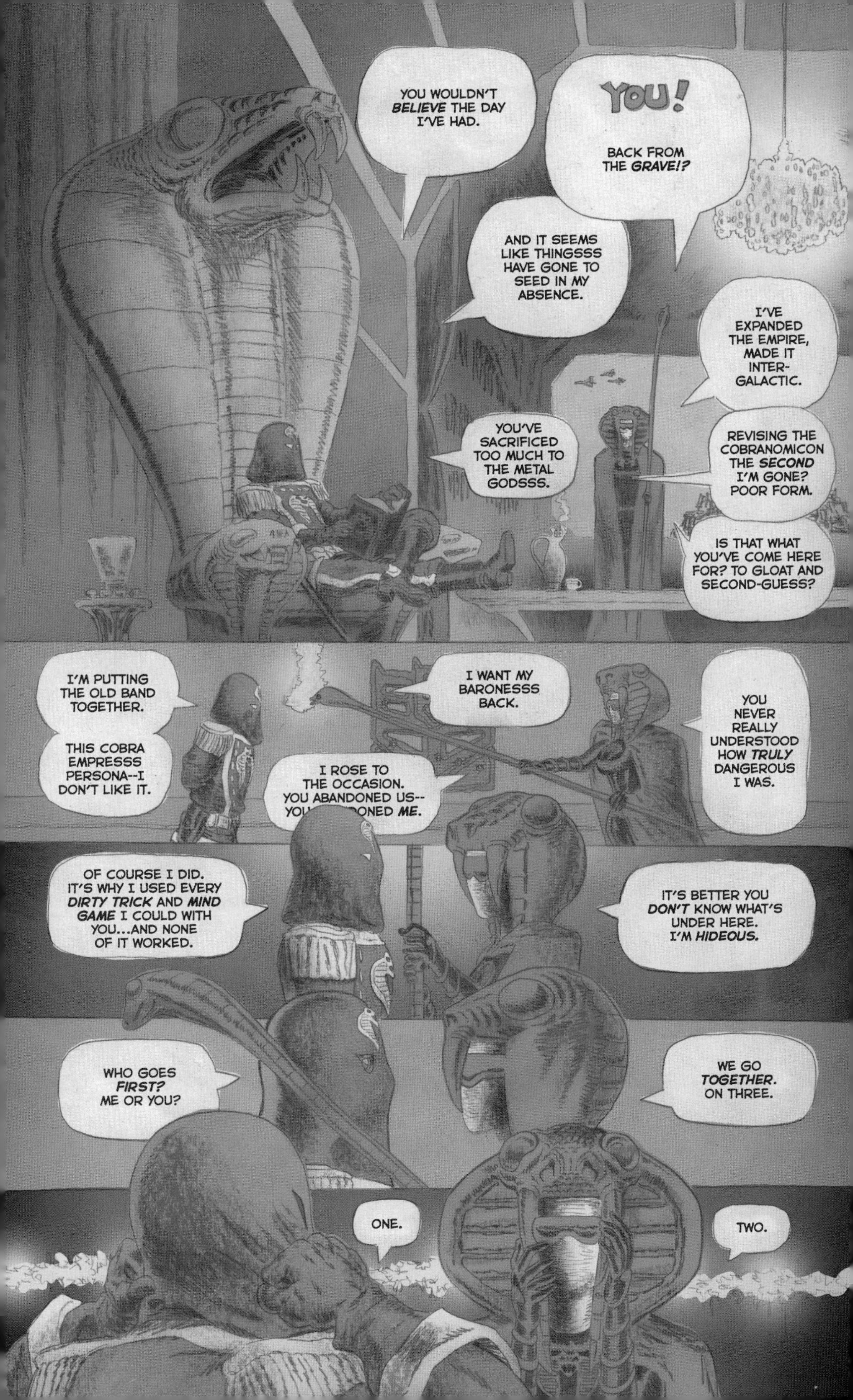
YOU!
BACK FROM THE GRAVE!?
YOU WOULDN'T BELIEVE THE DAY I'VE HAD.
AND IT SEEMS LIKE THINGSSS HAVE GONE TO SEED IN MY ABSENCE.
I'VE EXPANDED THE EMPIRE, MADE IT INTER-GALACTIC.
YOU'VE SACRIFICED TOO MUCH TO THE METAL GODSSS.
REVISING THE COBRANOMICON THE SECOND I'M GONE? POOR FORM.
IS THAT WHAT YOU'VE COME HERE FOR? TO GLOAT AND SECOND-GUESS?
I'M PUTTING THE OLD BAND TOGETHER.
THIS COBRA EMPRESSS PERSONA--I DON'T LIKE IT.
I WANT MY BARONESSS BACK.
I ROSE TO THE OCCASION. YOU ABANDONED US--
YOU NEVER REALLY UNDERSTOOD HOW TRULY DANGEROUS I WAS.
OF COURSE I DID. IT'S WHY I USED EVERY DIRTY TRICK AND MIND GAME I COULD WITH YOU...AND NONE OF IT WORKED.
IT'S BETTER YOU DON'T KNOW WHAT'S UNDER HERE. I'M HIDEOUS.
WHO GOES FIRST? ME OR YOU?
WE GO TOGETHER. ON THREE.
ONE.
TWO.

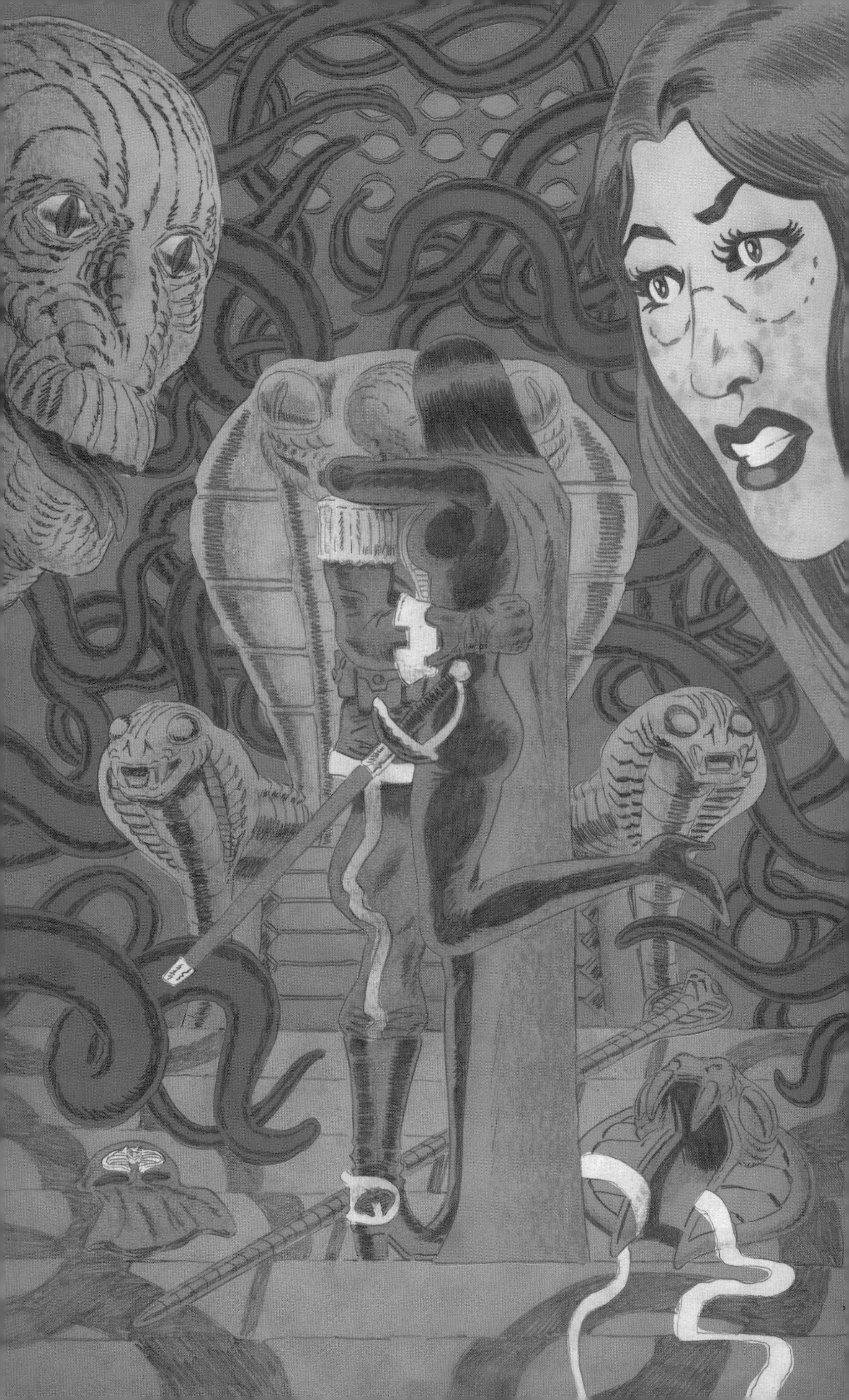

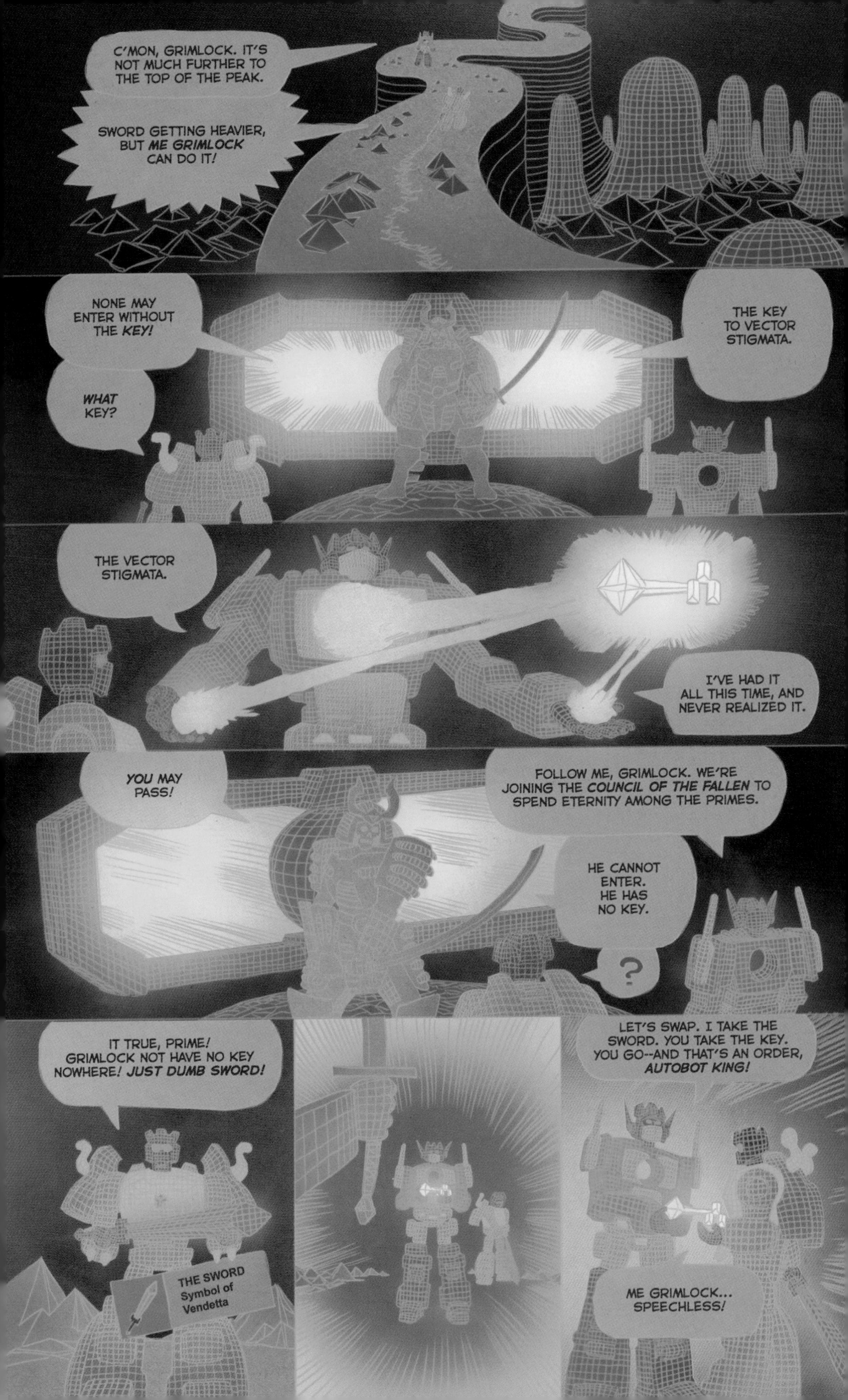
C'MON, GRIMLOCK. IT'S NOT MUCH FURTHER TO THE TOP OF THE PEAK.
SWORD GETTING HEAVIER, BUT *ME GRIMLOCK* CAN DO IT!
NONE MAY ENTER WITHOUT THE *KEY!*
WHAT KEY?
THE KEY TO VECTOR STIGMATA.
THE VECTOR STIGMATA.
I'VE HAD IT ALL THIS TIME, AND NEVER REALIZED IT.
YOU MAY PASS!
FOLLOW ME, GRIMLOCK. WE'RE JOINING THE *COUNCIL OF THE FALLEN* TO SPEND ETERNITY AMONG THE PRIMES.
HE CANNOT ENTER. HE HAS NO KEY.
?
IT TRUE, PRIME! GRIMLOCK NOT HAVE NO KEY NOWHERE! *JUST DUMB SWORD!*
THE SWORD
Symbol of Vendetta
LET'S SWAP. I TAKE THE SWORD. YOU TAKE THE KEY. YOU GO--AND THAT'S AN ORDER, *AUTOBOT KING!*
ME GRIMLOCK... SPEECHLESS!

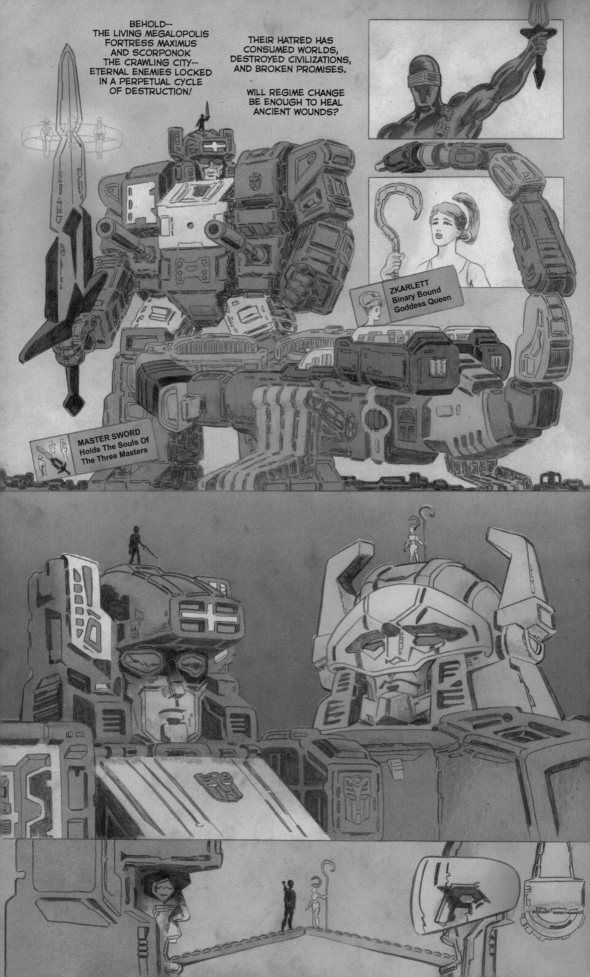

BEHOLD--
THE LIVING MEGALOPOLIS
FORTRESS MAXIMUS
AND SCORPONOK
THE CRAWLING CITY--
ETERNAL ENEMIES LOCKED
IN A PERPETUAL CYCLE
OF DESTRUCTION!

THEIR HATRED HAS
CONSUMED WORLDS,
DESTROYED CIVILIZATIONS,
AND BROKEN PROMISES.

WILL REGIME CHANGE
BE ENOUGH TO HEAL
ANCIENT WOUNDS?

ZKARLETT
Binary Bound
Goddess Queen

MASTER SWORD
Holds The Souls Of
The Three Masters

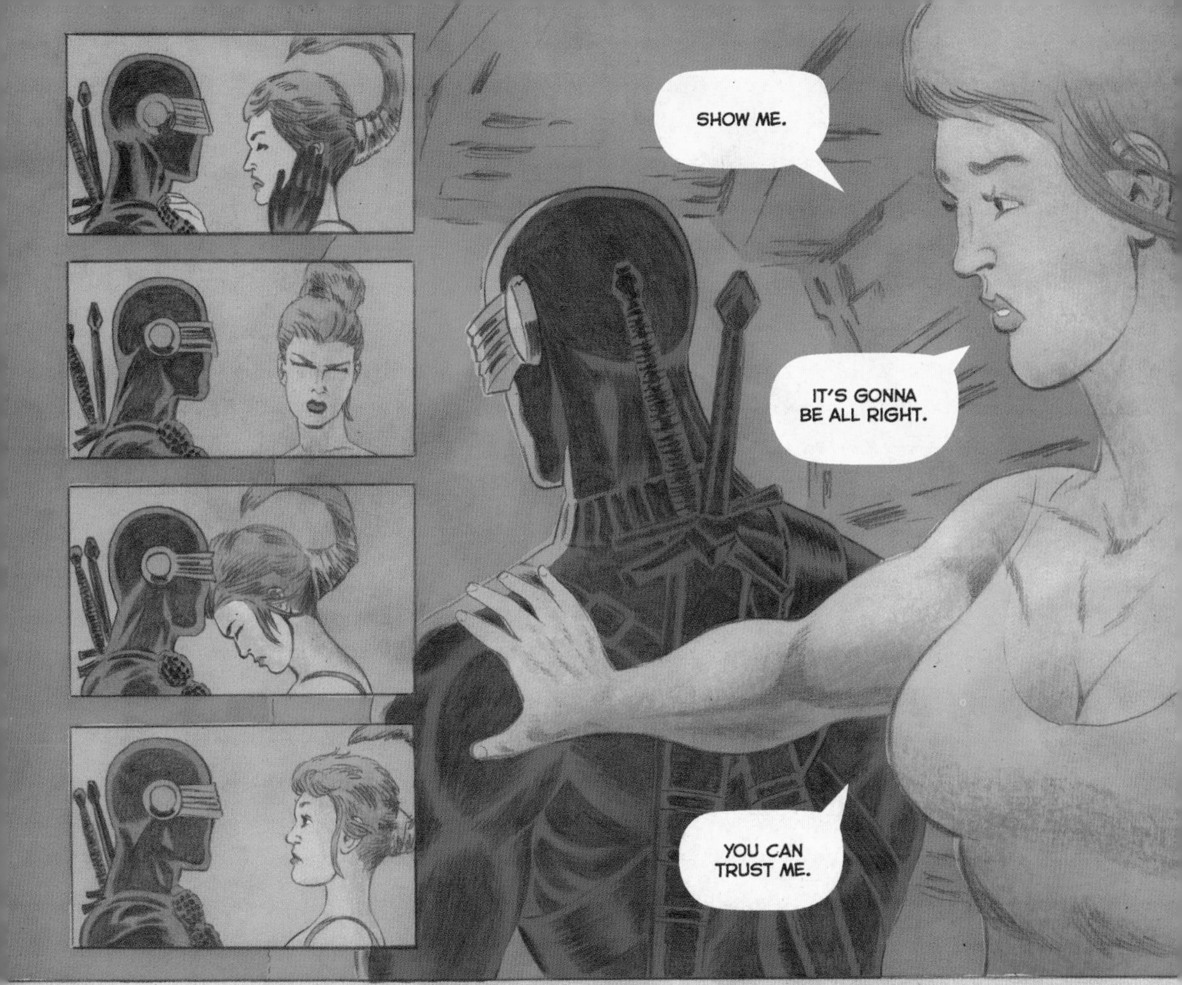
SHOW ME.
IT'S GONNA BE ALL RIGHT.
YOU CAN TRUST ME.

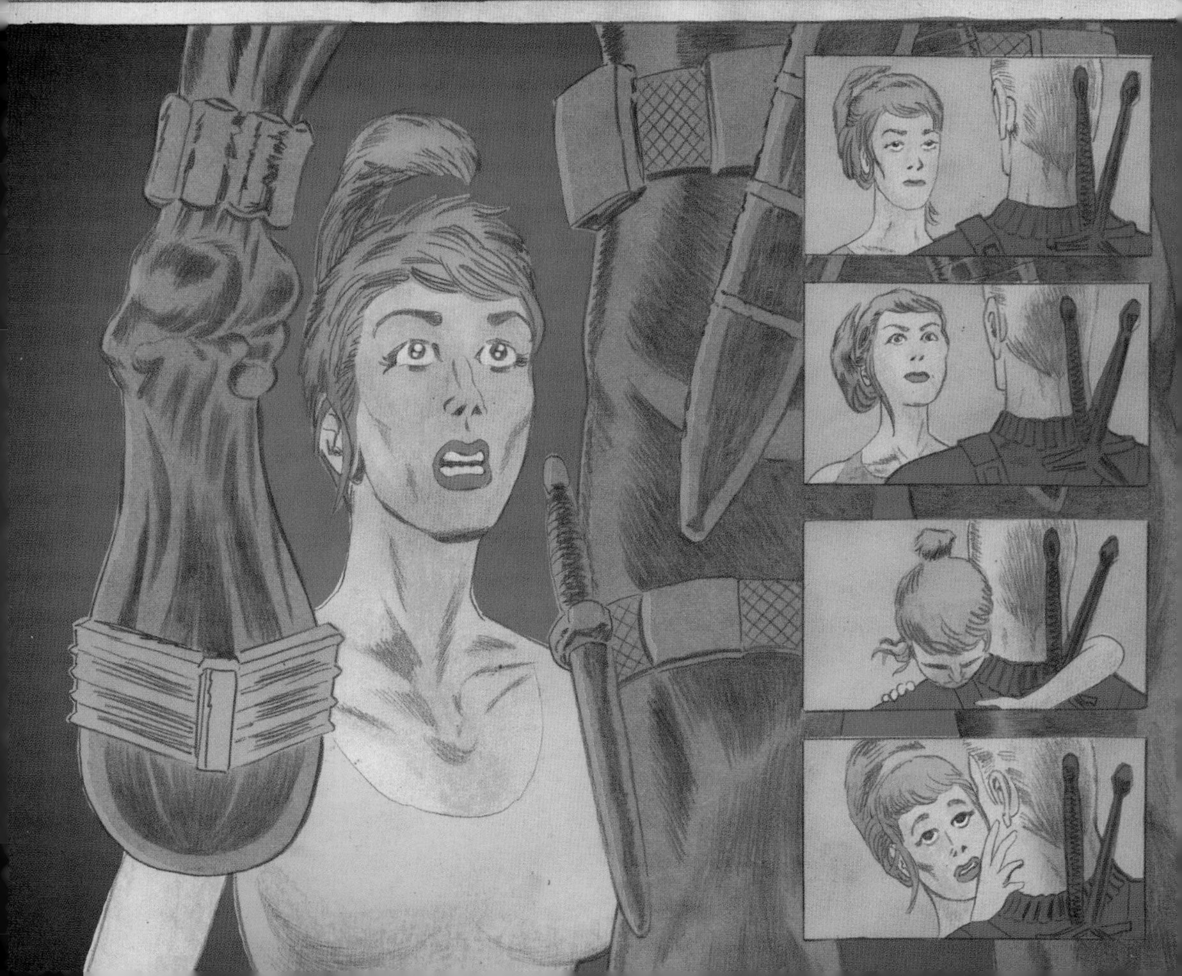

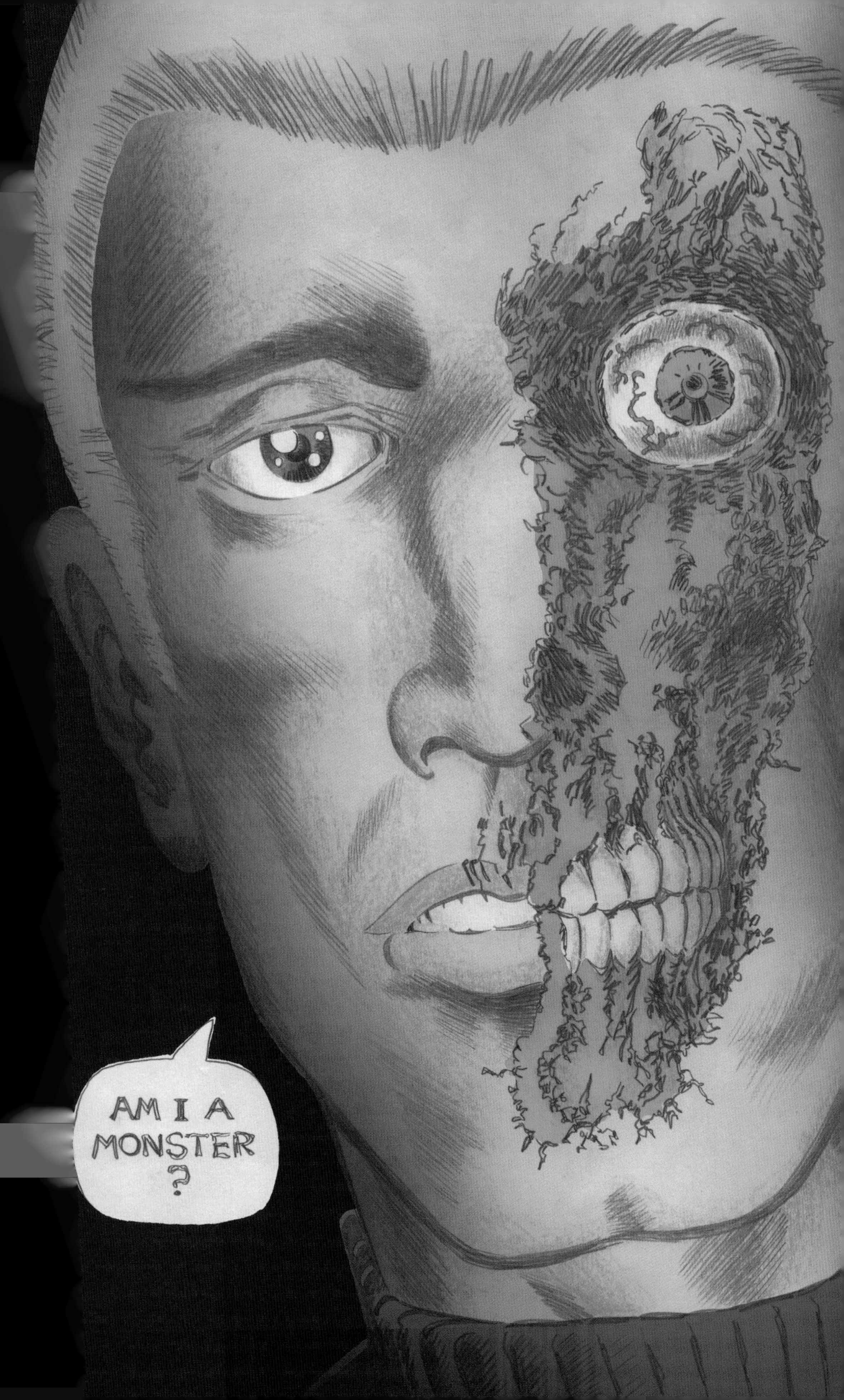
AM I A MONSTER ?

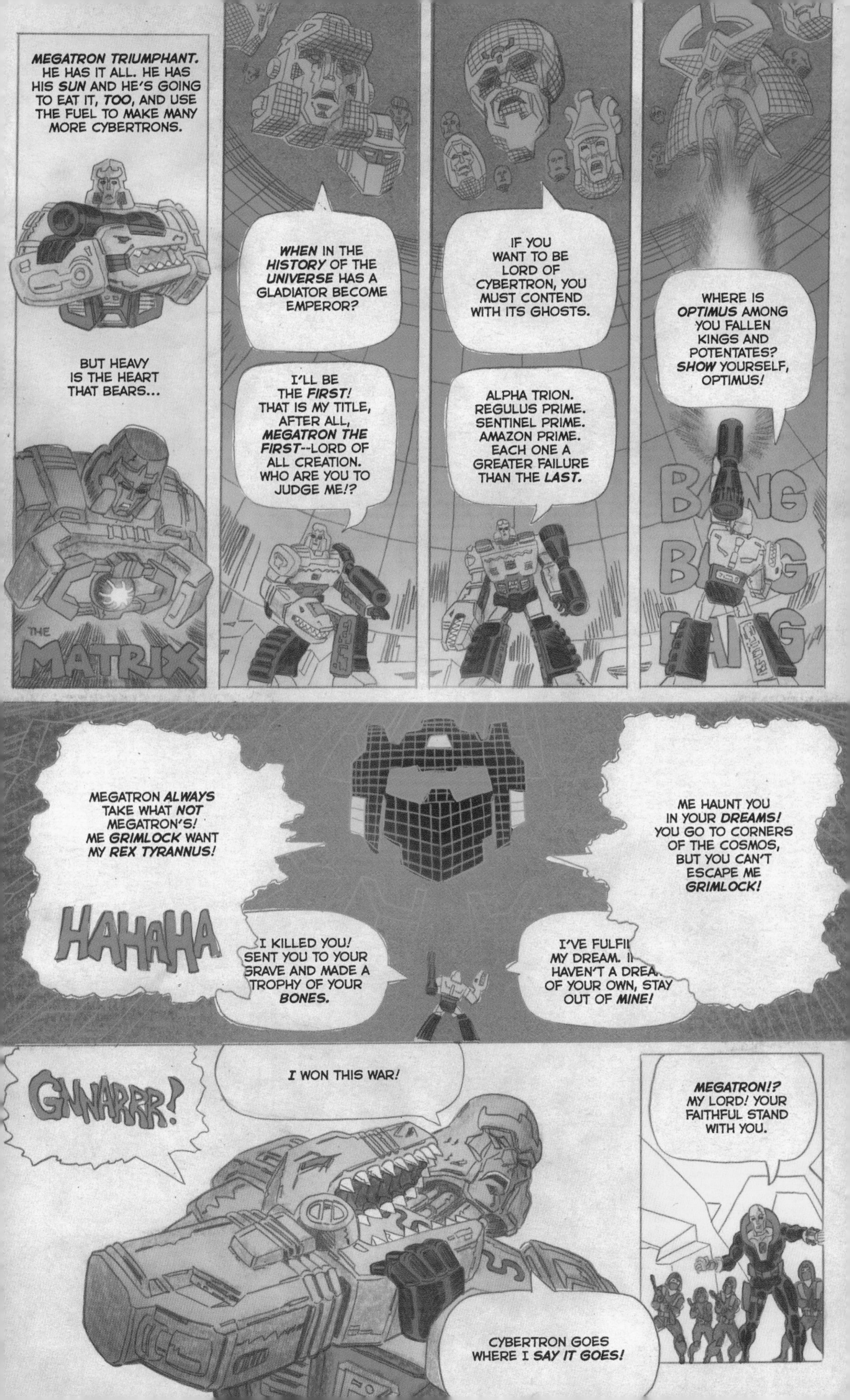
MEGATRON TRIUMPHANT. HE HAS IT ALL. HE HAS HIS SUN AND HE'S GOING TO EAT IT, TOO, AND USE THE FUEL TO MAKE MANY MORE CYBERTRONS.
BUT HEAVY IS THE HEART THAT BEARS...
THE MATRIX
WHEN IN THE HISTORY OF THE UNIVERSE HAS A GLADIATOR BECOME EMPEROR?
I'LL BE THE FIRST! THAT IS MY TITLE, AFTER ALL, MEGATRON THE FIRST--LORD OF ALL CREATION. WHO ARE YOU TO JUDGE ME!?
IF YOU WANT TO BE LORD OF CYBERTRON, YOU MUST CONTEND WITH ITS GHOSTS.
ALPHA TRION. REGULUS PRIME. SENTINEL PRIME. AMAZON PRIME. EACH ONE A GREATER FAILURE THAN THE LAST.
WHERE IS OPTIMUS AMONG YOU FALLEN KINGS AND POTENTATES? SHOW YOURSELF, OPTIMUS!
BANG
BANG
BANG
MEGATRON ALWAYS TAKE WHAT NOT MEGATRON'S! ME GRIMLOCK WANT MY REX TYRANNUS!
HAHAHA
ME HAUNT YOU IN YOUR DREAMS! YOU GO TO CORNERS OF THE COSMOS, BUT YOU CAN'T ESCAPE ME GRIMLOCK!
I KILLED YOU! SENT YOU TO YOUR GRAVE AND MADE A TROPHY OF YOUR BONES.
I'VE FULFIL MY DREAM. I HAVEN'T A DREA OF YOUR OWN, STAY OUT OF MINE!
GNNARRR!
I WON THIS WAR!
CYBERTRON GOES WHERE I SAY IT GOES!
MEGATRON!? MY LORD! YOUR FAITHFUL STAND WITH YOU.

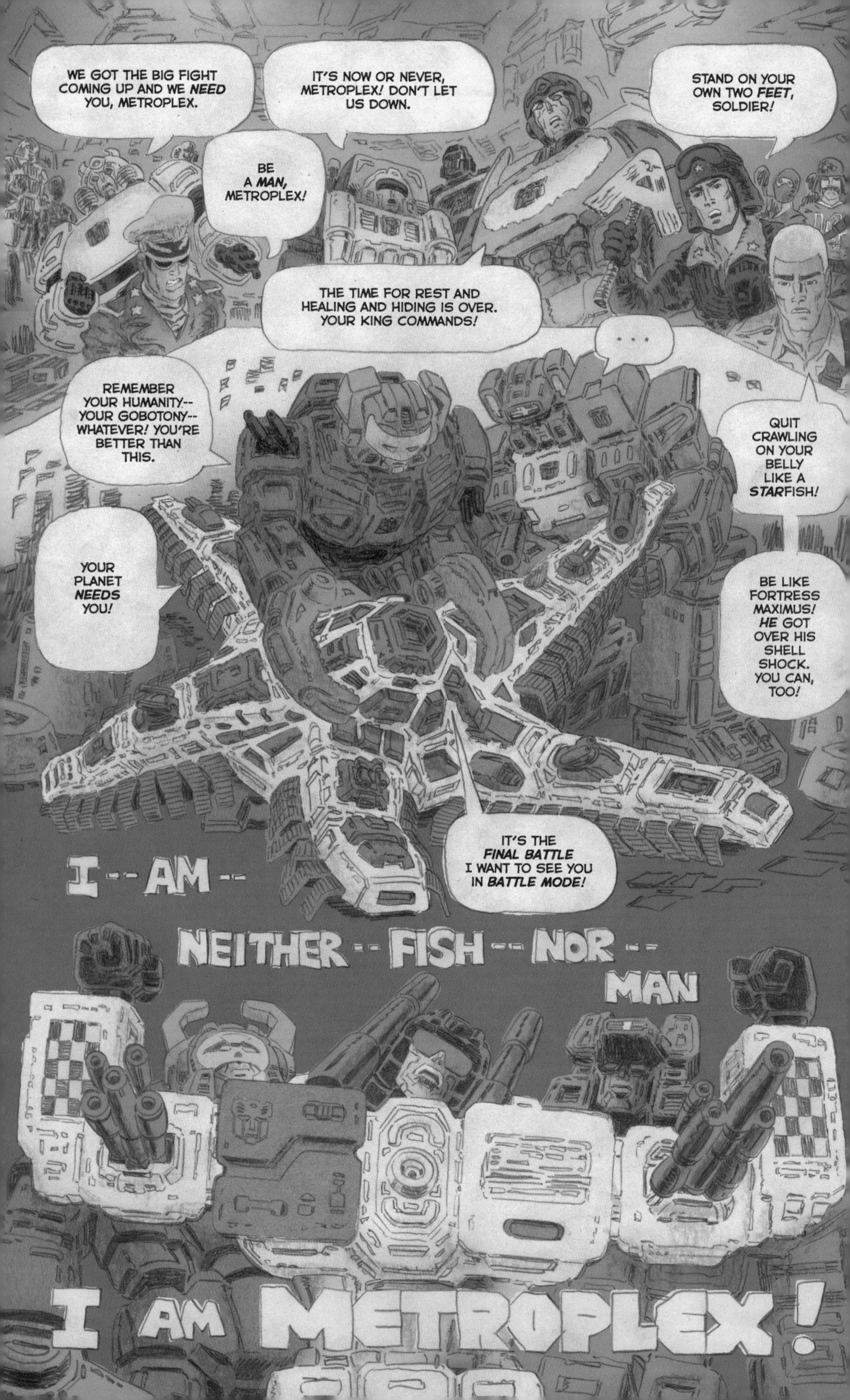
WE GOT THE BIG FIGHT COMING UP AND WE *NEED* YOU, METROPLEX.
IT'S NOW OR NEVER, METROPLEX! DON'T LET US DOWN.
STAND ON YOUR OWN TWO *FEET*, SOLDIER!
BE A *MAN*, METROPLEX!
THE TIME FOR REST AND HEALING AND HIDING IS OVER. YOUR KING COMMANDS!
. . .
REMEMBER YOUR HUMANITY-- YOUR GOBOTONY-- WHATEVER! YOU'RE BETTER THAN THIS.
QUIT CRAWLING ON YOUR BELLY LIKE A *STAR*FISH!
YOUR PLANET *NEEDS* YOU!
BE LIKE FORTRESS MAXIMUS! *HE* GOT OVER HIS SHELL SHOCK. YOU CAN, TOO!
IT'S THE *FINAL BATTLE* I WANT TO SEE YOU IN *BATTLE MODE!*
I -- AM --
NEITHER -- FISH -- NOR -- MAN
I AM METROPLEX!

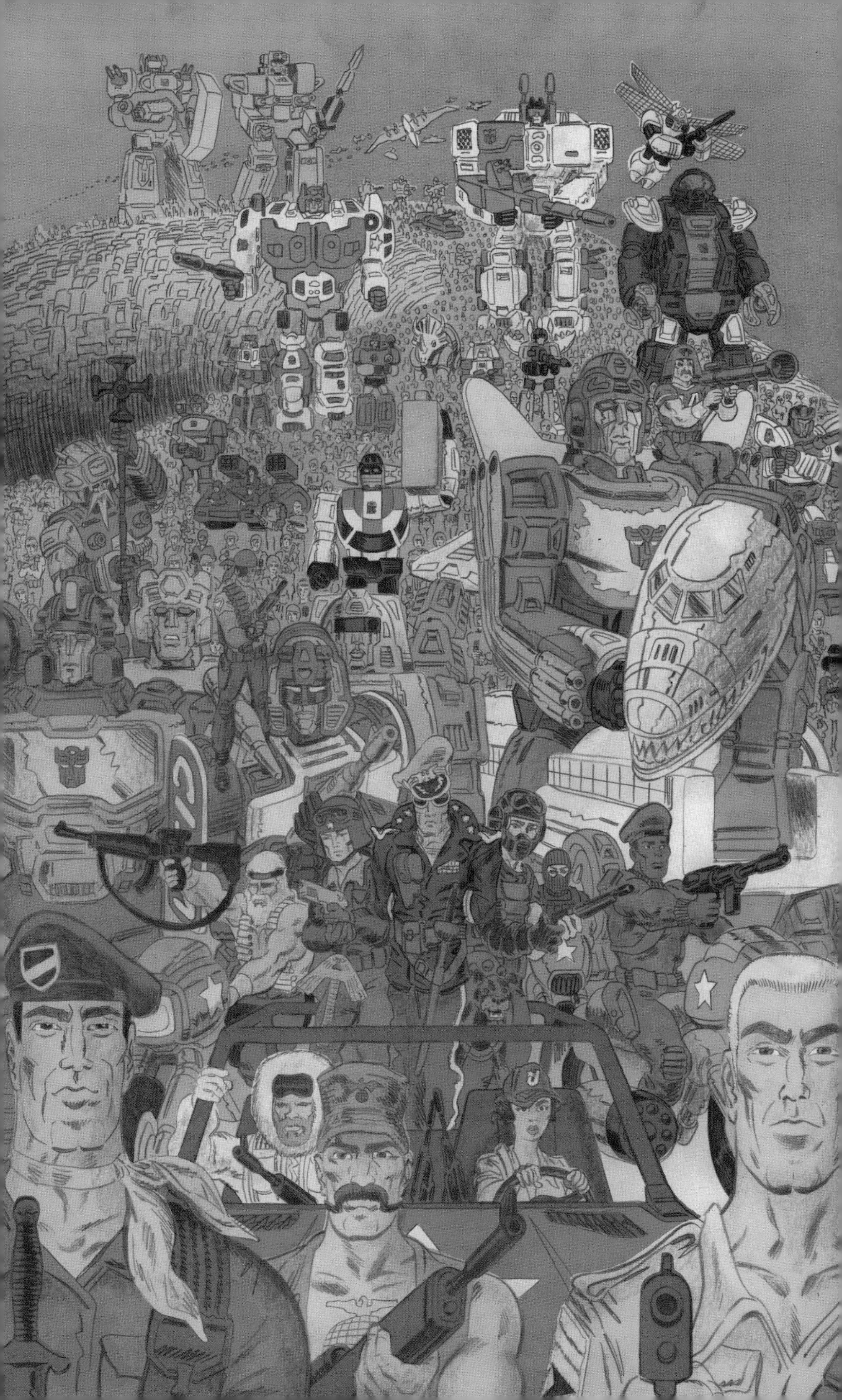

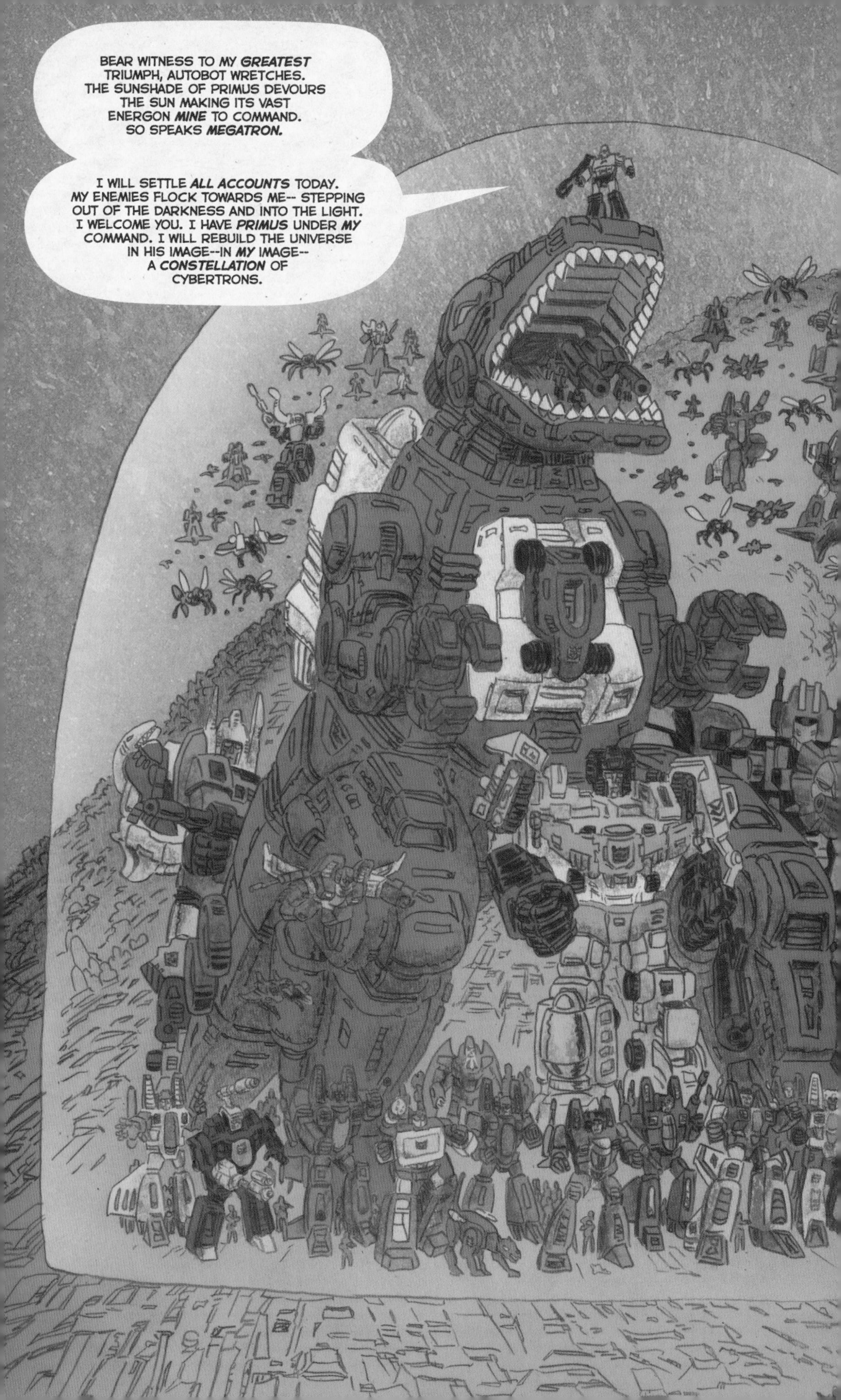

BEAR WITNESS TO MY *GREATEST* TRIUMPH, AUTOBOT WRETCHES. THE SUNSHADE OF PRIMUS DEVOURS THE SUN *MAKING* ITS VAST ENERGON *MINE* TO COMMAND. SO SPEAKS *MEGATRON.*
I WILL SETTLE *ALL ACCOUNTS* TODAY. MY ENEMIES FLOCK TOWARDS ME-- STEPPING OUT OF THE DARKNESS AND INTO THE LIGHT. I WELCOME YOU. I HAVE *PRIMUS* UNDER *MY* COMMAND. I WILL REBUILD THE UNIVERSE IN HIS IMAGE--IN *MY* IMAGE-- A *CONSTELLATION* OF CYBERTRONS.

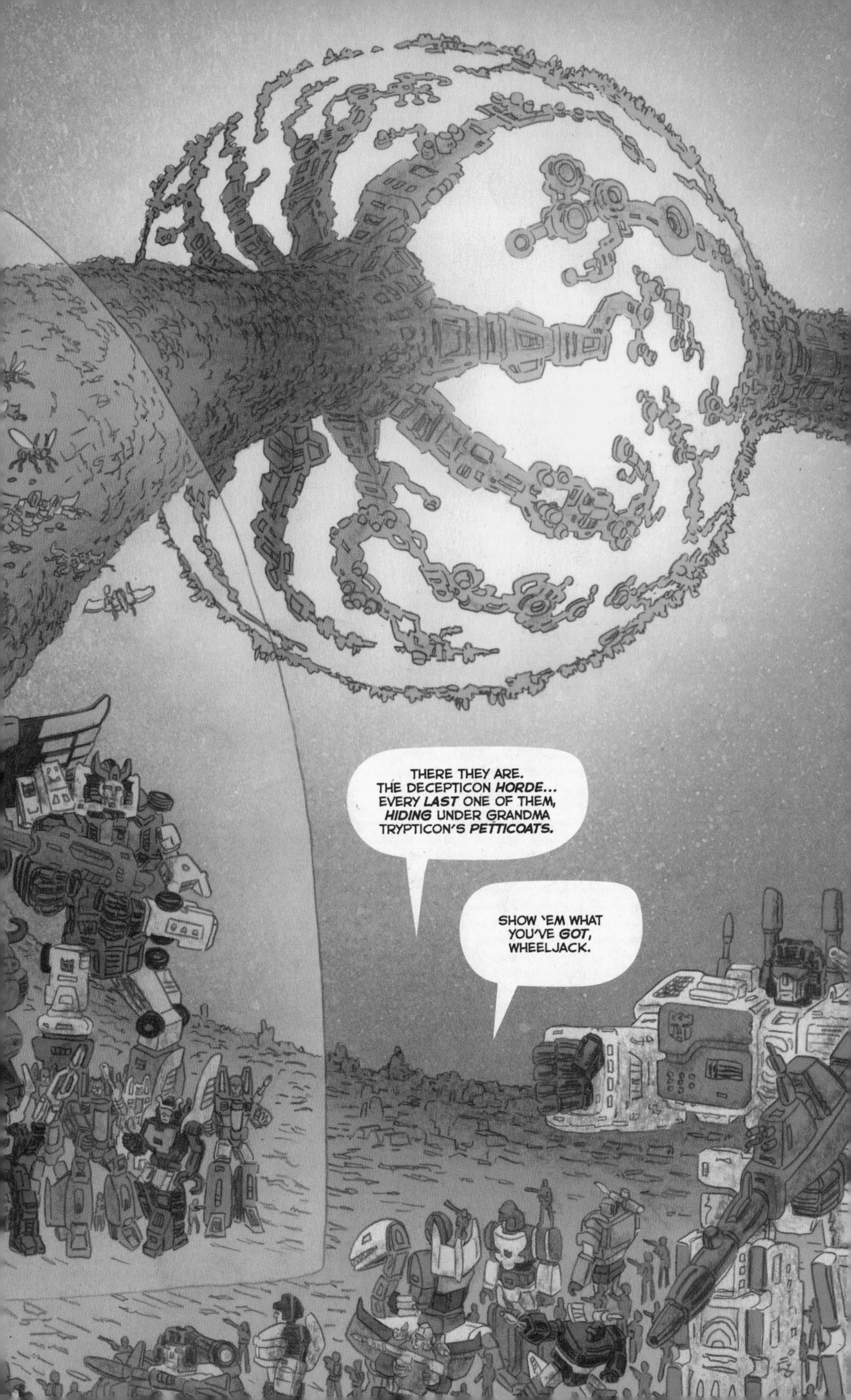
THERE THEY ARE. THE DECEPTICON HORDE... EVERY LAST ONE OF THEM, HIDING UNDER GRANDMA TRYPTICON'S PETTICOATS.
SHOW 'EM WHAT YOU'VE GOT, WHEELJACK.

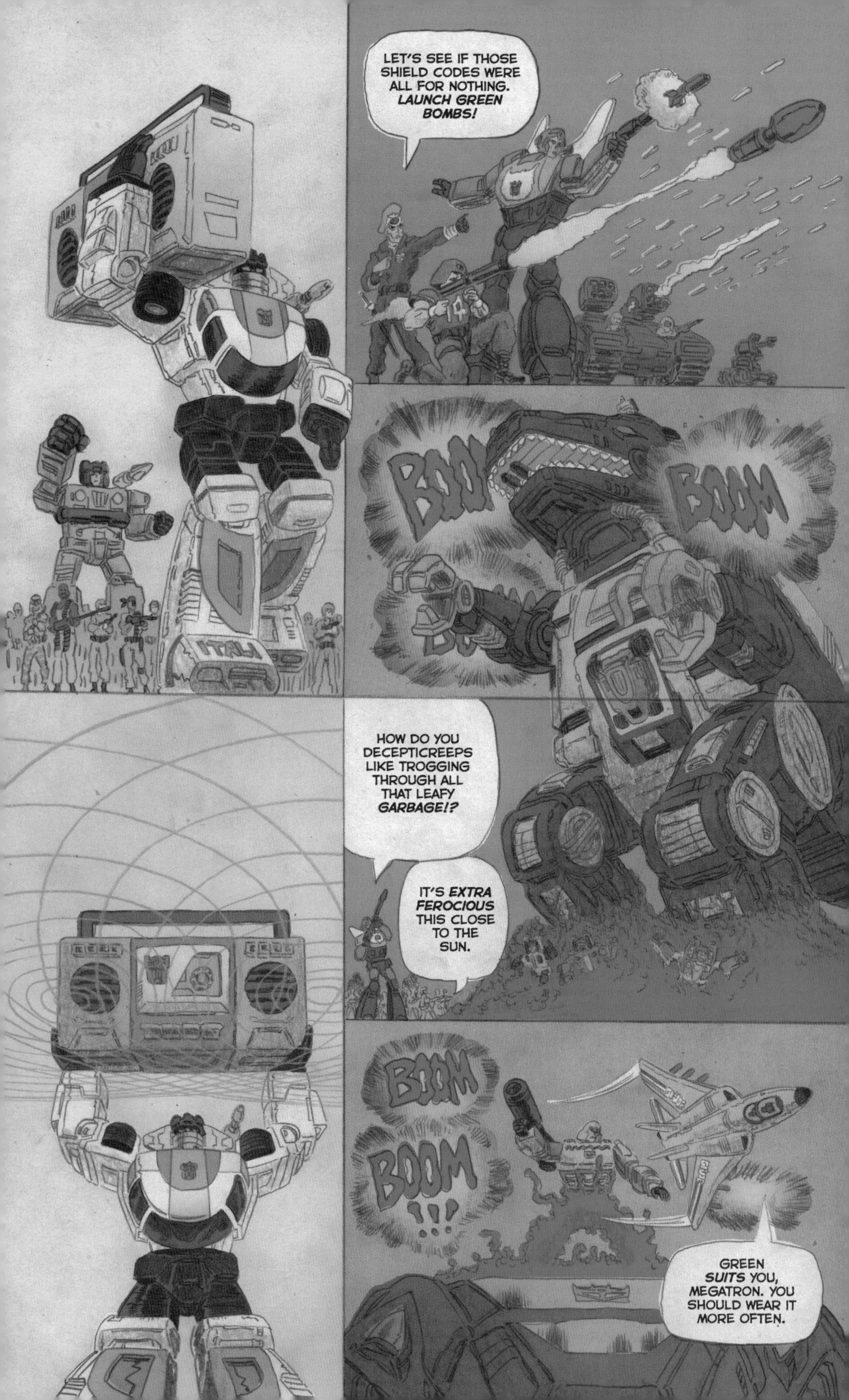
LET'S SEE IF THOSE SHIELD CODES WERE ALL FOR NOTHING. *LAUNCH GREEN BOMBS!*
14
BOOM
BOOM
ITALI
HOW DO YOU DECEPTICREEPS LIKE TROGGING THROUGH ALL THAT LEAFY *GARBAGE!?*
IT'S *EXTRA FEROCIOUS* THIS CLOSE TO THE SUN.
BOOM
BOOM
!!!
GREEN *SUITS* YOU, MEGATRON. YOU SHOULD WEAR IT MORE OFTEN.

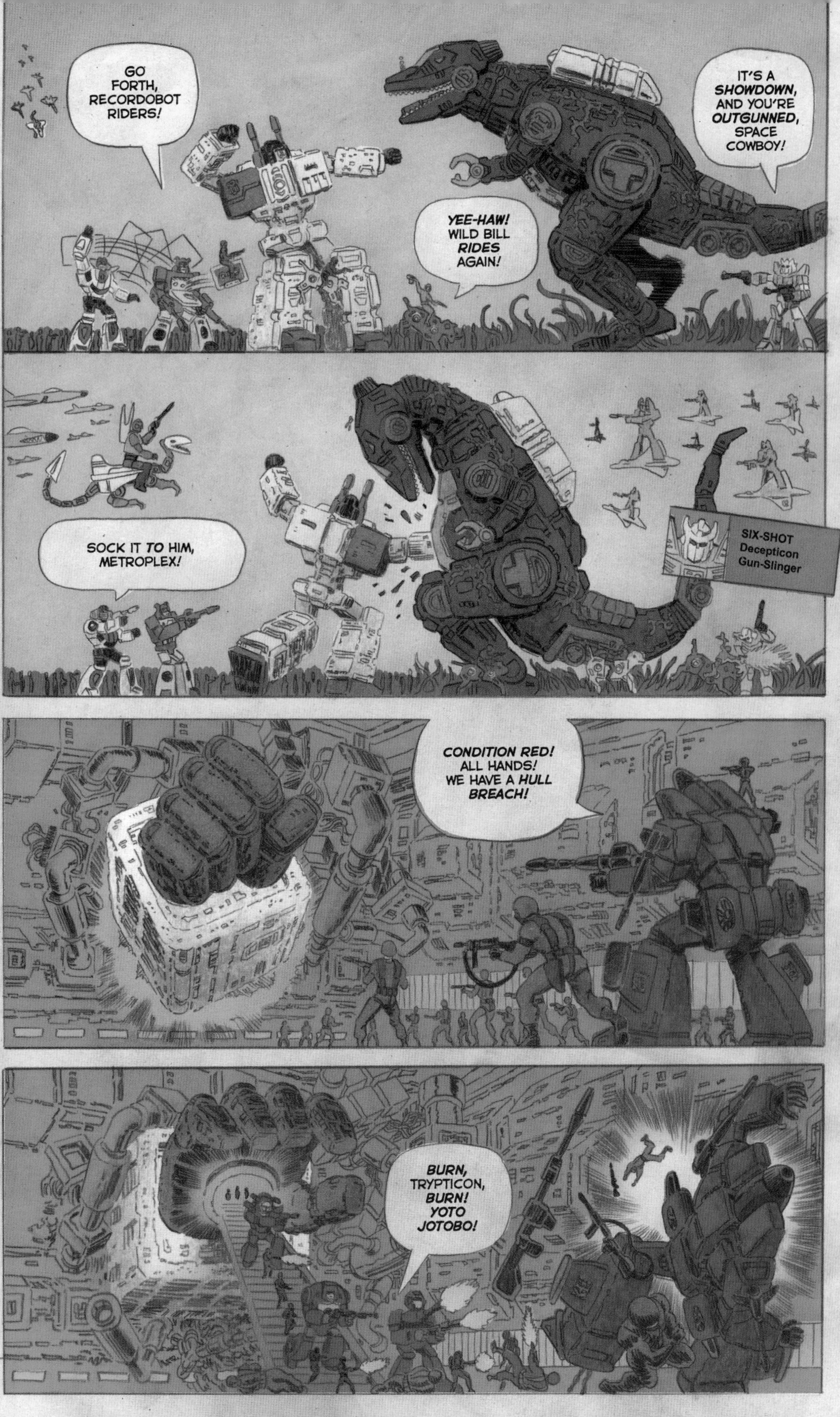
GO FORTH, RECORDOBOT RIDERS!
IT'S A SHOWDOWN, AND YOU'RE OUTGUNNED, SPACE COWBOY!
YEE-HAW! WILD BILL RIDES AGAIN!
SOCK IT TO HIM, METROPLEX!
SIX-SHOT Decepticon Gun-Slinger
CONDITION RED! ALL HANDS! WE HAVE A HULL BREACH!
BURN, TRYPTICON, BURN! YOTO JOTOBO!

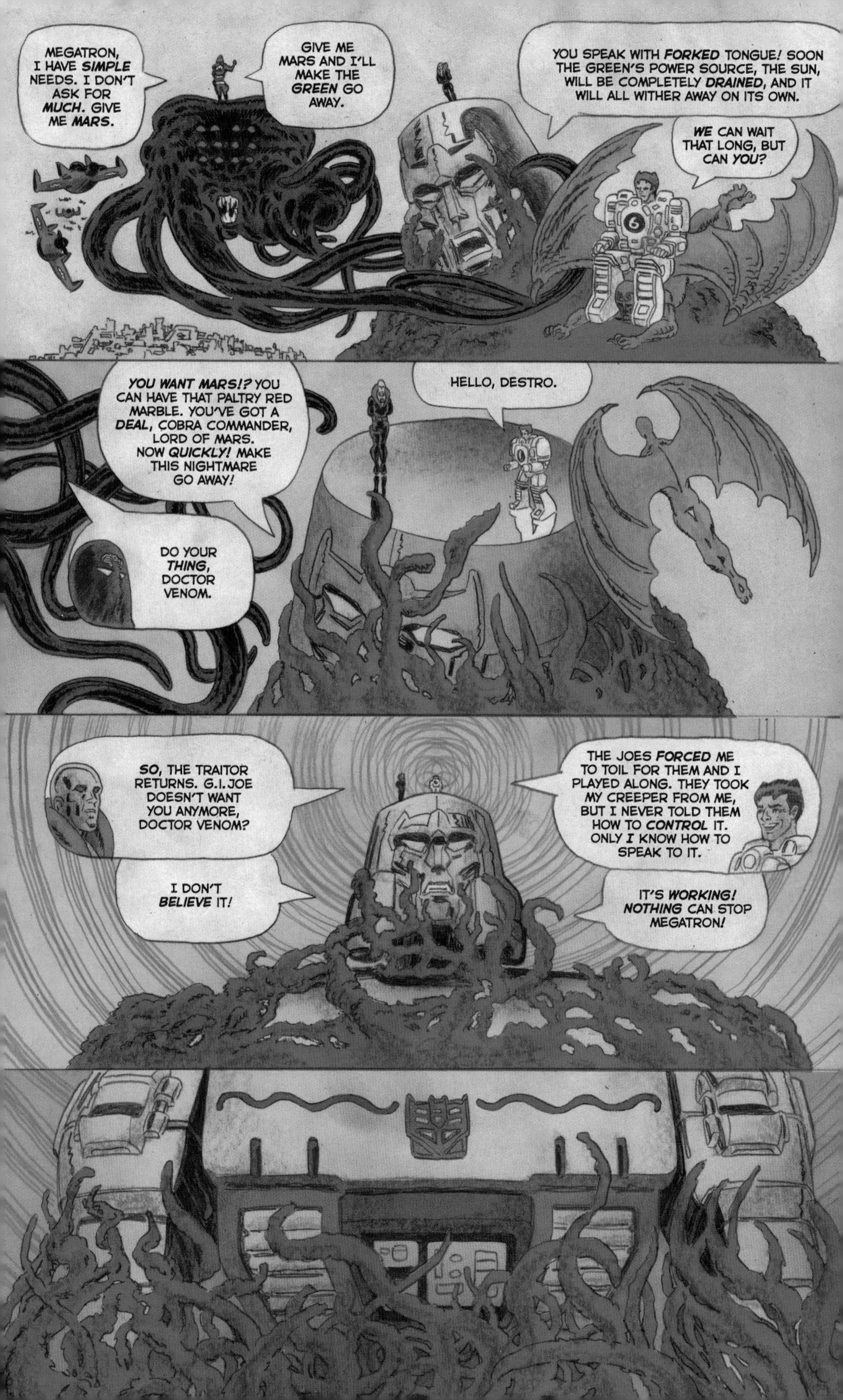
MEGATRON, I HAVE SIMPLE NEEDS. I DON'T ASK FOR MUCH. GIVE ME MARS.
GIVE ME MARS AND I'LL MAKE THE GREEN GO AWAY.
YOU SPEAK WITH FORKED TONGUE! SOON THE GREEN'S POWER SOURCE, THE SUN, WILL BE COMPLETELY DRAINED, AND IT WILL ALL WITHER AWAY ON ITS OWN.
WE CAN WAIT THAT LONG, BUT CAN YOU?
YOU WANT MARS!? YOU CAN HAVE THAT PALTRY RED MARBLE. YOU'VE GOT A DEAL, COBRA COMMANDER, LORD OF MARS. NOW QUICKLY! MAKE THIS NIGHTMARE GO AWAY!
HELLO, DESTRO.
DO YOUR THING, DOCTOR VENOM.
SO, THE TRAITOR RETURNS. G.I. JOE DOESN'T WANT YOU ANYMORE, DOCTOR VENOM?
THE JOES FORCED ME TO TOIL FOR THEM AND I PLAYED ALONG. THEY TOOK MY CREEPER FROM ME, BUT I NEVER TOLD THEM HOW TO CONTROL IT. ONLY I KNOW HOW TO SPEAK TO IT.
I DON'T BELIEVE IT!
IT'S WORKING! NOTHING CAN STOP MEGATRON!

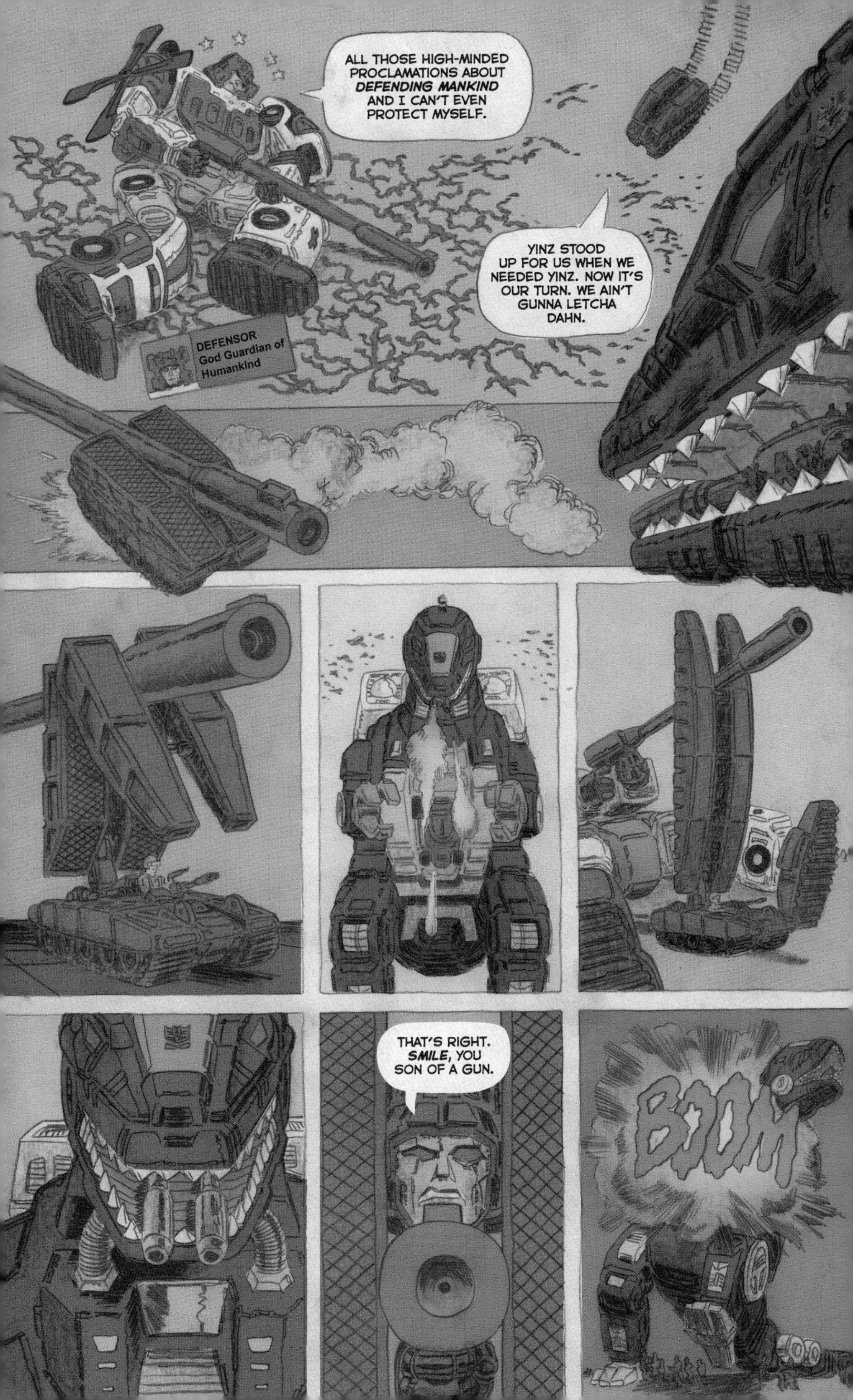
ALL THOSE HIGH-MINDED PROCLAMATIONS ABOUT ***DEFENDING MANKIND*** AND I CAN'T EVEN PROTECT MYSELF.
YINZ STOOD UP FOR US WHEN WE NEEDED YINZ. NOW IT'S OUR TURN. WE AIN'T GUNNA LETCHA DAHN.
DEFENSOR
God Guardian of Humankind
THAT'S RIGHT. ***SMILE***, YOU SON OF A GUN.
BOOM

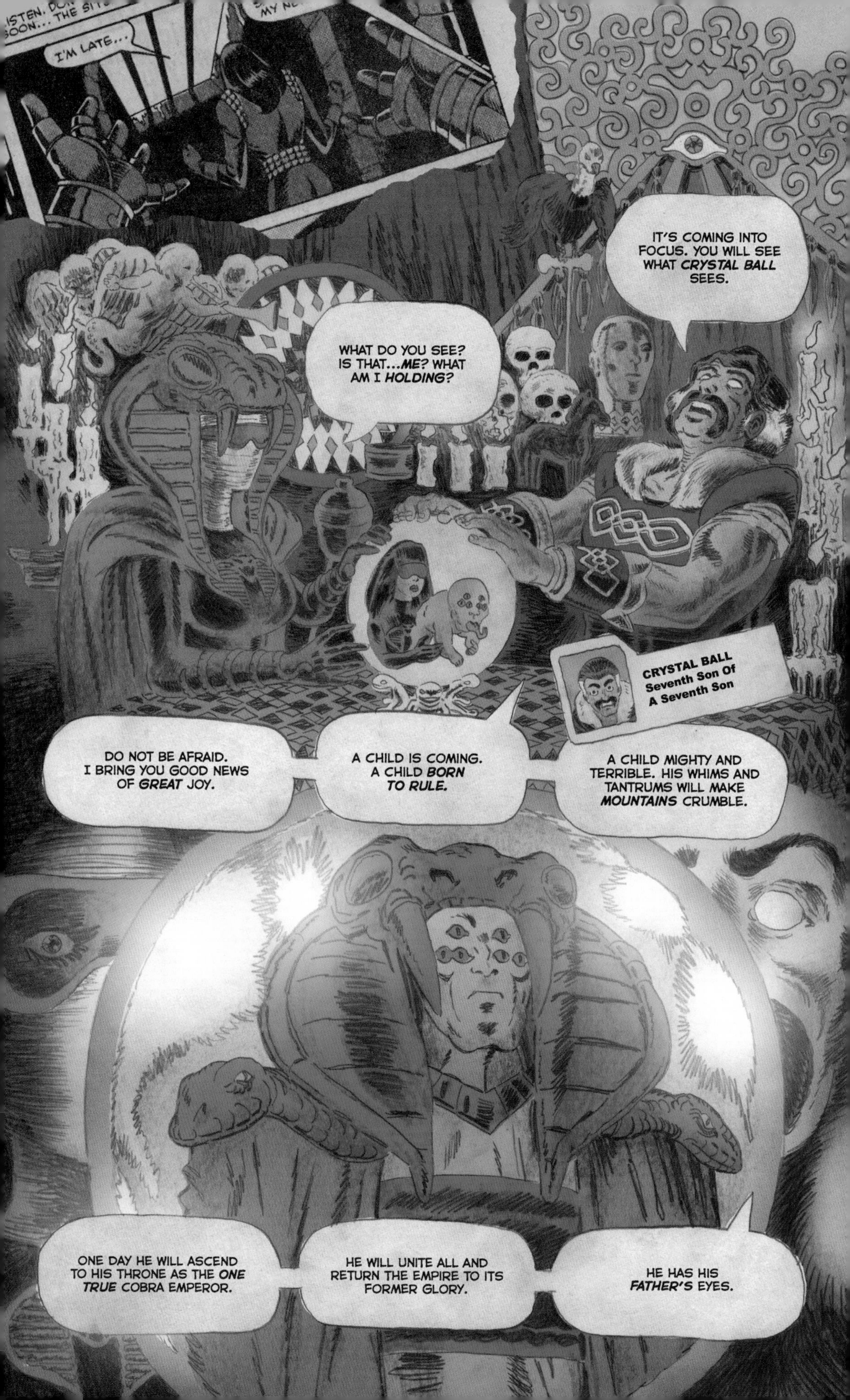
I'M LATE...
IT'S COMING INTO FOCUS. YOU WILL SEE WHAT CRYSTAL BALL SEES.
WHAT DO YOU SEE? IS THAT...ME? WHAT AM I HOLDING?
CRYSTAL BALL Seventh Son Of A Seventh Son
DO NOT BE AFRAID. I BRING YOU GOOD NEWS OF GREAT JOY.
A CHILD IS COMING. A CHILD BORN TO RULE.
A CHILD MIGHTY AND TERRIBLE. HIS WHIMS AND TANTRUMS WILL MAKE MOUNTAINS CRUMBLE.
ONE DAY HE WILL ASCEND TO HIS THRONE AS THE ONE TRUE COBRA EMPEROR.
HE WILL UNITE ALL AND RETURN THE EMPIRE TO ITS FORMER GLORY.
HE HAS HIS FATHER'S EYES.

ARTWORK BY TOM SCIOLI

CHAPTER 13

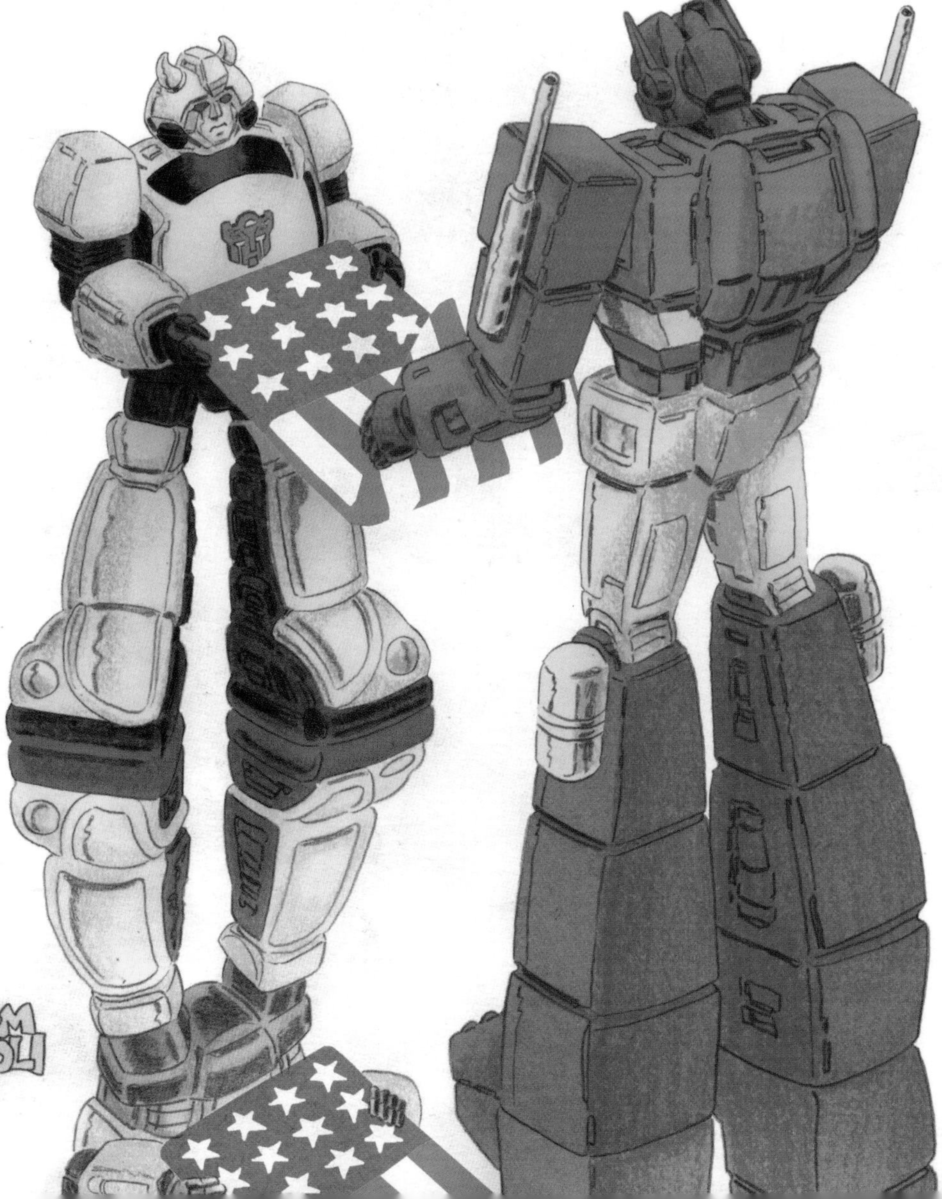
TOM SCIOLI

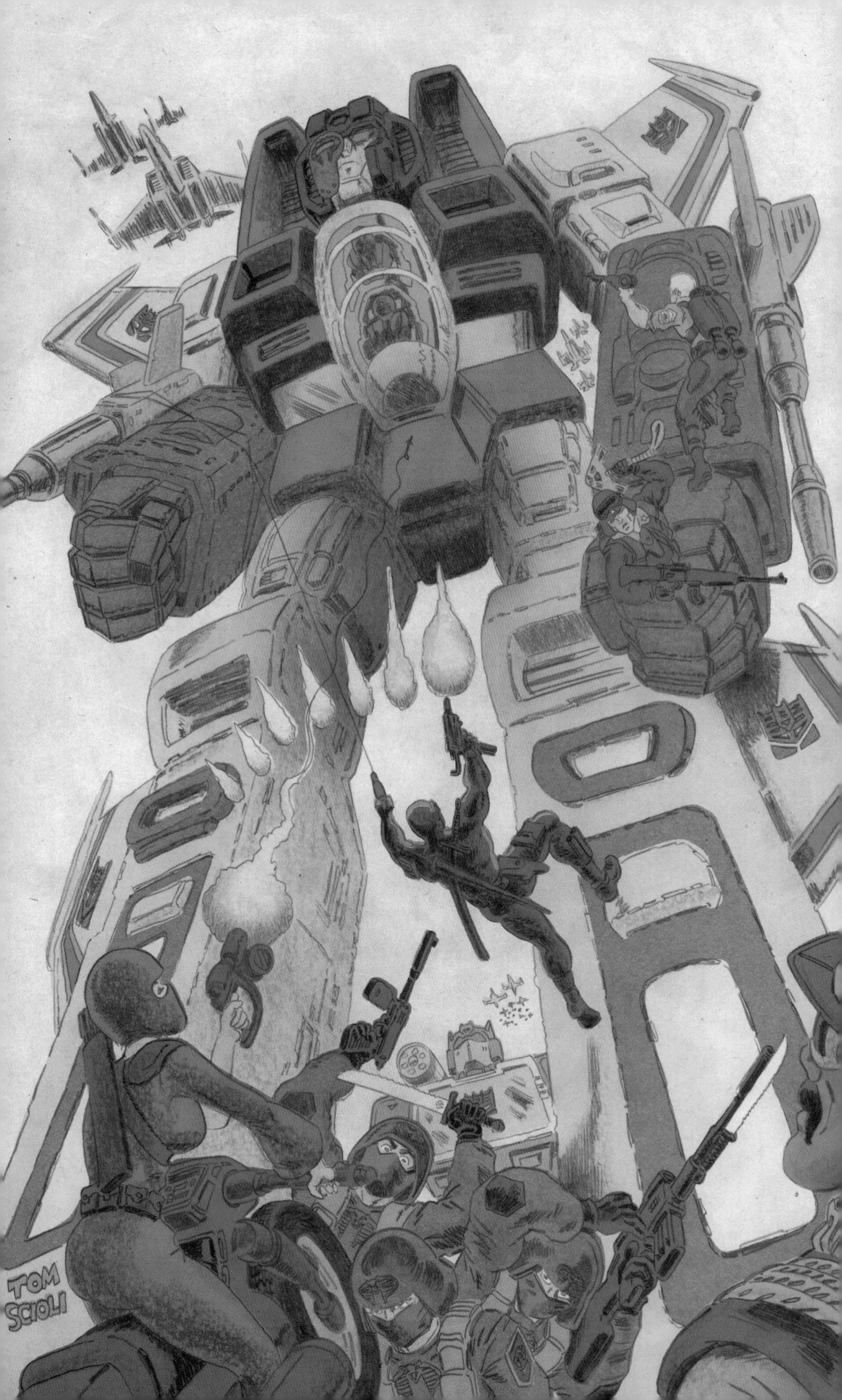
TOM
SCIOLI

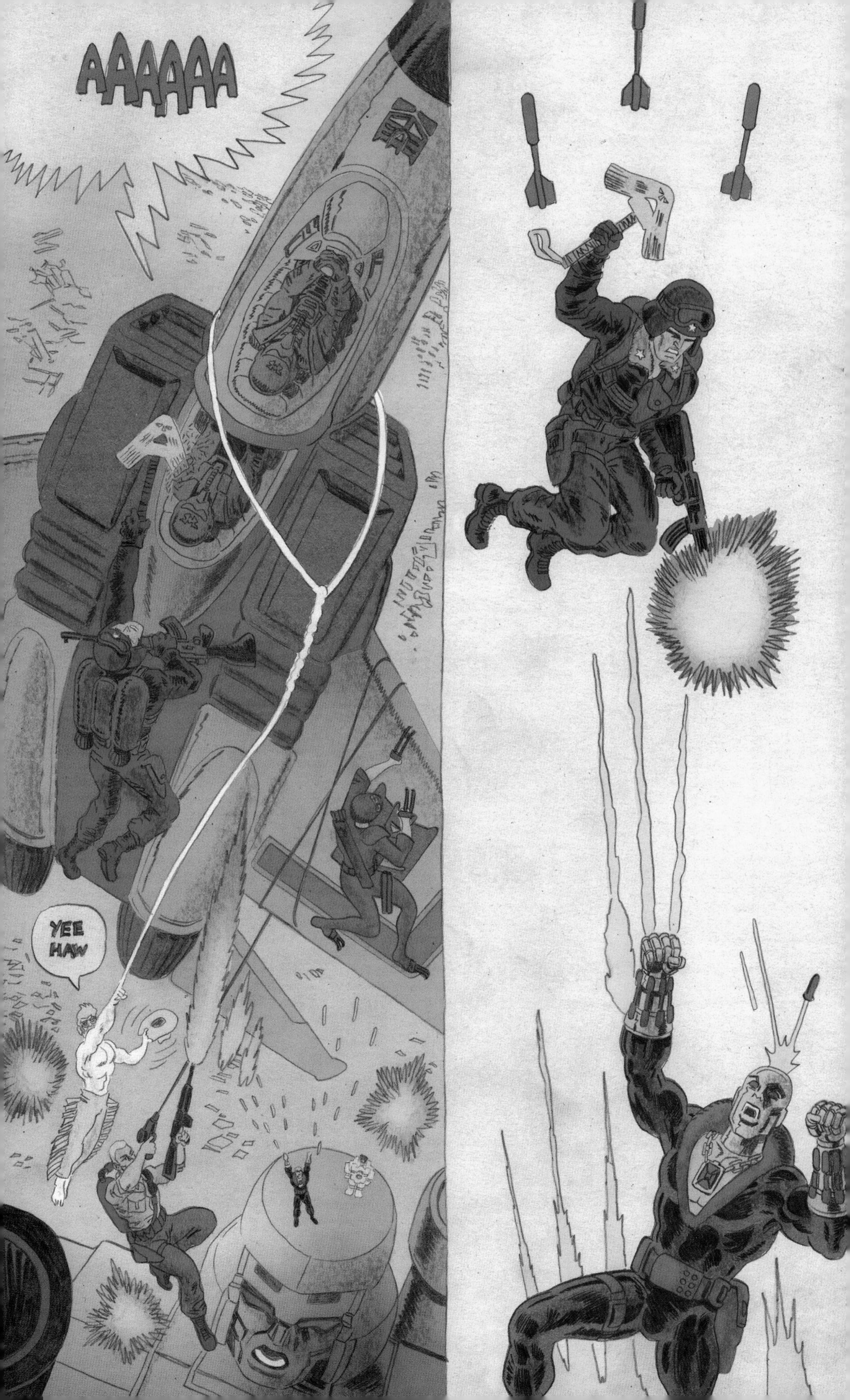
AAAAAA
YEE HAW

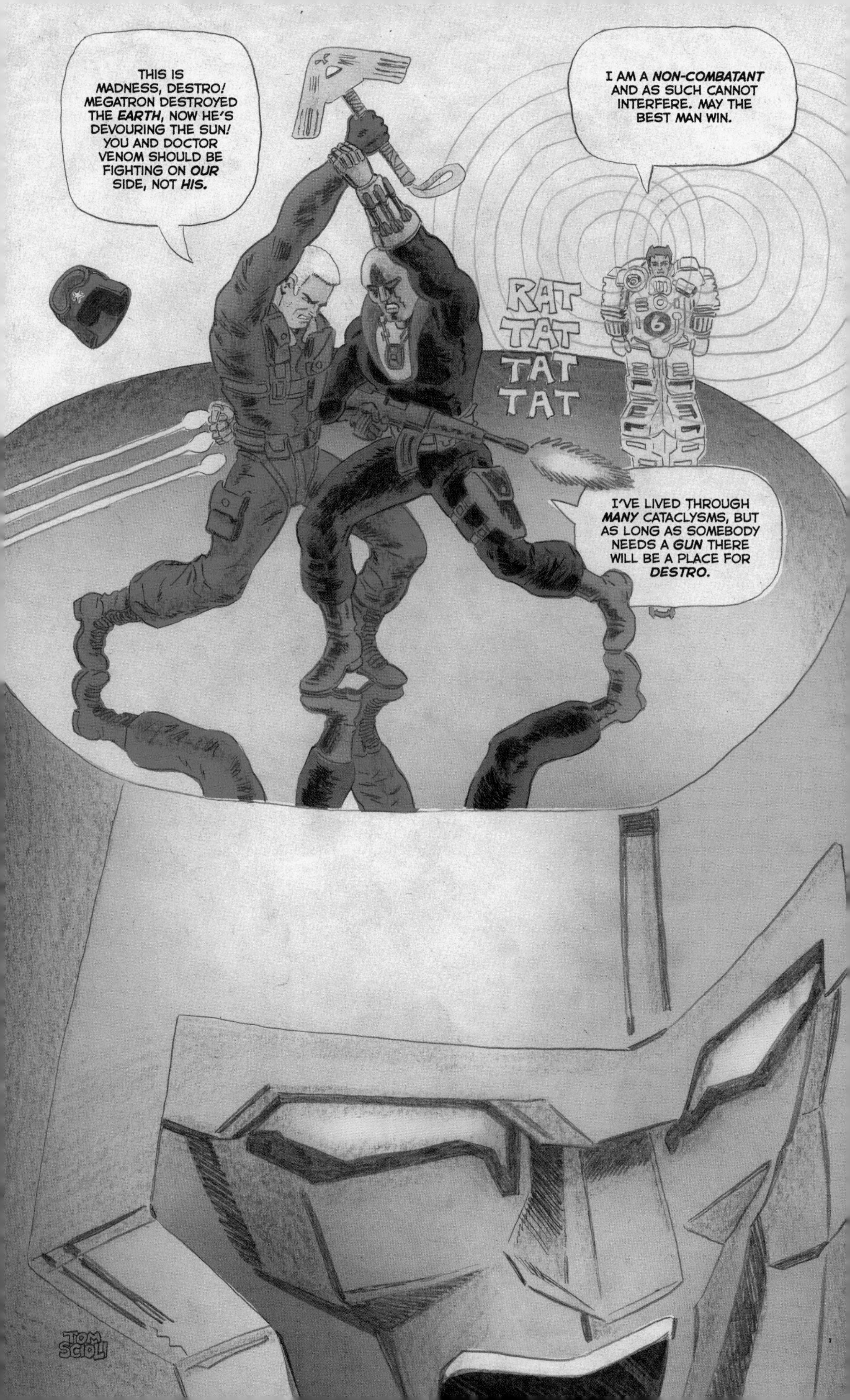
THIS IS MADNESS, DESTRO! MEGATRON DESTROYED THE EARTH, NOW HE'S DEVOURING THE SUN! YOU AND DOCTOR VENOM SHOULD BE FIGHTING ON OUR SIDE, NOT HIS.
I AM A NON-COMBATANT AND AS SUCH CANNOT INTERFERE. MAY THE BEST MAN WIN.
RAT TAT TAT TAT
I'VE LIVED THROUGH MANY CATACLYSMS, BUT AS LONG AS SOMEBODY NEEDS A GUN THERE WILL BE A PLACE FOR DESTRO.
TOM SCIOLI

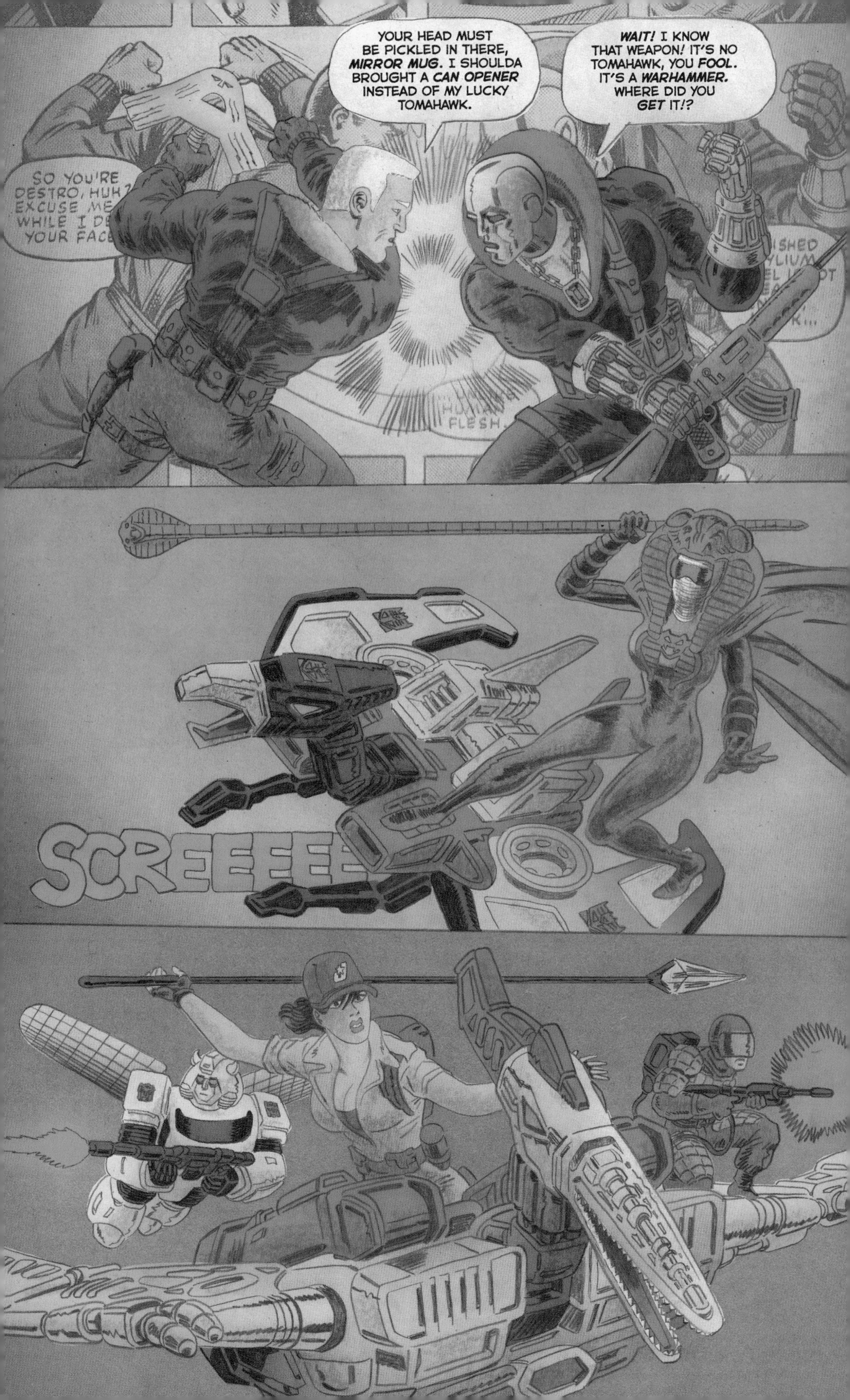
YOUR HEAD MUST BE PICKLED IN THERE, MIRROR MUG. I SHOULDA BROUGHT A CAN OPENER INSTEAD OF MY LUCKY TOMAHAWK.
WAIT! I KNOW THAT WEAPON! IT'S NO TOMAHAWK, YOU FOOL. IT'S A WARHAMMER. WHERE DID YOU GET IT!?
SCREEEEE

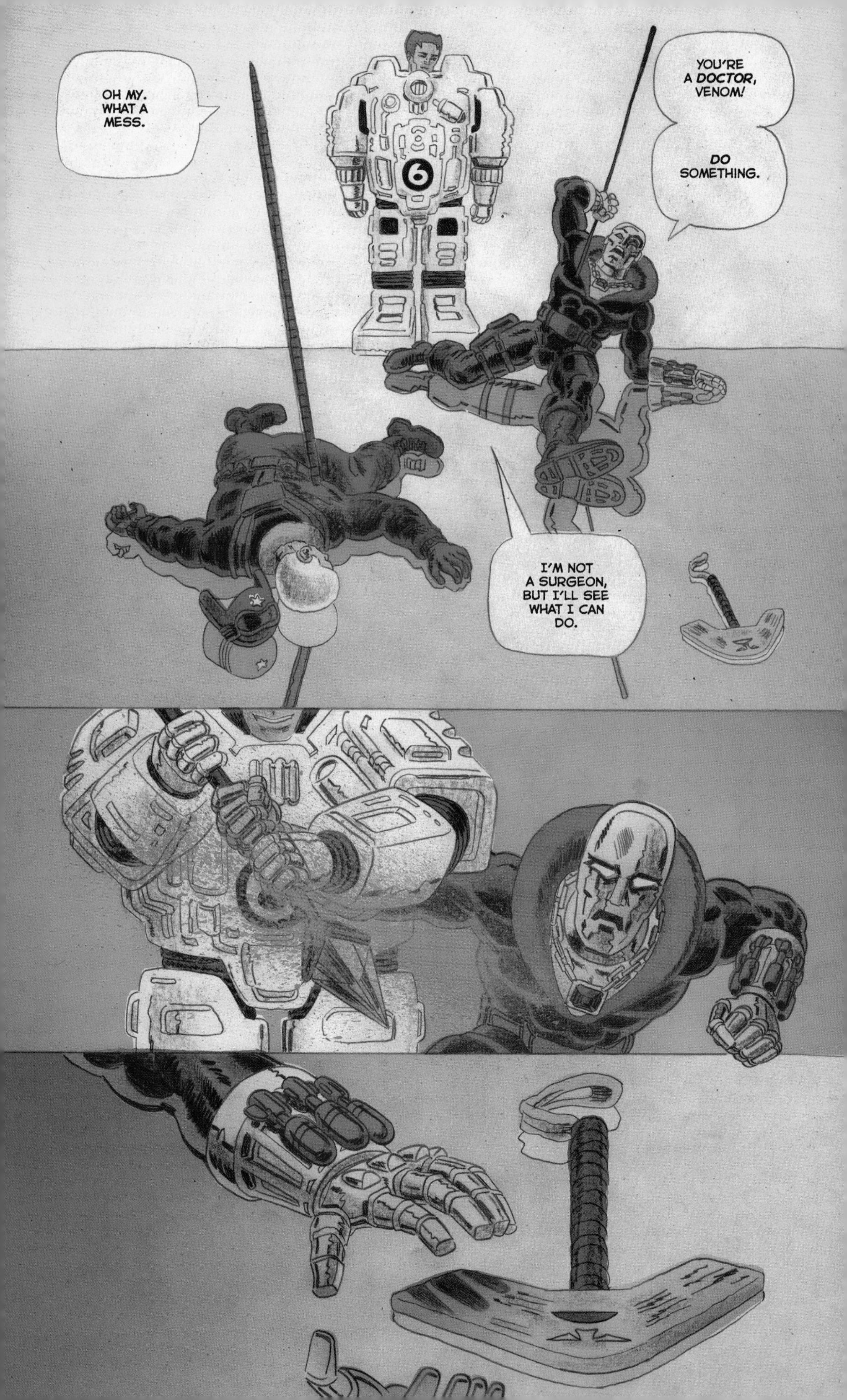
OH MY. WHAT A MESS.
YOU'RE A *DOCTOR*, VENOM!
DO SOMETHING.
I'M NOT A SURGEON, BUT I'LL SEE WHAT I CAN DO.

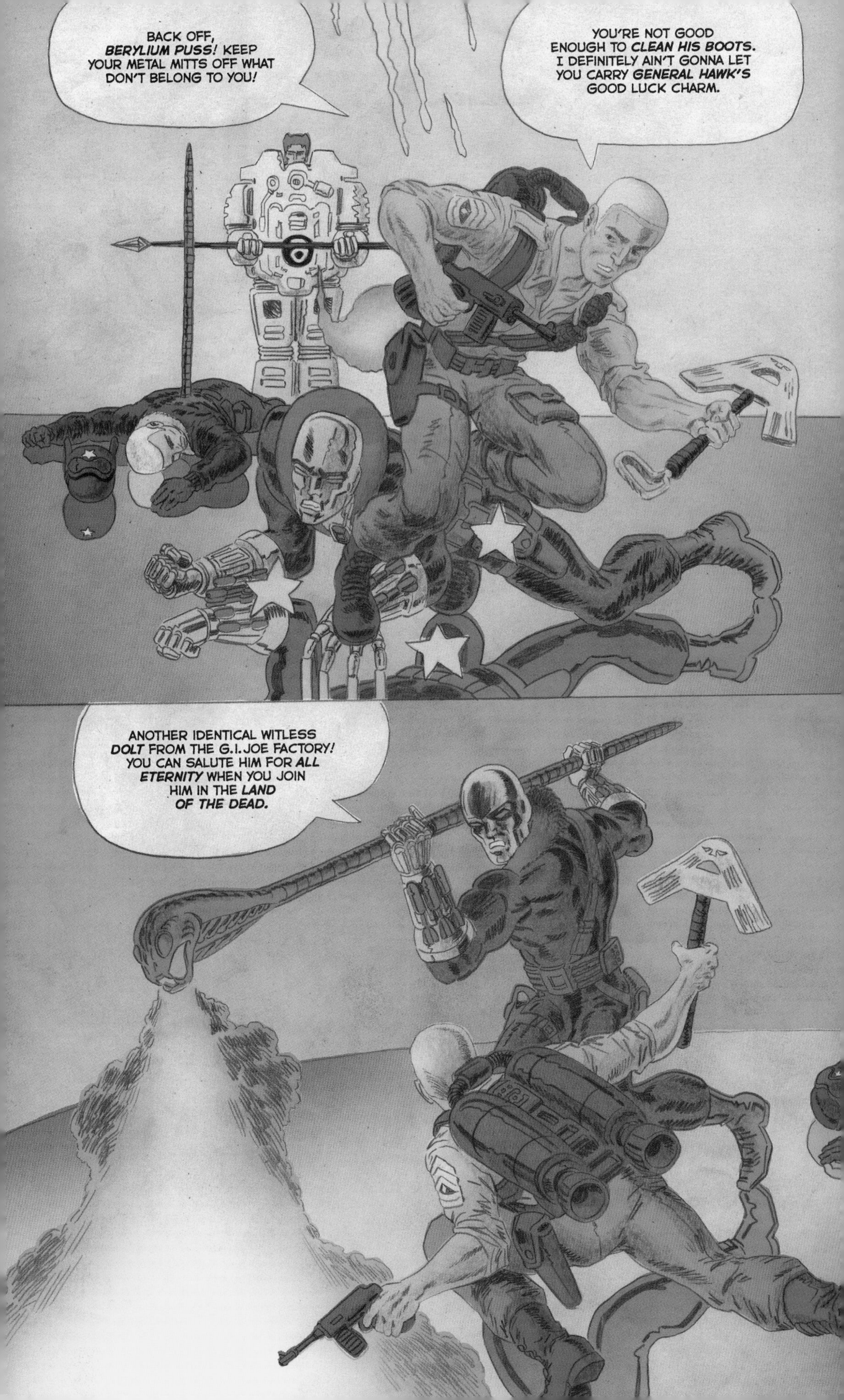
BACK OFF, *BERYLIUM PUSS!* KEEP YOUR METAL MITTS OFF WHAT DON'T BELONG TO YOU!
YOU'RE NOT GOOD ENOUGH TO *CLEAN HIS BOOTS.* I DEFINITELY AIN'T GONNA LET YOU CARRY *GENERAL HAWK'S* GOOD LUCK CHARM.
ANOTHER IDENTICAL WITLESS *DOLT* FROM THE G.I. JOE FACTORY! YOU CAN SALUTE HIM FOR *ALL ETERNITY* WHEN YOU JOIN HIM IN THE *LAND OF THE DEAD.*

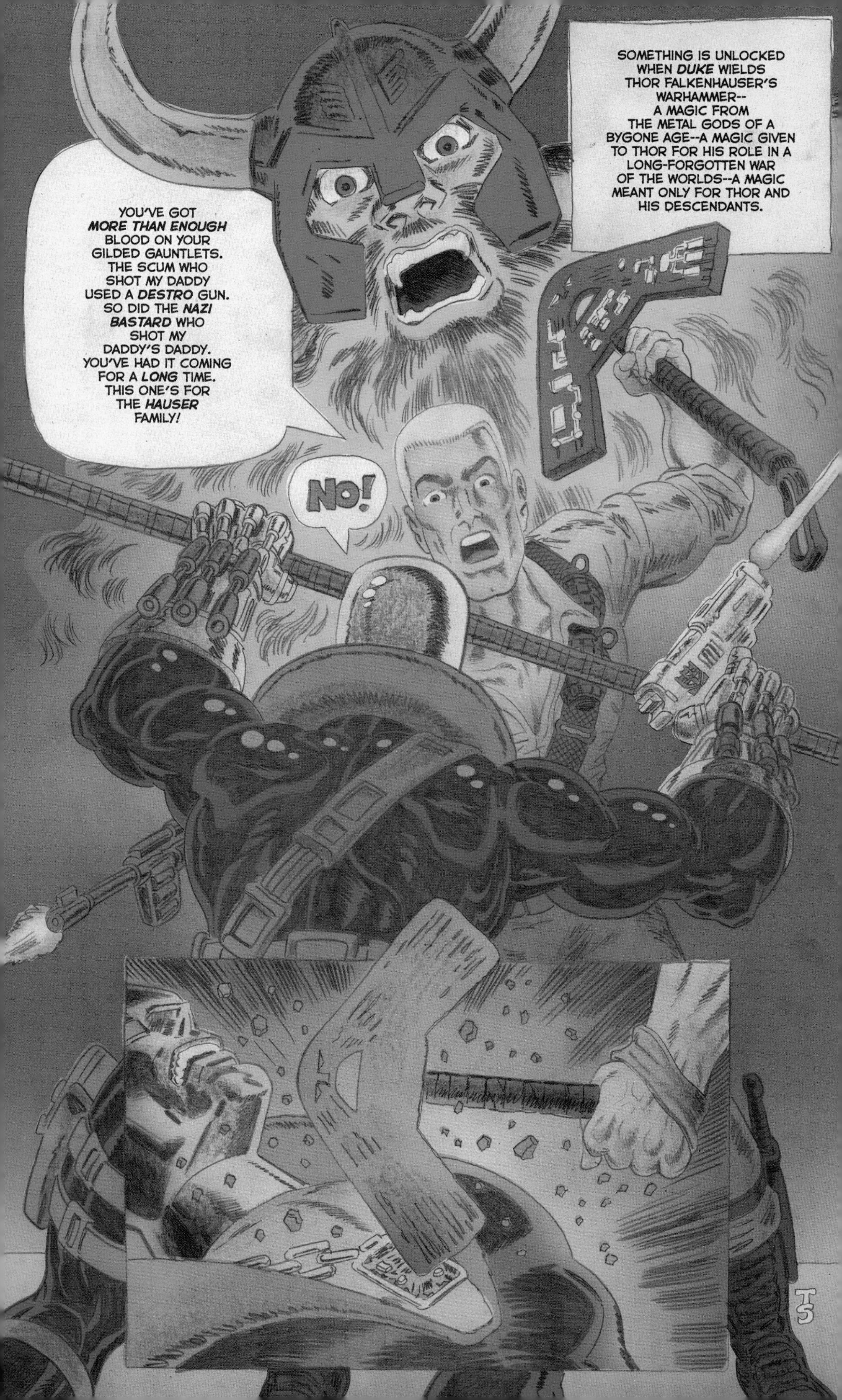

SOMETHING IS UNLOCKED WHEN *DUKE* WIELDS THOR FALKENHAUSER'S WARHAMMER-- A MAGIC FROM THE METAL GODS OF A BYGONE AGE--A MAGIC GIVEN TO THOR FOR HIS ROLE IN A LONG-FORGOTTEN WAR OF THE WORLDS--A MAGIC MEANT ONLY FOR THOR AND HIS DESCENDANTS.
YOU'VE GOT ***MORE THAN ENOUGH*** BLOOD ON YOUR GILDED GAUNTLETS. THE SCUM WHO SHOT MY DADDY USED A *DESTRO* GUN. SO DID THE ***NAZI BASTARD*** WHO SHOT MY DADDY'S DADDY. YOU'VE HAD IT COMING FOR A *LONG* TIME. THIS ONE'S FOR THE *HAUSER* FAMILY!
NO!

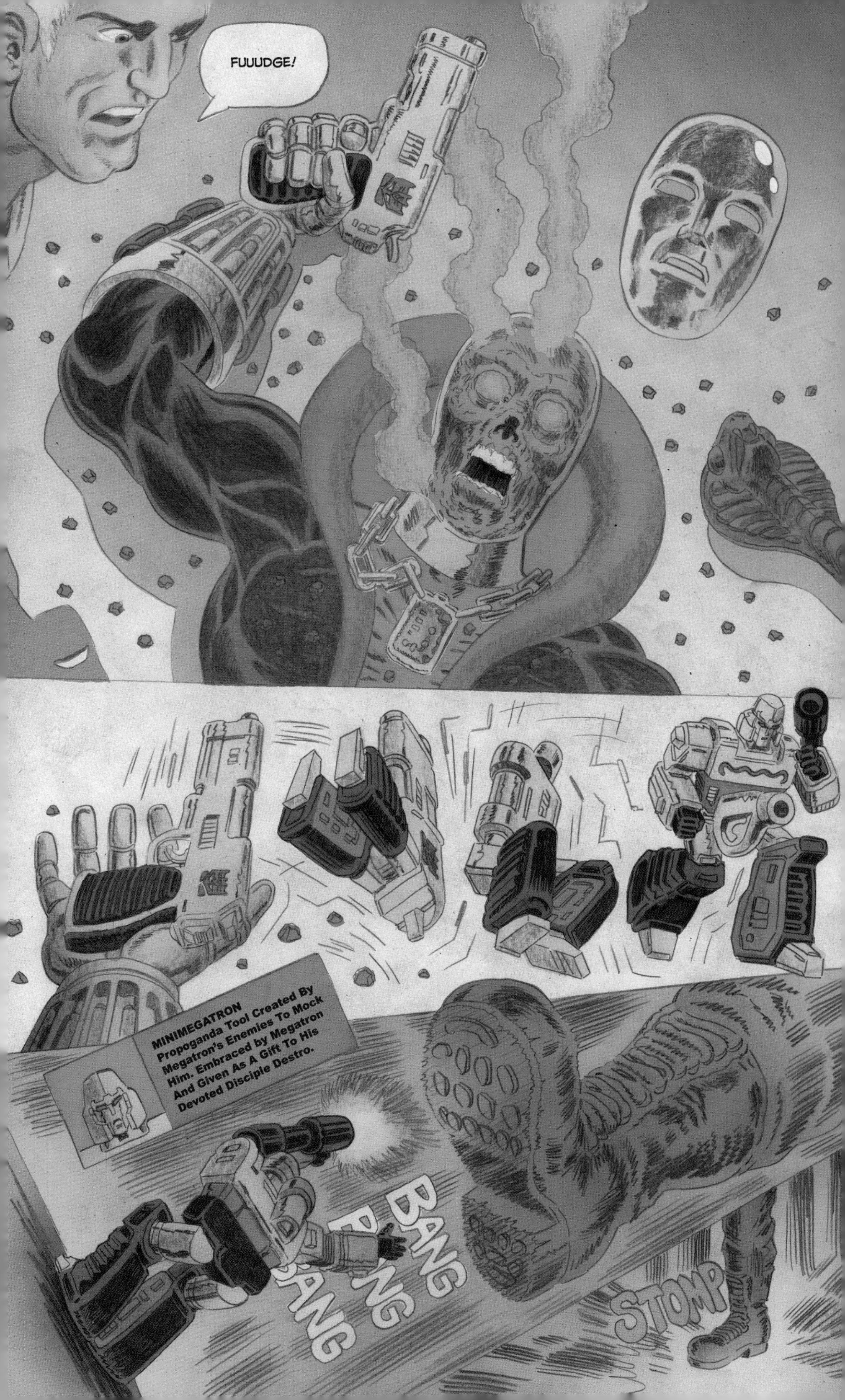
FUUUDGE!
MINIMEGATRON
Propoganda Tool Created By Megatron's Enemies To Mock Him. Embraced by Megatron And Given As A Gift To His Devoted Disciple Destro.
BANG
BANG
BANG
STOMP

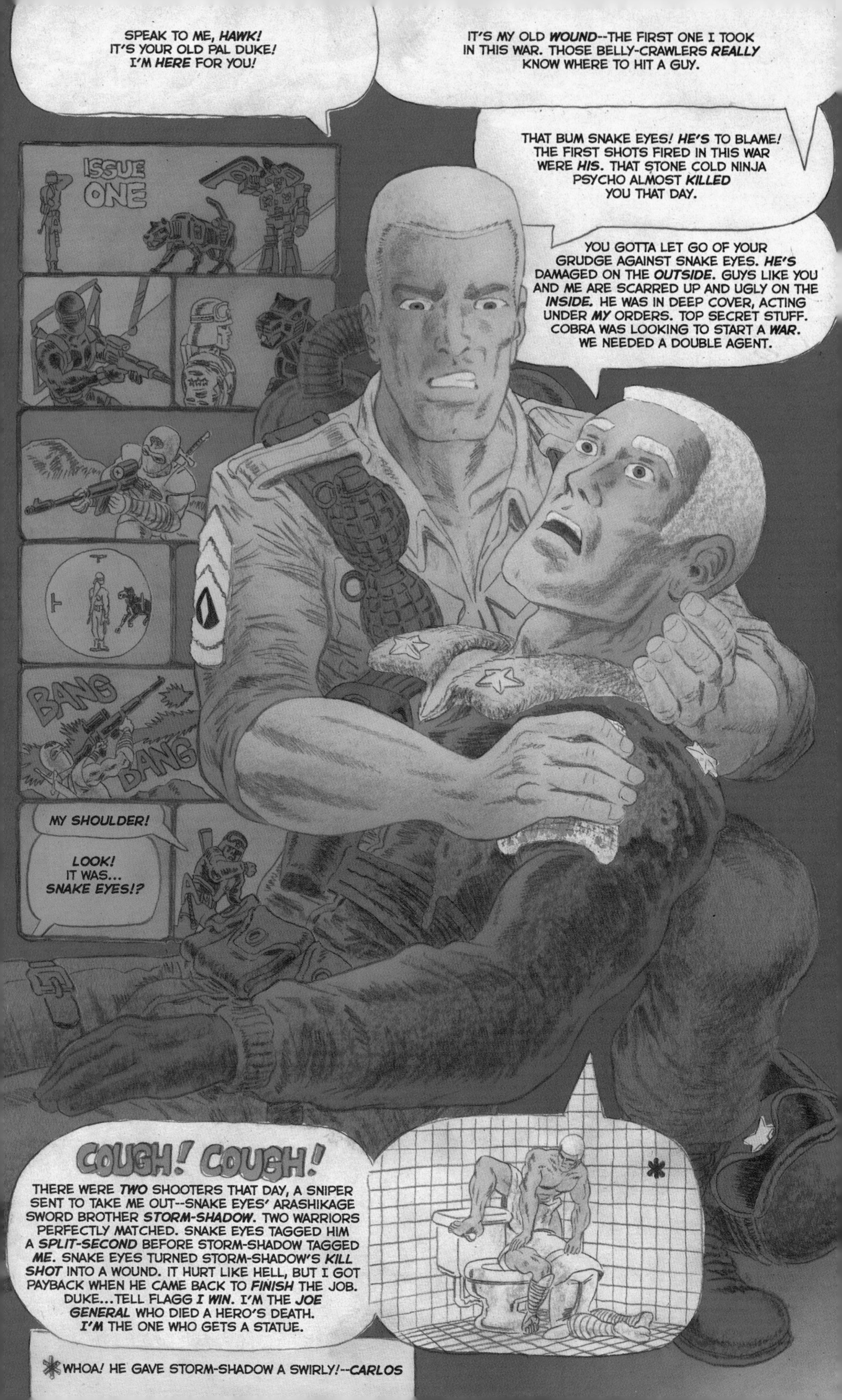

SPEAK TO ME, HAWK! IT'S YOUR OLD PAL DUKE! I'M HERE FOR YOU!
IT'S MY OLD WOUND--THE FIRST ONE I TOOK IN THIS WAR. THOSE BELLY-CRAWLERS REALLY KNOW WHERE TO HIT A GUY.
THAT BUM SNAKE EYES! HE'S TO BLAME! THE FIRST SHOTS FIRED IN THIS WAR WERE HIS. THAT STONE COLD NINJA PSYCHO ALMOST KILLED YOU THAT DAY.
YOU GOTTA LET GO OF YOUR GRUDGE AGAINST SNAKE EYES. HE'S DAMAGED ON THE OUTSIDE. GUYS LIKE YOU AND ME ARE SCARRED UP AND UGLY ON THE INSIDE. HE WAS IN DEEP COVER, ACTING UNDER MY ORDERS. TOP SECRET STUFF. COBRA WAS LOOKING TO START A WAR. WE NEEDED A DOUBLE AGENT.
ISSUE ONE
BANG
BANG
MY SHOULDER!
LOOK! IT WAS... SNAKE EYES!?
COUGH! COUGH!
THERE WERE TWO SHOOTERS THAT DAY, A SNIPER SENT TO TAKE ME OUT--SNAKE EYES' ARASHIKAGE SWORD BROTHER STORM-SHADOW. TWO WARRIORS PERFECTLY MATCHED. SNAKE EYES TAGGED HIM A SPLIT-SECOND BEFORE STORM-SHADOW TAGGED ME. SNAKE EYES TURNED STORM-SHADOW'S KILL SHOT INTO A WOUND. IT HURT LIKE HELL, BUT I GOT PAYBACK WHEN HE CAME BACK TO FINISH THE JOB. DUKE...TELL FLAGG I WIN. I'M THE JOE GENERAL WHO DIED A HERO'S DEATH. I'M THE ONE WHO GETS A STATUE.
*
* WHOA! HE GAVE STORM-SHADOW A SWIRLY!--CARLOS

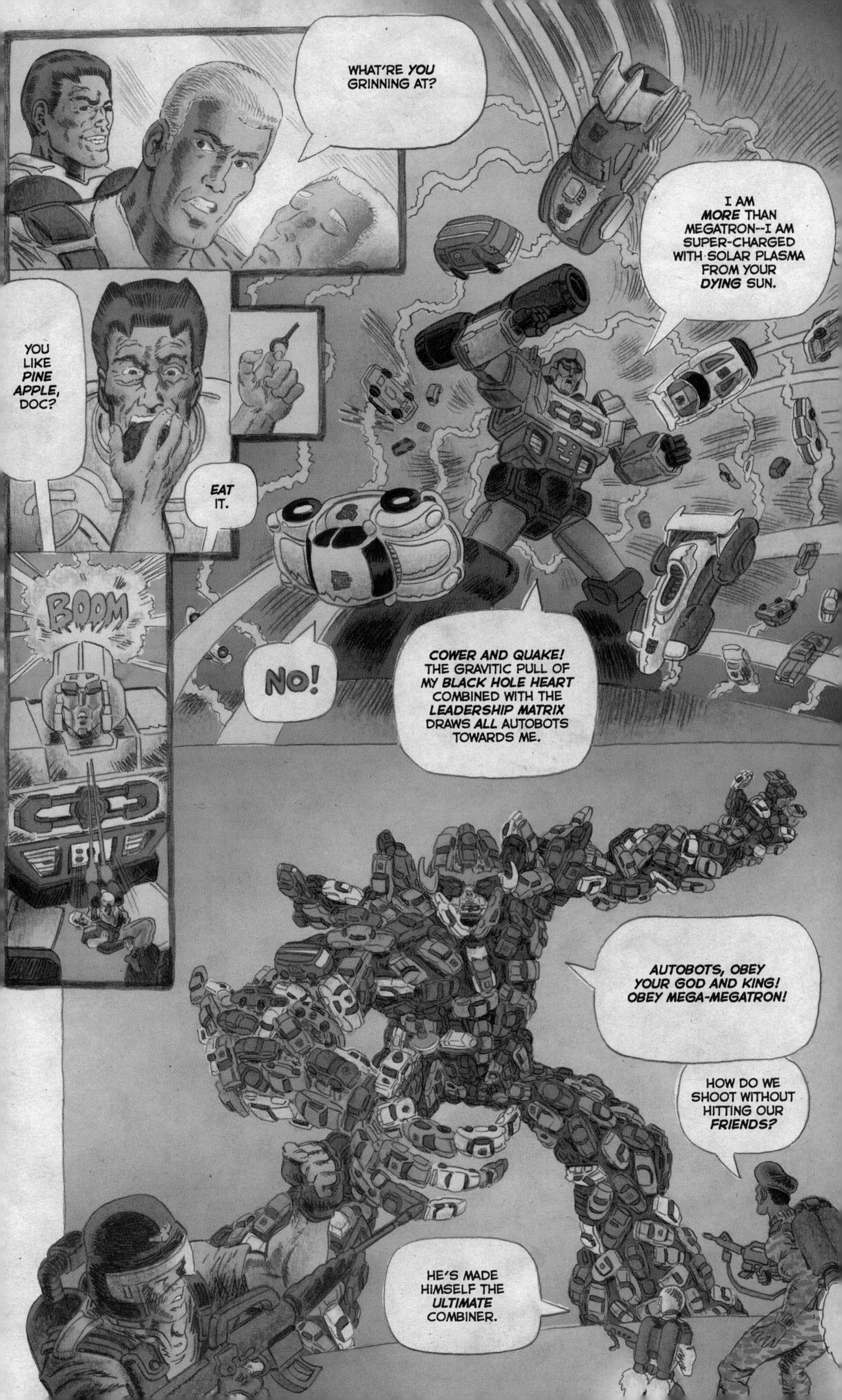
WHAT'RE YOU GRINNING AT?
YOU LIKE PINE APPLE, DOC?
EAT IT.
BOOM
I AM MORE THAN MEGATRON--I AM SUPER-CHARGED WITH SOLAR PLASMA FROM YOUR DYING SUN.
COWER AND QUAKE! THE GRAVITIC PULL OF MY BLACK HOLE HEART COMBINED WITH THE LEADERSHIP MATRIX DRAWS ALL AUTOBOTS TOWARDS ME.
NO!
AUTOBOTS, OBEY YOUR GOD AND KING! OBEY MEGA-MEGATRON!
HOW DO WE SHOOT WITHOUT HITTING OUR FRIENDS?
HE'S MADE HIMSELF THE ULTIMATE COMBINER.

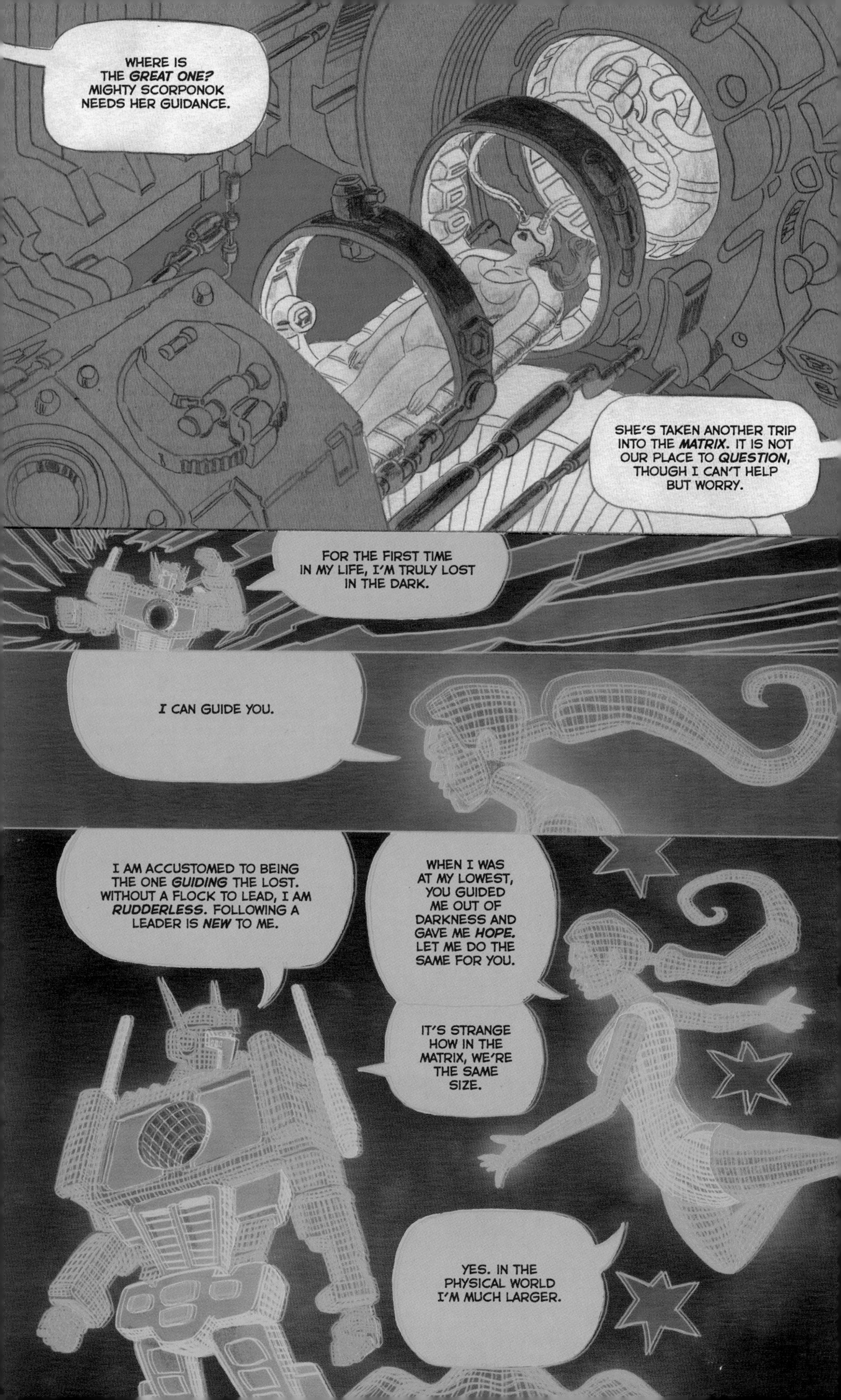

WHERE IS THE *GREAT ONE?* MIGHTY SCORPONOK NEEDS HER GUIDANCE.
SHE'S TAKEN ANOTHER TRIP INTO THE *MATRIX*. IT IS NOT OUR PLACE TO *QUESTION*, THOUGH I CAN'T HELP BUT WORRY.
FOR THE FIRST TIME IN MY LIFE, I'M TRULY LOST IN THE DARK.
I CAN GUIDE *YOU*.
I AM ACCUSTOMED TO BEING THE ONE *GUIDING* THE LOST. WITHOUT A FLOCK TO LEAD, I AM *RUDDERLESS*. FOLLOWING A LEADER IS *NEW* TO ME.
WHEN I WAS AT MY LOWEST, YOU GUIDED ME OUT OF DARKNESS AND GAVE ME *HOPE*. LET ME DO THE SAME FOR YOU.
IT'S STRANGE HOW IN THE MATRIX, WE'RE THE SAME SIZE.
YES. IN THE PHYSICAL WORLD I'M MUCH LARGER.

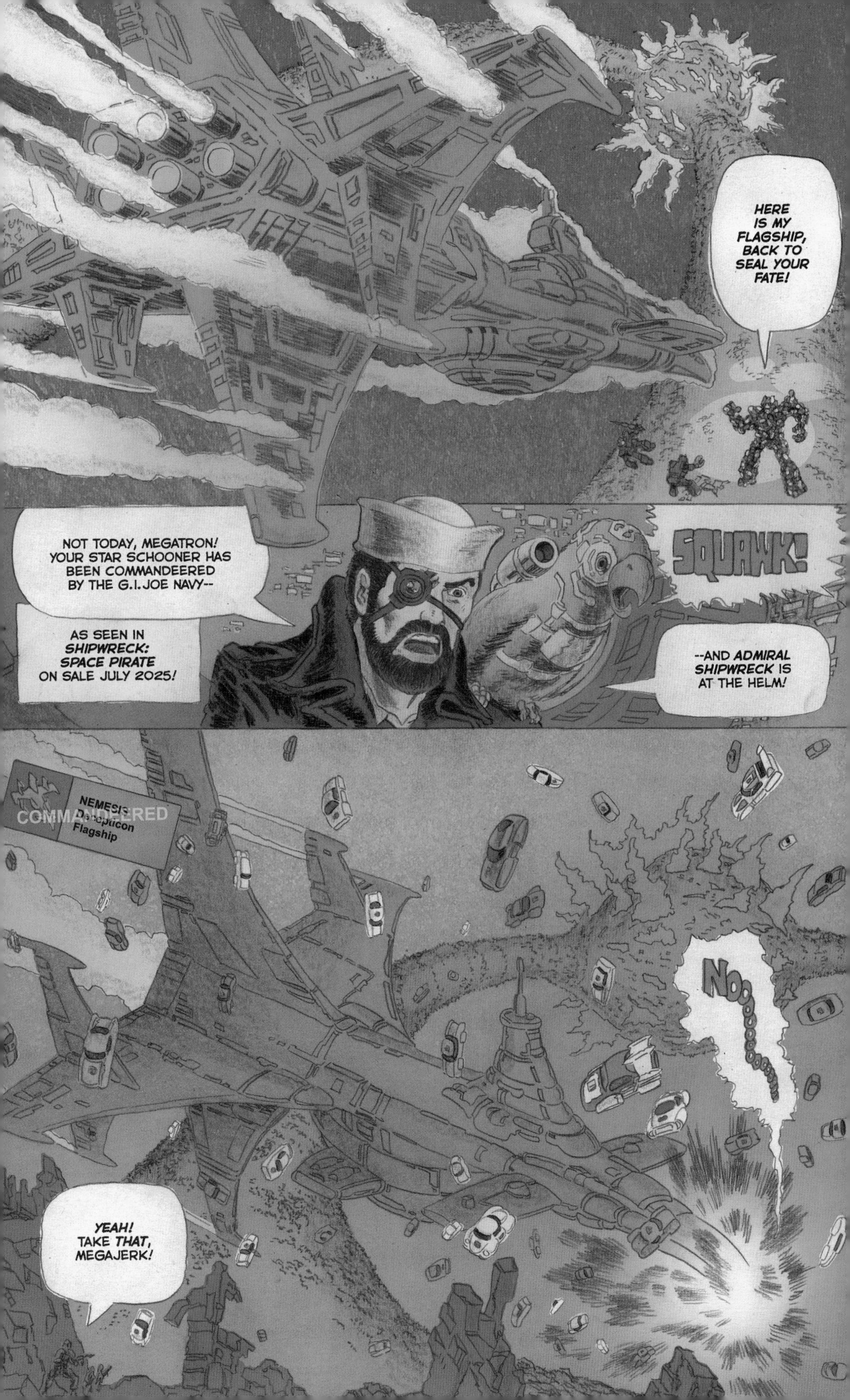
HERE IS MY FLAGSHIP, BACK TO SEAL YOUR FATE!
NOT TODAY, MEGATRON! YOUR STAR SCHOONER HAS BEEN COMMANDEERED BY THE G.I.JOE NAVY--
AS SEEN IN *SHIPWRECK: SPACE PIRATE* ON SALE JULY 2025!
SQUAWK!
--AND *ADMIRAL SHIPWRECK* IS AT THE HELM!
NEMESIS
COMMANDEERED
Flagship
YEAH! TAKE *THAT,* MEGAJERK!

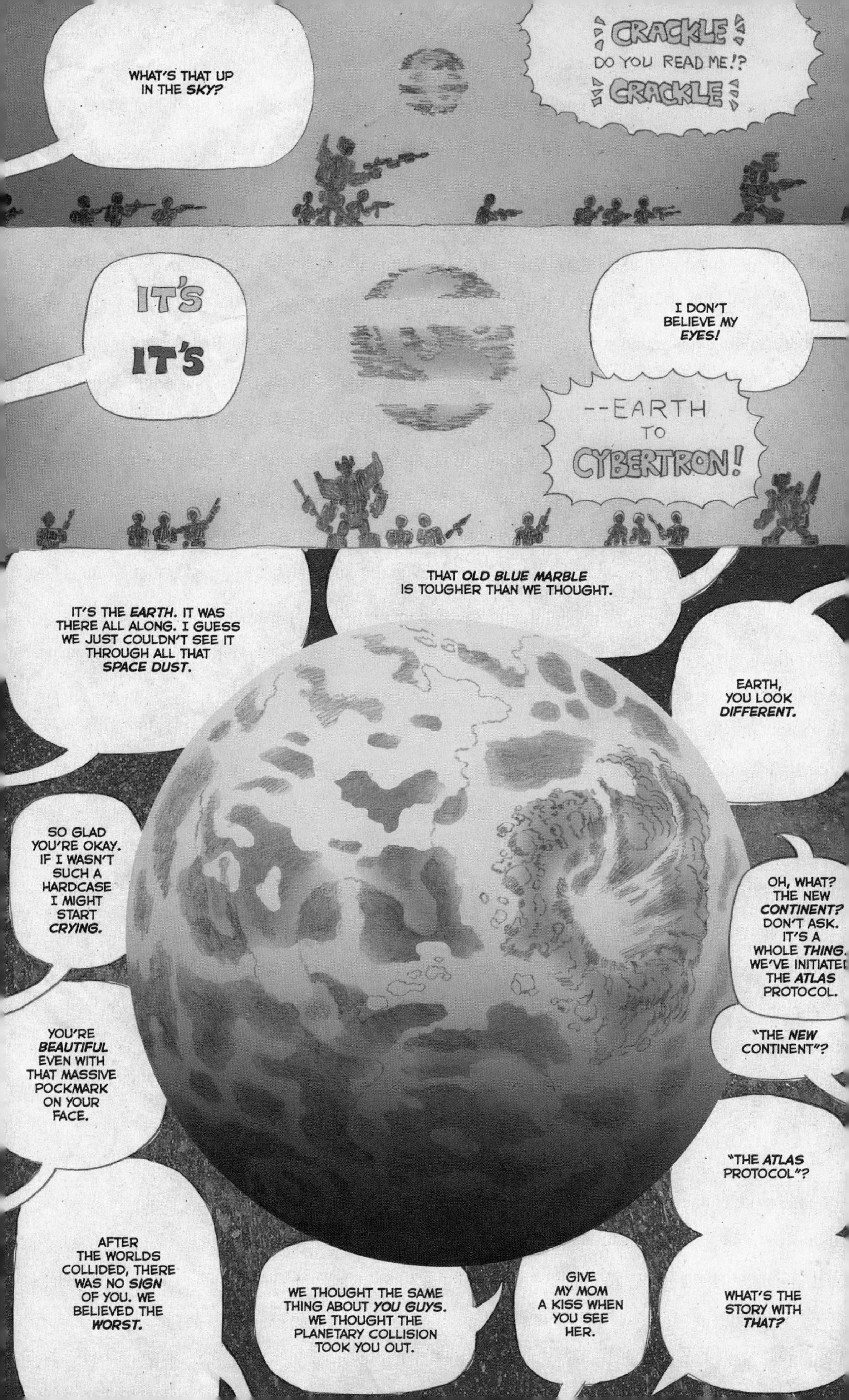
WHAT'S THAT UP IN THE SKY?
CRACKLE DO YOU READ ME!? CRACKLE
IT'S IT'S
I DON'T BELIEVE MY EYES!
--EARTH TO CYBERTRON!
IT'S THE EARTH. IT WAS THERE ALL ALONG. I GUESS WE JUST COULDN'T SEE IT THROUGH ALL THAT SPACE DUST.
THAT OLD BLUE MARBLE IS TOUGHER THAN WE THOUGHT.
EARTH, YOU LOOK DIFFERENT.
SO GLAD YOU'RE OKAY. IF I WASN'T SUCH A HARDCASE I MIGHT START CRYING.
OH, WHAT? THE NEW CONTINENT? DON'T ASK. IT'S A WHOLE THING. WE'VE INITIATED THE ATLAS PROTOCOL.
YOU'RE BEAUTIFUL EVEN WITH THAT MASSIVE POCKMARK ON YOUR FACE.
"THE NEW CONTINENT"?
"THE ATLAS PROTOCOL"?
AFTER THE WORLDS COLLIDED, THERE WAS NO SIGN OF YOU. WE BELIEVED THE WORST.
WE THOUGHT THE SAME THING ABOUT YOU GUYS. WE THOUGHT THE PLANETARY COLLISION TOOK YOU OUT.
GIVE MY MOM A KISS WHEN YOU SEE HER.
WHAT'S THE STORY WITH THAT?

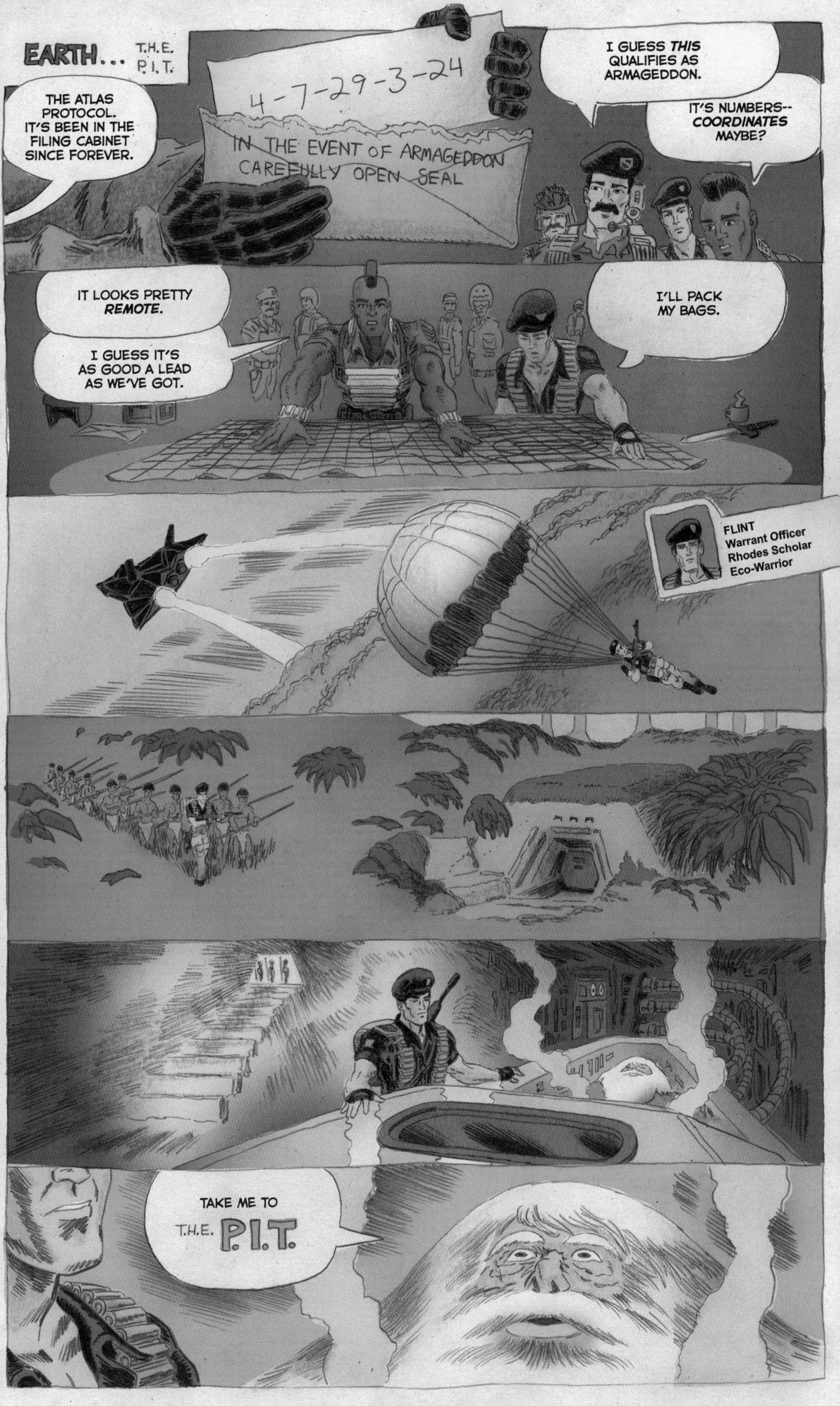
EARTH... T.H.E. P.I.T.
4-7-29-3-24
IN THE EVENT OF ARMAGEDDON CAREFULLY OPEN SEAL
THE ATLAS PROTOCOL. IT'S BEEN IN THE FILING CABINET SINCE FOREVER.
I GUESS THIS QUALIFIES AS ARMAGEDDON.
IT'S NUMBERS-- COORDINATES MAYBE?
IT LOOKS PRETTY REMOTE.
I GUESS IT'S AS GOOD A LEAD AS WE'VE GOT.
I'LL PACK MY BAGS.
FLINT
Warrant Officer
Rhodes Scholar
Eco-Warrior
TAKE ME TO T.H.E. P.I.T.

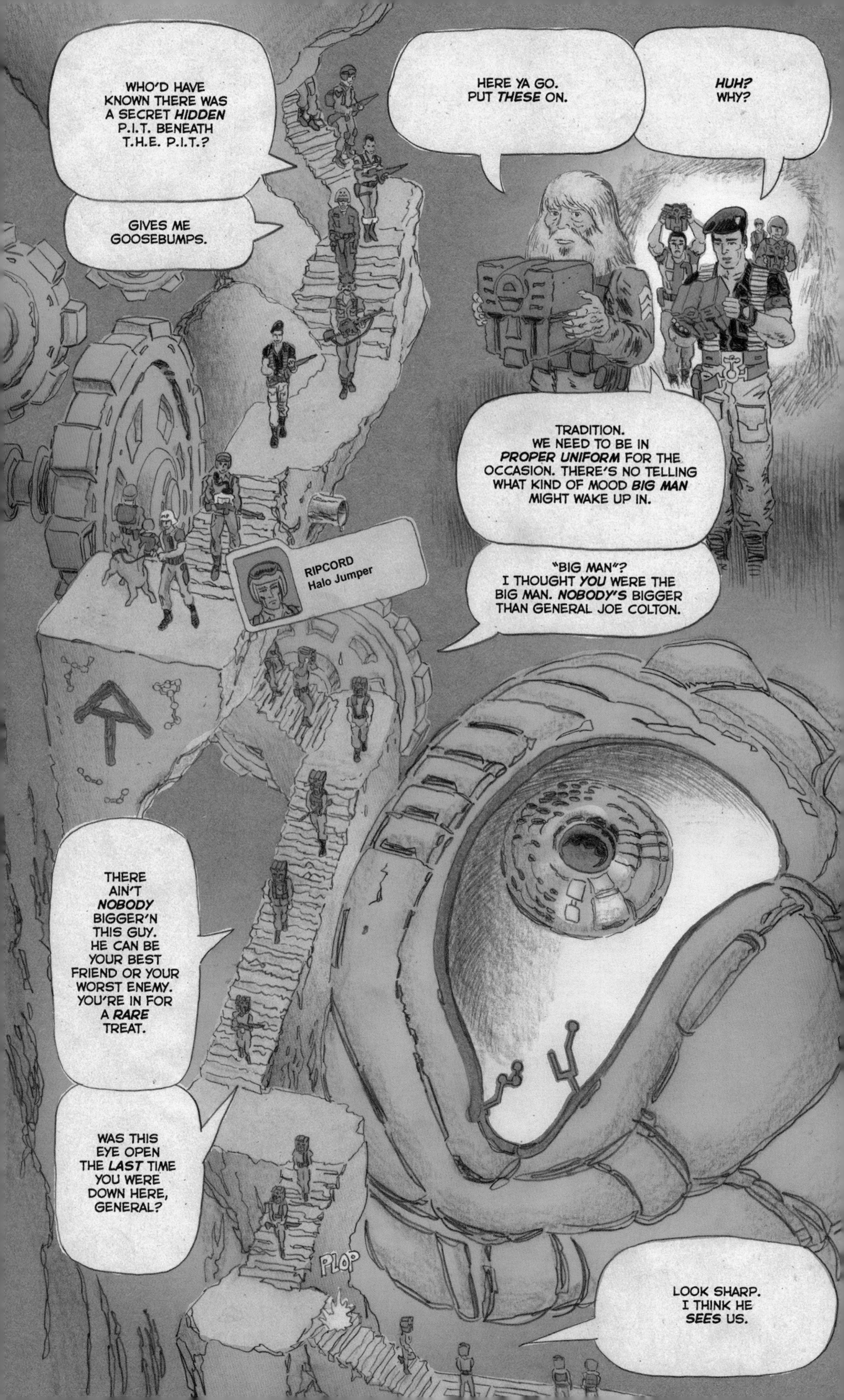
WHO'D HAVE KNOWN THERE WAS A SECRET HIDDEN P.I.T. BENEATH T.H.E. P.I.T.?
GIVES ME GOOSEBUMPS.
HERE YA GO. PUT THESE ON.
HUH? WHY?
TRADITION. WE NEED TO BE IN PROPER UNIFORM FOR THE OCCASION. THERE'S NO TELLING WHAT KIND OF MOOD BIG MAN MIGHT WAKE UP IN.
RIPCORD
Halo Jumper
"BIG MAN"? I THOUGHT YOU WERE THE BIG MAN. NOBODY'S BIGGER THAN GENERAL JOE COLTON.
THERE AIN'T NOBODY BIGGER'N THIS GUY. HE CAN BE YOUR BEST FRIEND OR YOUR WORST ENEMY. YOU'RE IN FOR A RARE TREAT.
WAS THIS EYE OPEN THE LAST TIME YOU WERE DOWN HERE, GENERAL?
PLOP
LOOK SHARP. I THINK HE SEES US.

DRAT! SOMEBODY FETCH ME A MASSSK.
ONE OF THOSE ACCURSED U.S.7 BEASTS SNATCHED IT FROM ME.
HUH?
SNAKE EYES?
MY OLD HELMET. YOU SAVED IT FOR ME. YOU'RE NEVER SHORT ON SURPRISES, SNAKE EYESSS.
I GAVE THAT TO HIM AS AN ENGAGEMENT GIFT.
I KNEW HE WAS A RAT!

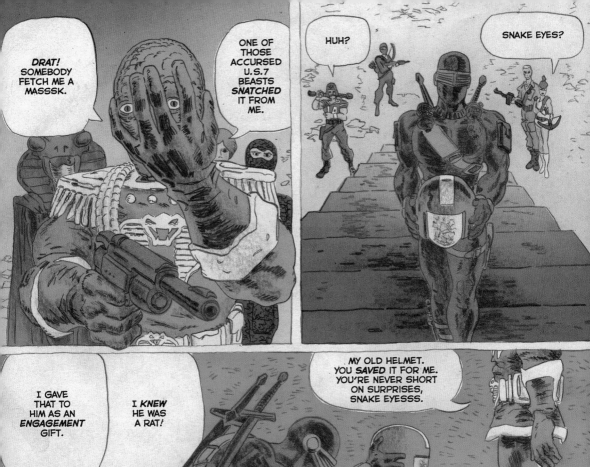

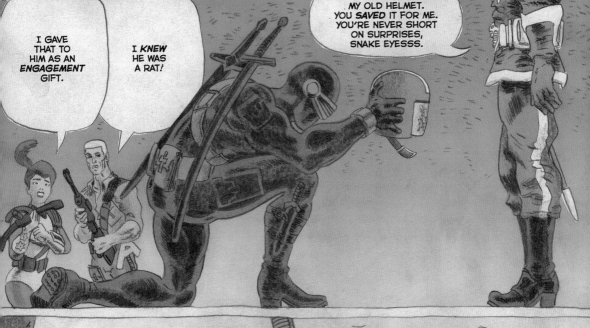

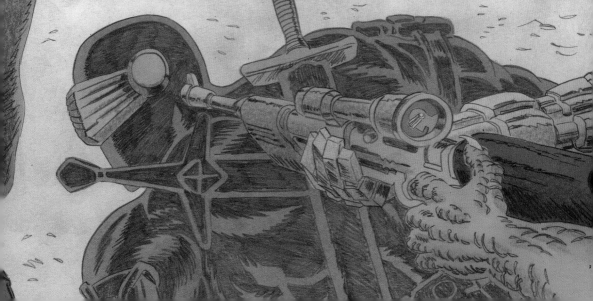

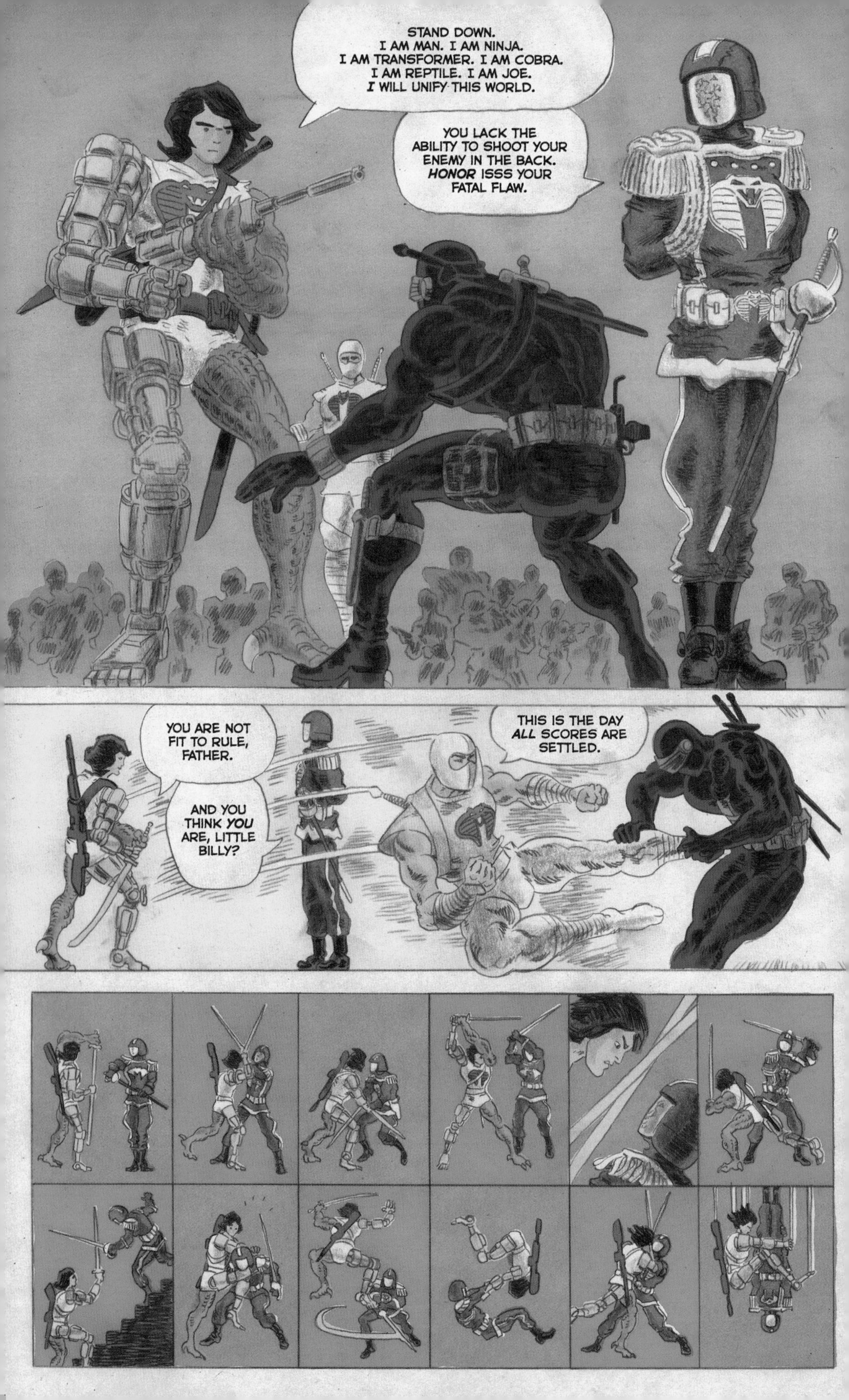
STAND DOWN. I AM MAN. I AM NINJA. I AM TRANSFORMER. I AM COBRA. I AM REPTILE. I AM JOE. *I* WILL UNIFY THIS WORLD.
YOU LACK THE ABILITY TO SHOOT YOUR ENEMY IN THE BACK. ***HONOR*** ISSS YOUR FATAL FLAW.
YOU ARE NOT FIT TO RULE, FATHER.
AND YOU THINK *YOU* ARE, LITTLE BILLY?
THIS IS THE DAY *ALL* SCORES ARE SETTLED.

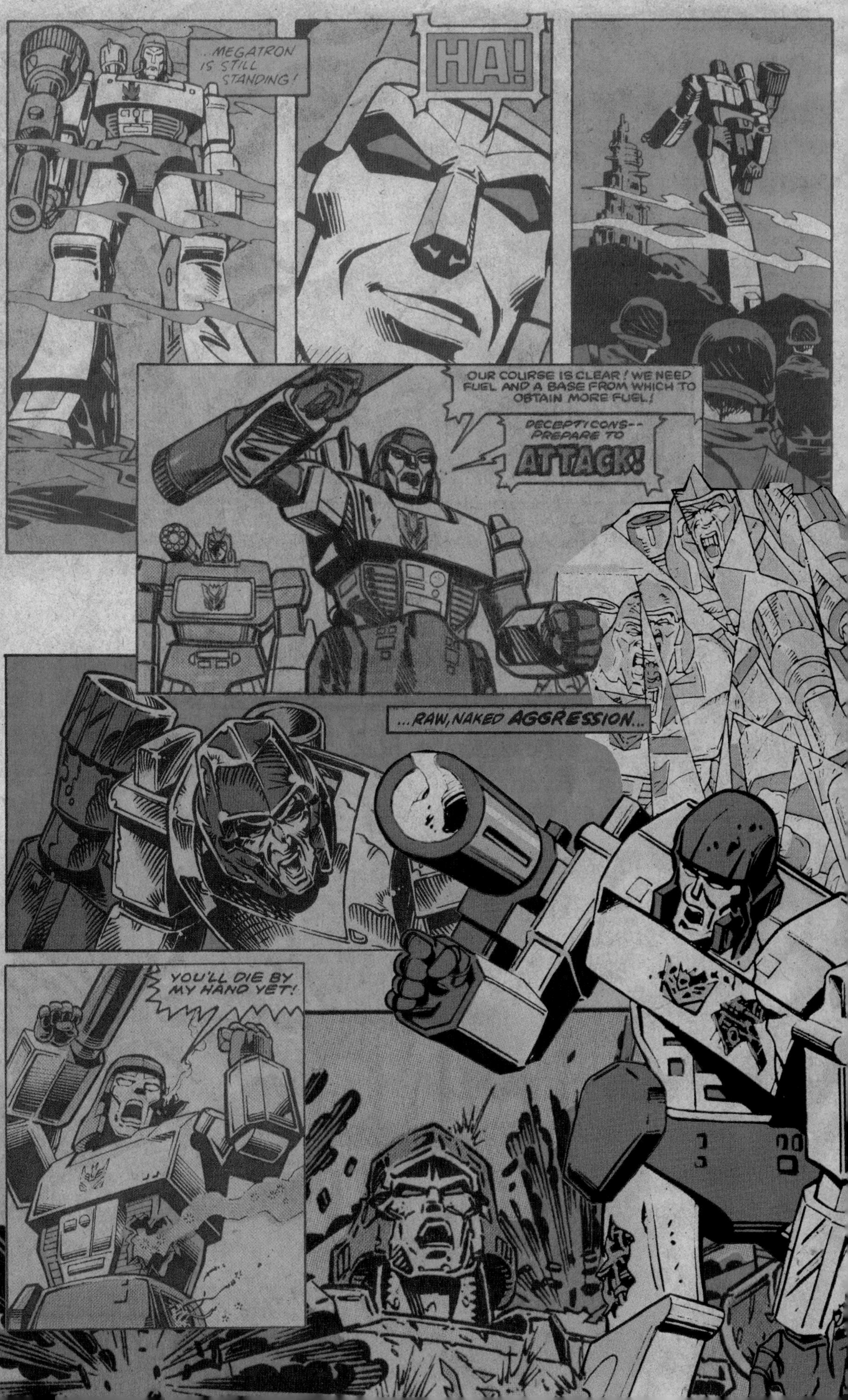
...MEGATRON IS STILL STANDING!
HA!
OUR COURSE IS CLEAR! WE NEED FUEL AND A BASE FROM WHICH TO OBTAIN MORE FUEL!
DECEPTICONS-- PREPARE TO
ATTACK!
...RAW, NAKED AGGRESSION...
YOU'LL DIE BY MY HAND YET!

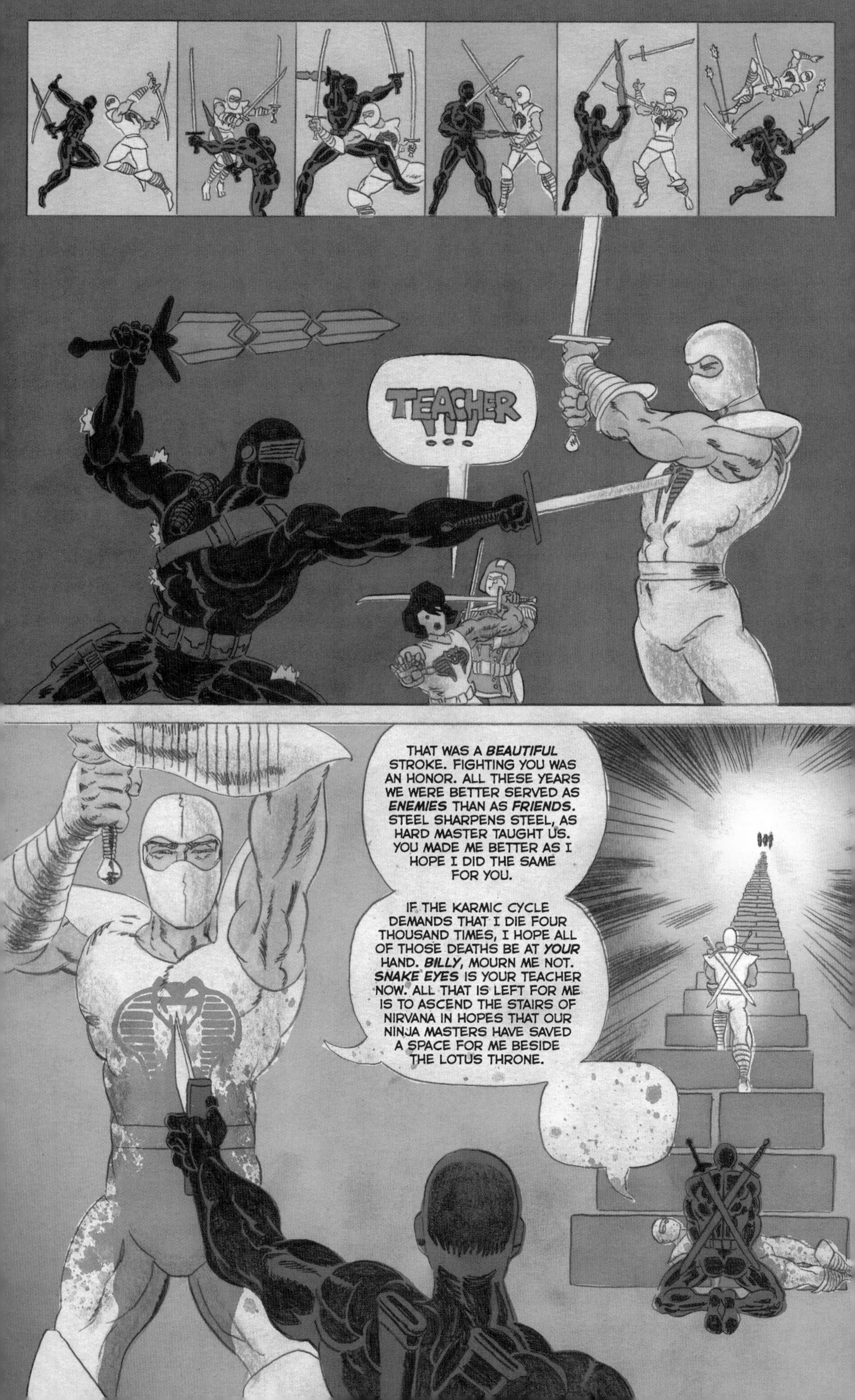

TEACHER
...
THAT WAS A BEAUTIFUL STROKE. FIGHTING YOU WAS AN HONOR. ALL THESE YEARS WE WERE BETTER SERVED AS ENEMIES THAN AS FRIENDS. STEEL SHARPENS STEEL, AS HARD MASTER TAUGHT US. YOU MADE ME BETTER AS I HOPE I DID THE SAME FOR YOU.
IF THE KARMIC CYCLE DEMANDS THAT I DIE FOUR THOUSAND TIMES, I HOPE ALL OF THOSE DEATHS BE AT YOUR HAND. BILLY, MOURN ME NOT. SNAKE EYES IS YOUR TEACHER NOW. ALL THAT IS LEFT FOR ME IS TO ASCEND THE STAIRS OF NIRVANA IN HOPES THAT OUR NINJA MASTERS HAVE SAVED A SPACE FOR ME BESIDE THE LOTUS THRONE.

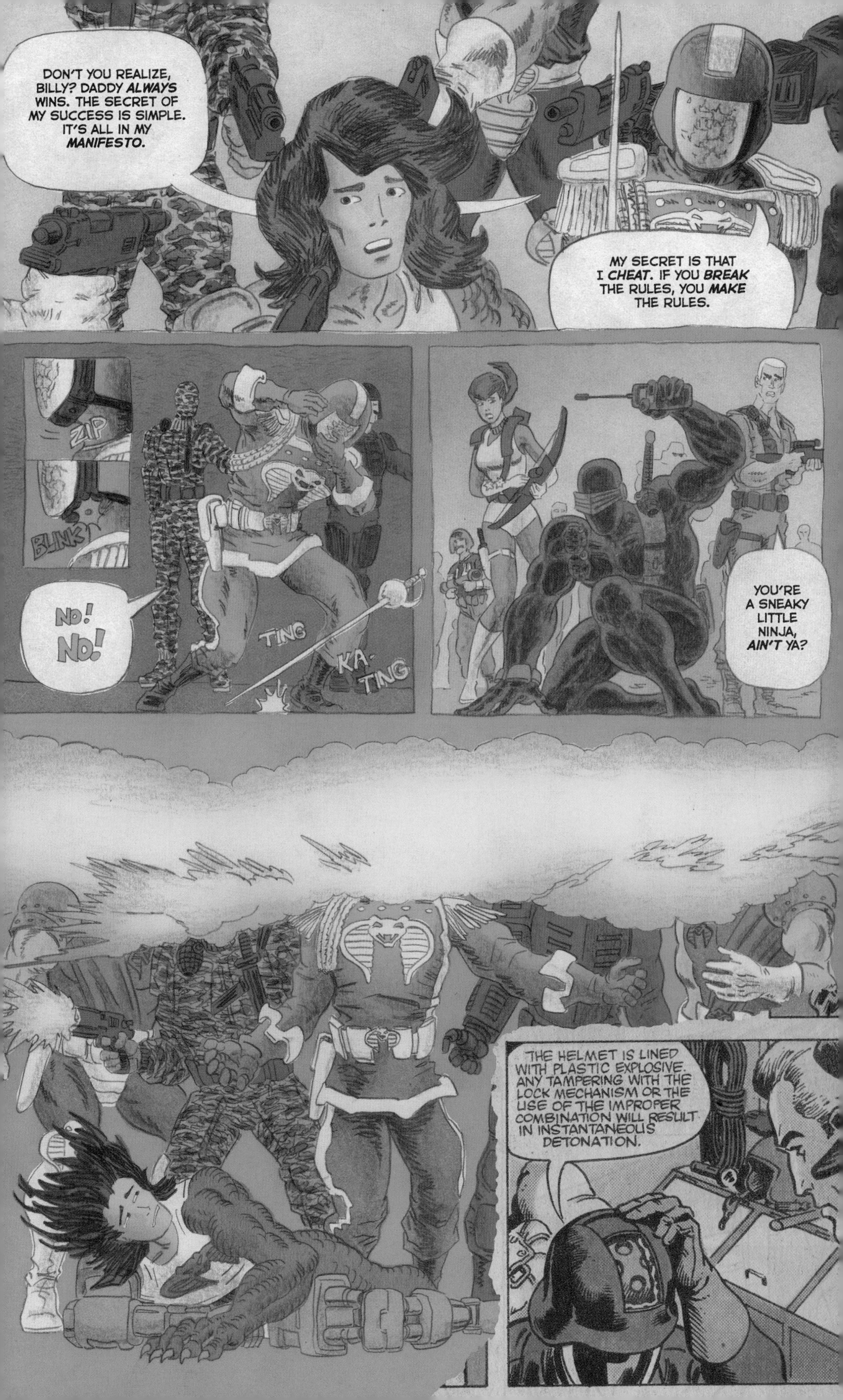
DON'T YOU REALIZE, BILLY? DADDY ALWAYS WINS. THE SECRET OF MY SUCCESS IS SIMPLE. IT'S ALL IN MY MANIFESTO.
MY SECRET IS THAT I CHEAT. IF YOU BREAK THE RULES, YOU MAKE THE RULES.
ZIP
BLINK
NO! NO!
TING
KA-TING
YOU'RE A SNEAKY LITTLE NINJA, AIN'T YA?
THE HELMET IS LINED WITH PLASTIC EXPLOSIVE. ANY TAMPERING WITH THE LOCK MECHANISM OR THE USE OF THE IMPROPER COMBINATION WILL RESULT IN INSTANTANEOUS DETONATION.

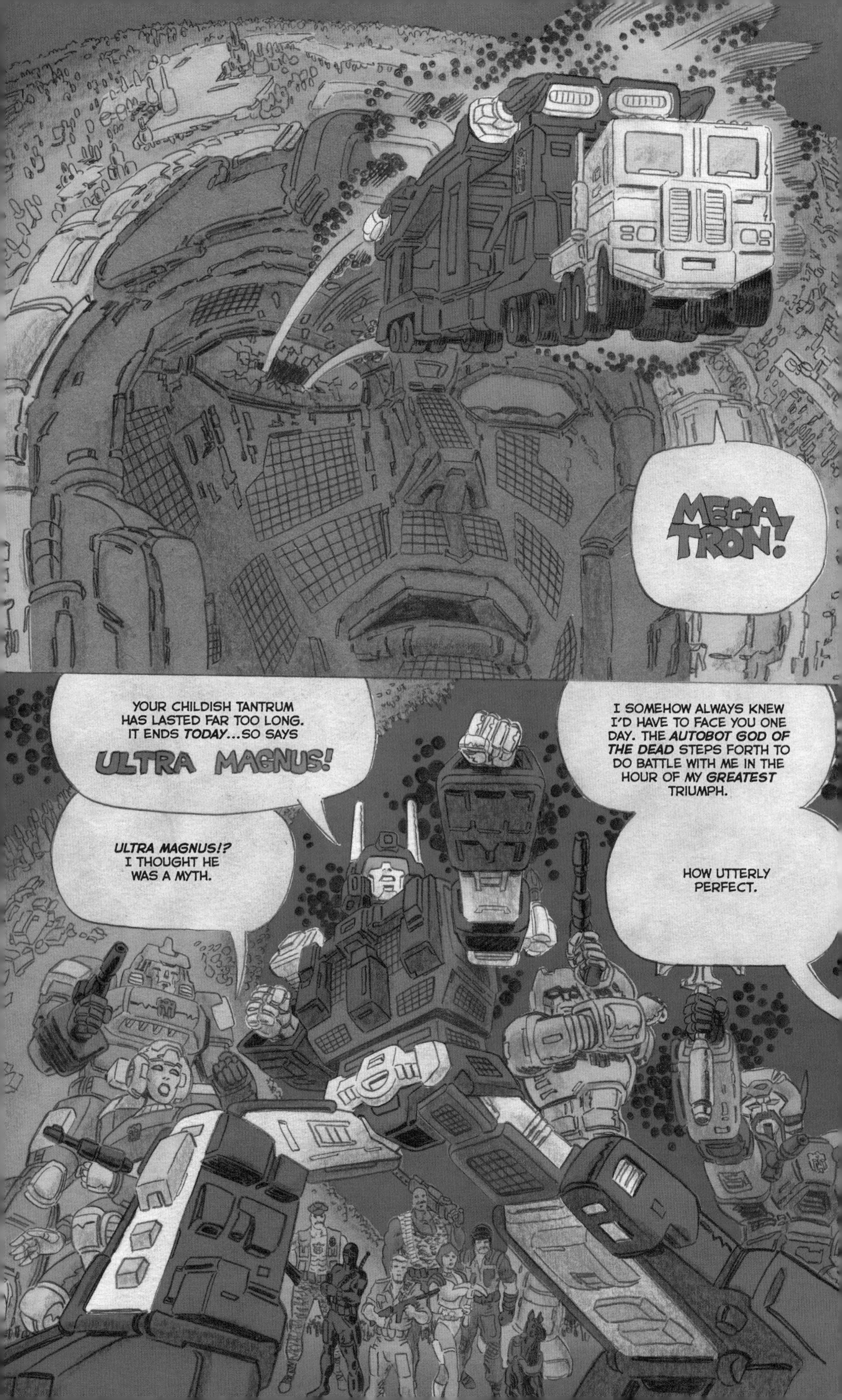

MEGATRON!
YOUR CHILDISH TANTRUM HAS LASTED FAR TOO LONG. IT ENDS TODAY...SO SAYS ULTRA MAGNUS!
ULTRA MAGNUS!? I THOUGHT HE WAS A MYTH.
I SOMEHOW ALWAYS KNEW I'D HAVE TO FACE YOU ONE DAY. THE AUTOBOT GOD OF THE DEAD STEPS FORTH TO DO BATTLE WITH ME IN THE HOUR OF MY GREATEST TRIUMPH.
HOW UTTERLY PERFECT.

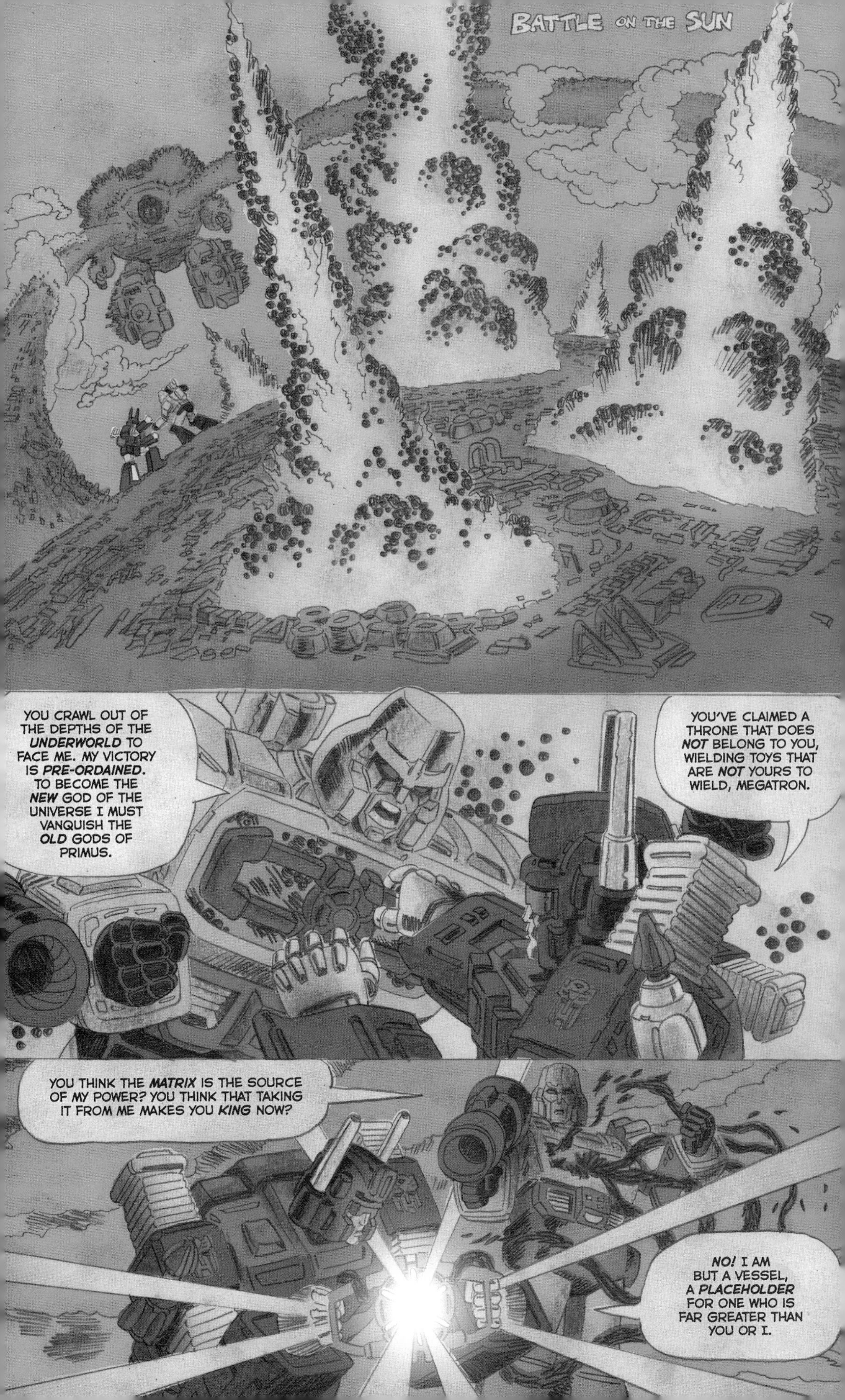
BATTLE ON THE SUN
YOU CRAWL OUT OF THE DEPTHS OF THE UNDERWORLD TO FACE ME. MY VICTORY IS PRE-ORDAINED. TO BECOME THE NEW GOD OF THE UNIVERSE I MUST VANQUISH THE OLD GODS OF PRIMUS.
YOU'VE CLAIMED A THRONE THAT DOES NOT BELONG TO YOU, WIELDING TOYS THAT ARE NOT YOURS TO WIELD, MEGATRON.
YOU THINK THE MATRIX IS THE SOURCE OF MY POWER? YOU THINK THAT TAKING IT FROM ME MAKES YOU KING NOW?
NO! I AM BUT A VESSEL, A PLACEHOLDER FOR ONE WHO IS FAR GREATER THAN YOU OR I.

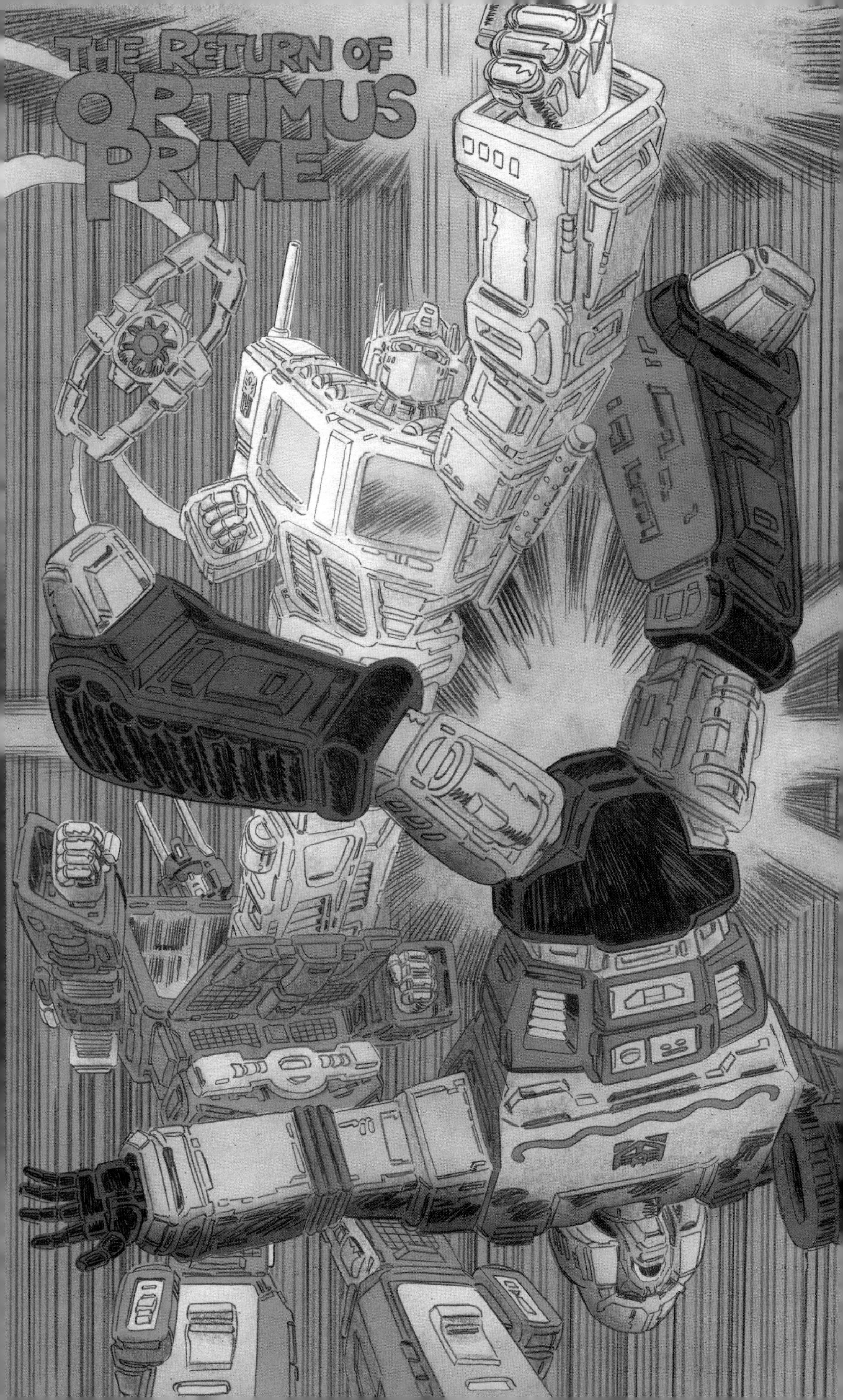
THE RETURN OF
OPTIMUS
PRIME

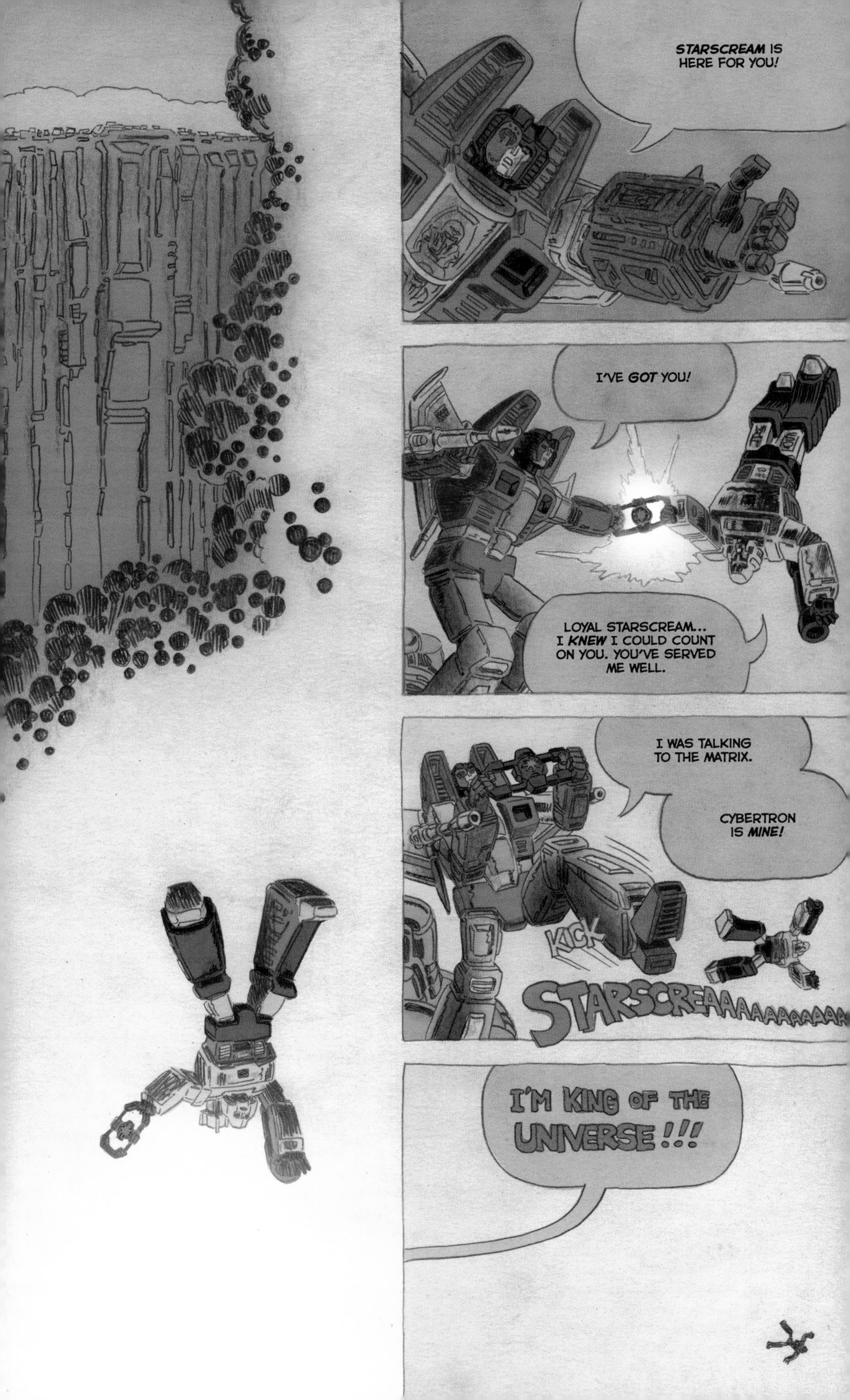
STARSCREAM IS HERE FOR YOU!
I'VE GOT YOU!
LOYAL STARSCREAM... I KNEW I COULD COUNT ON YOU. YOU'VE SERVED ME WELL.
I WAS TALKING TO THE MATRIX.
CYBERTRON IS MINE!
KICK
STARSCREAAAAAAAAAAA
I'M KING OF THE UNIVERSE!!!

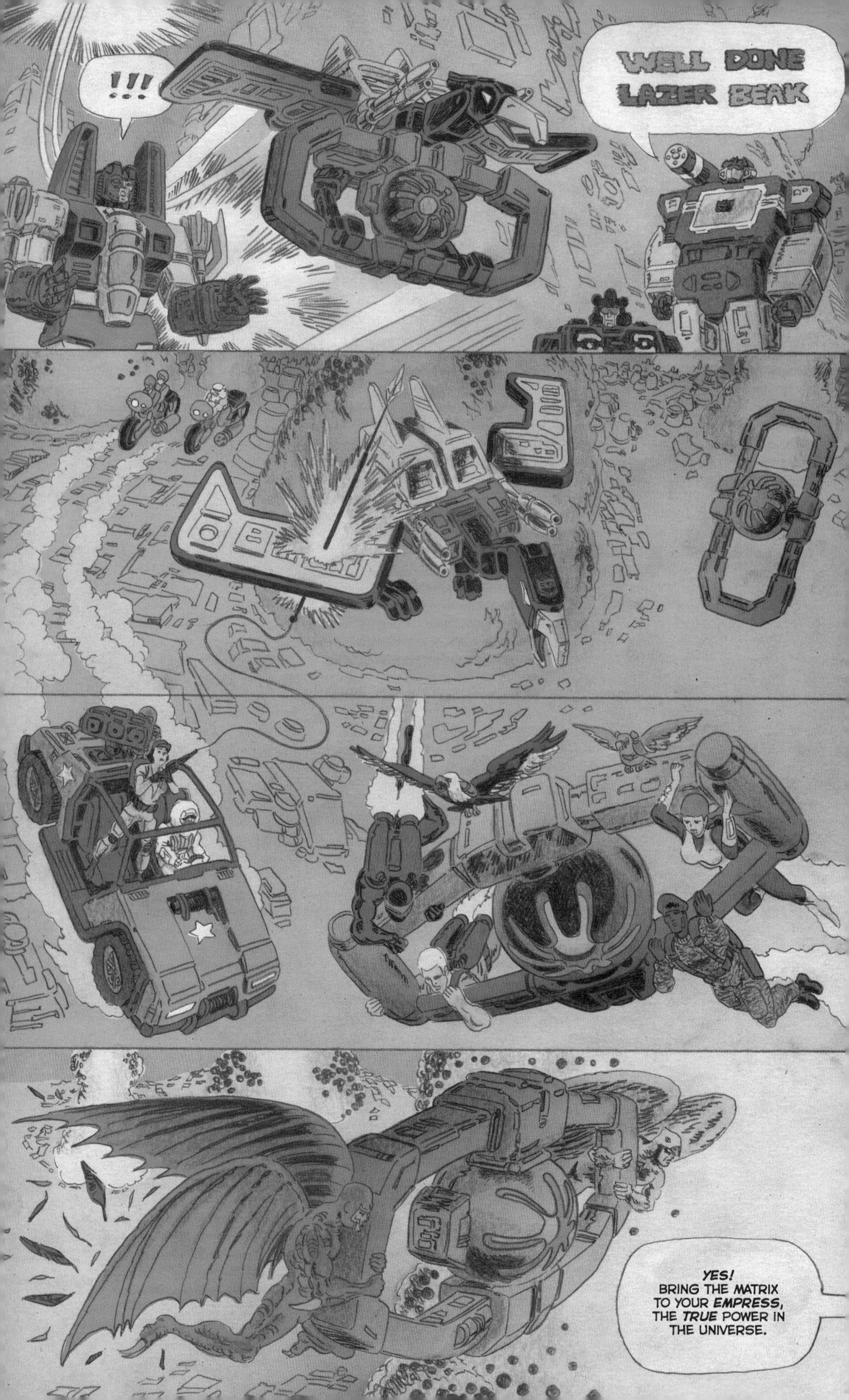
!!!
WELL DONE LAZER BEAK
YES! BRING THE MATRIX TO YOUR *EMPRESS*, THE *TRUE* POWER IN THE UNIVERSE.

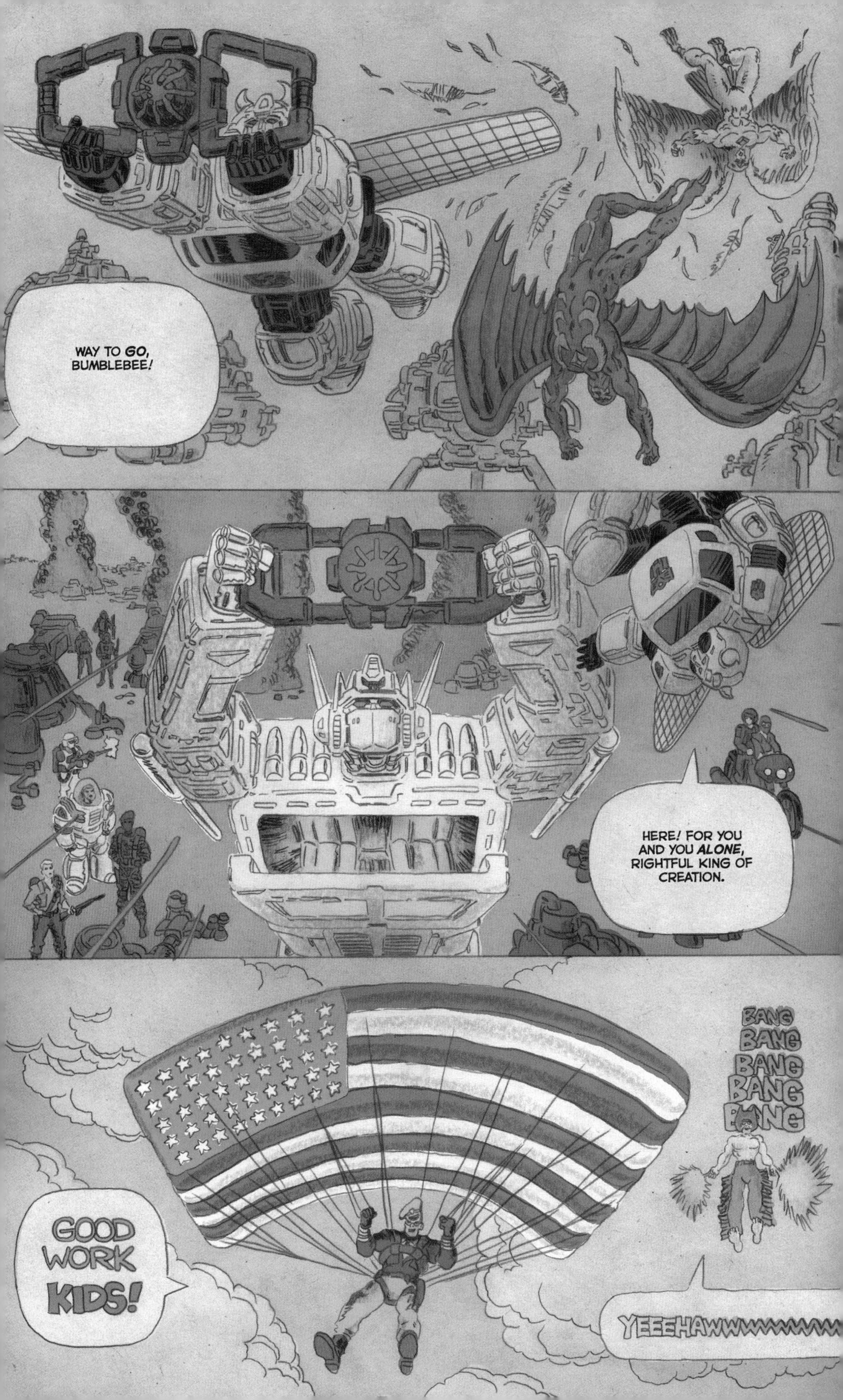
WAY TO GO, BUMBLEBEE!
HERE! FOR YOU AND YOU ALONE, RIGHTFUL KING OF CREATION.
GOOD WORK KIDS!
BANG BANG BANG BANG BANG
YEEEHAWWWWWWWW

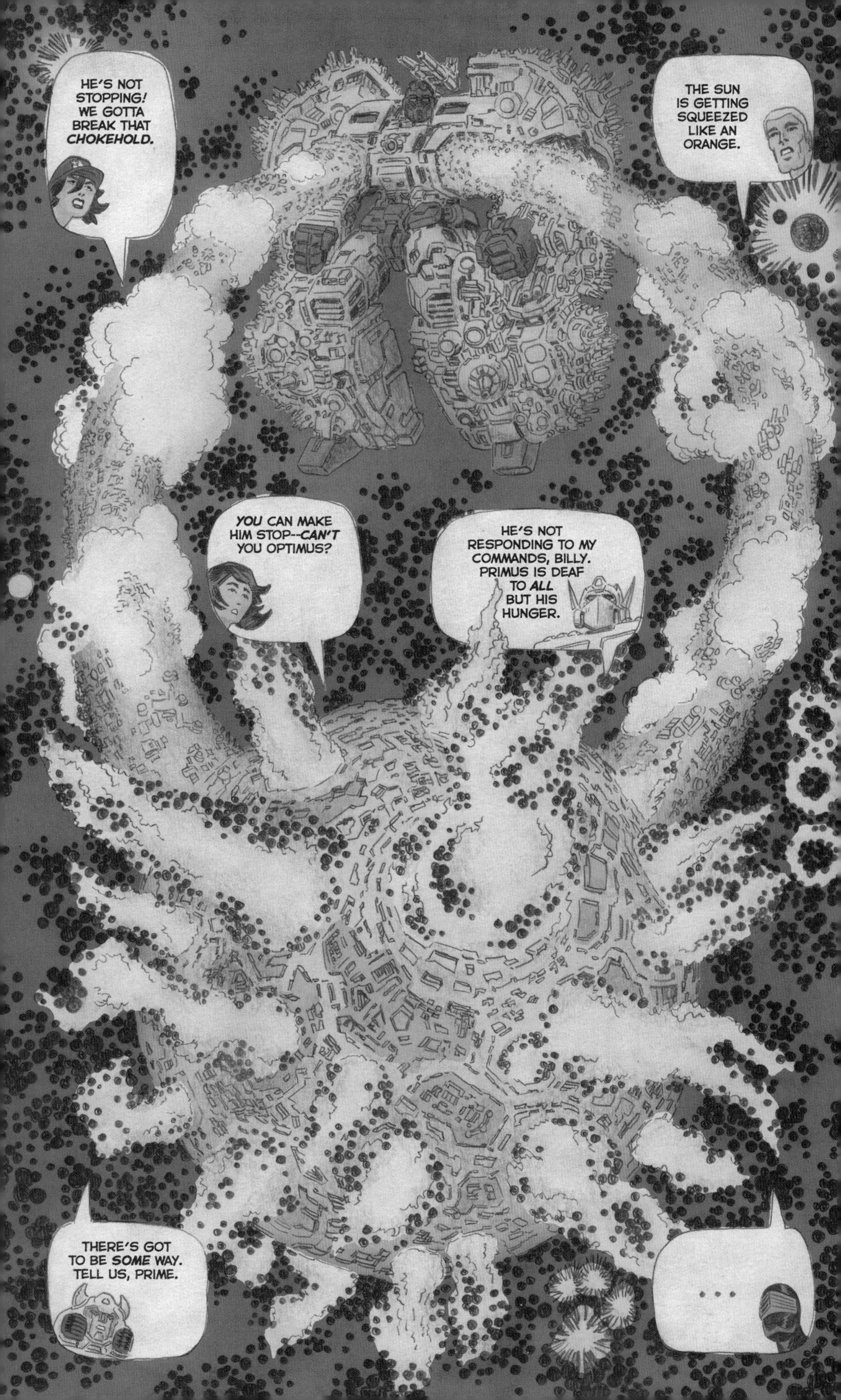
HE'S NOT STOPPING! WE GOTTA BREAK THAT CHOKEHOLD.
THE SUN IS GETTING SQUEEZED LIKE AN ORANGE.
YOU CAN MAKE HIM STOP--CAN'T YOU OPTIMUS?
HE'S NOT RESPONDING TO MY COMMANDS, BILLY. PRIMUS IS DEAF TO ALL BUT HIS HUNGER.
THERE'S GOT TO BE SOME WAY. TELL US, PRIME.
...

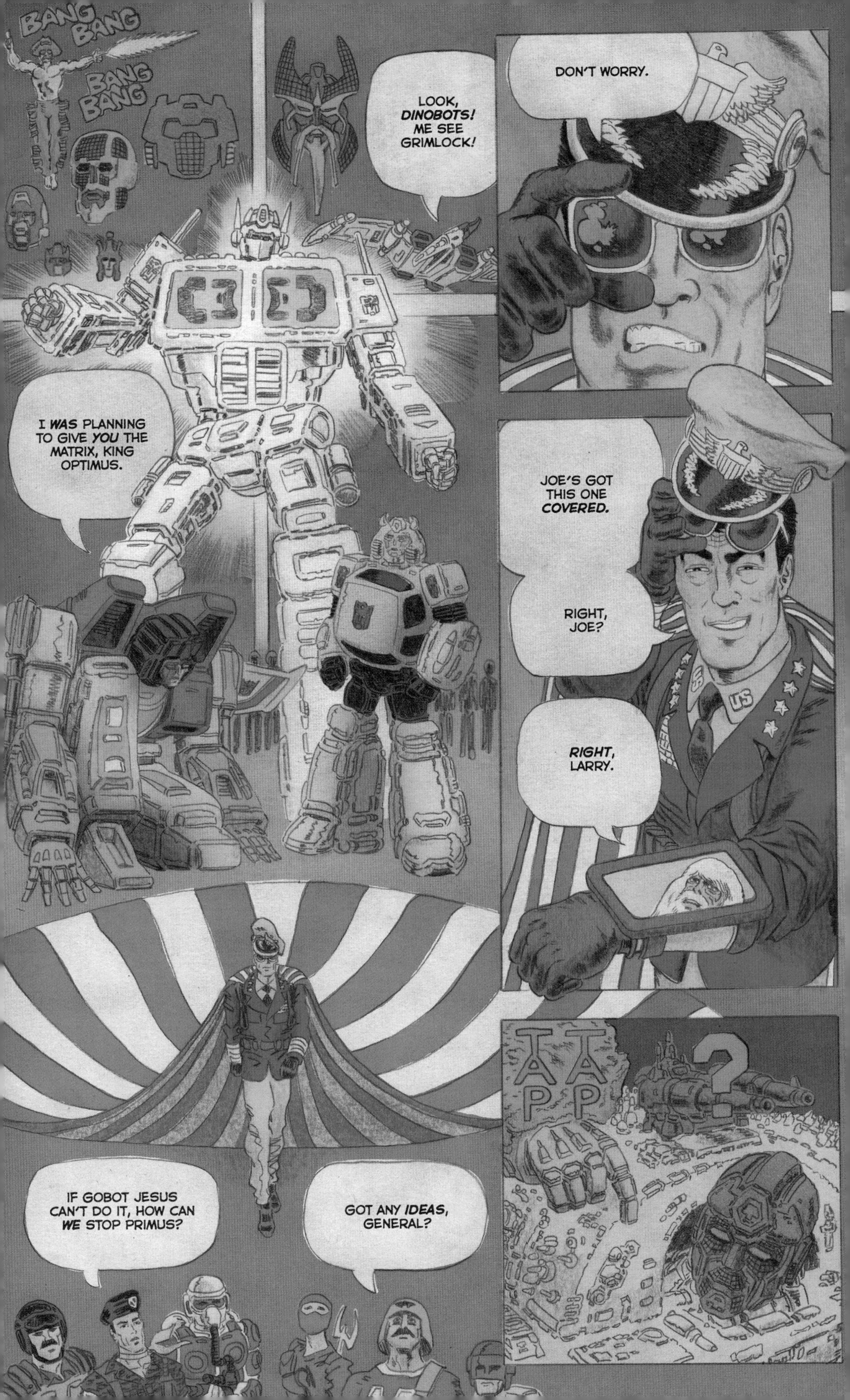
BANG BANG
BANG BANG
LOOK, *DINOBOTS!* ME SEE GRIMLOCK!
I *WAS* PLANNING TO GIVE *YOU* THE MATRIX, KING OPTIMUS.
DON'T WORRY.
JOE'S GOT THIS ONE *COVERED.*
RIGHT, JOE?
RIGHT, LARRY.
IF GOBOT JESUS CAN'T DO IT, HOW CAN *WE* STOP PRIMUS?
GOT ANY *IDEAS,* GENERAL?
TAP TAP
?

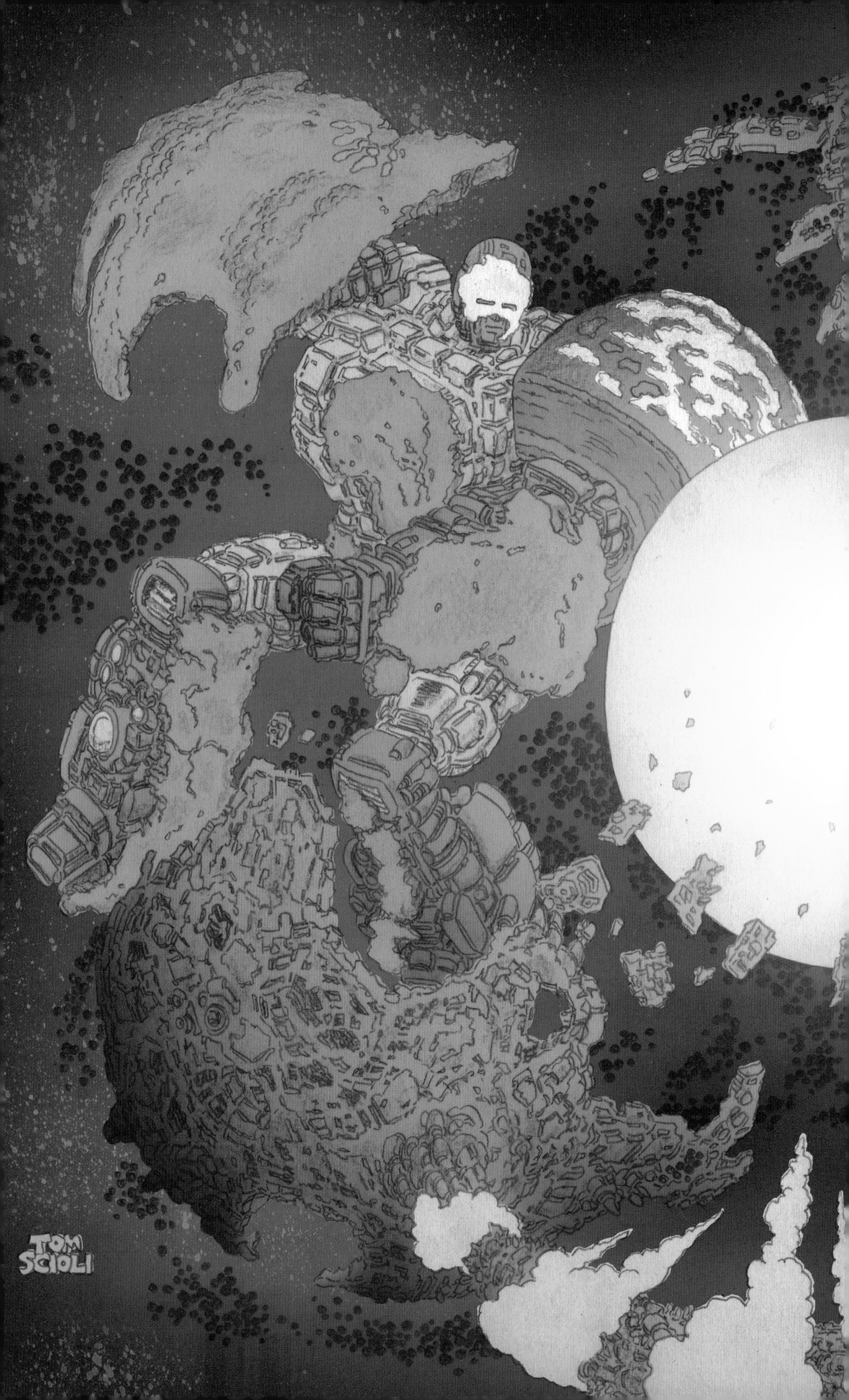
TOM
SCIOLI

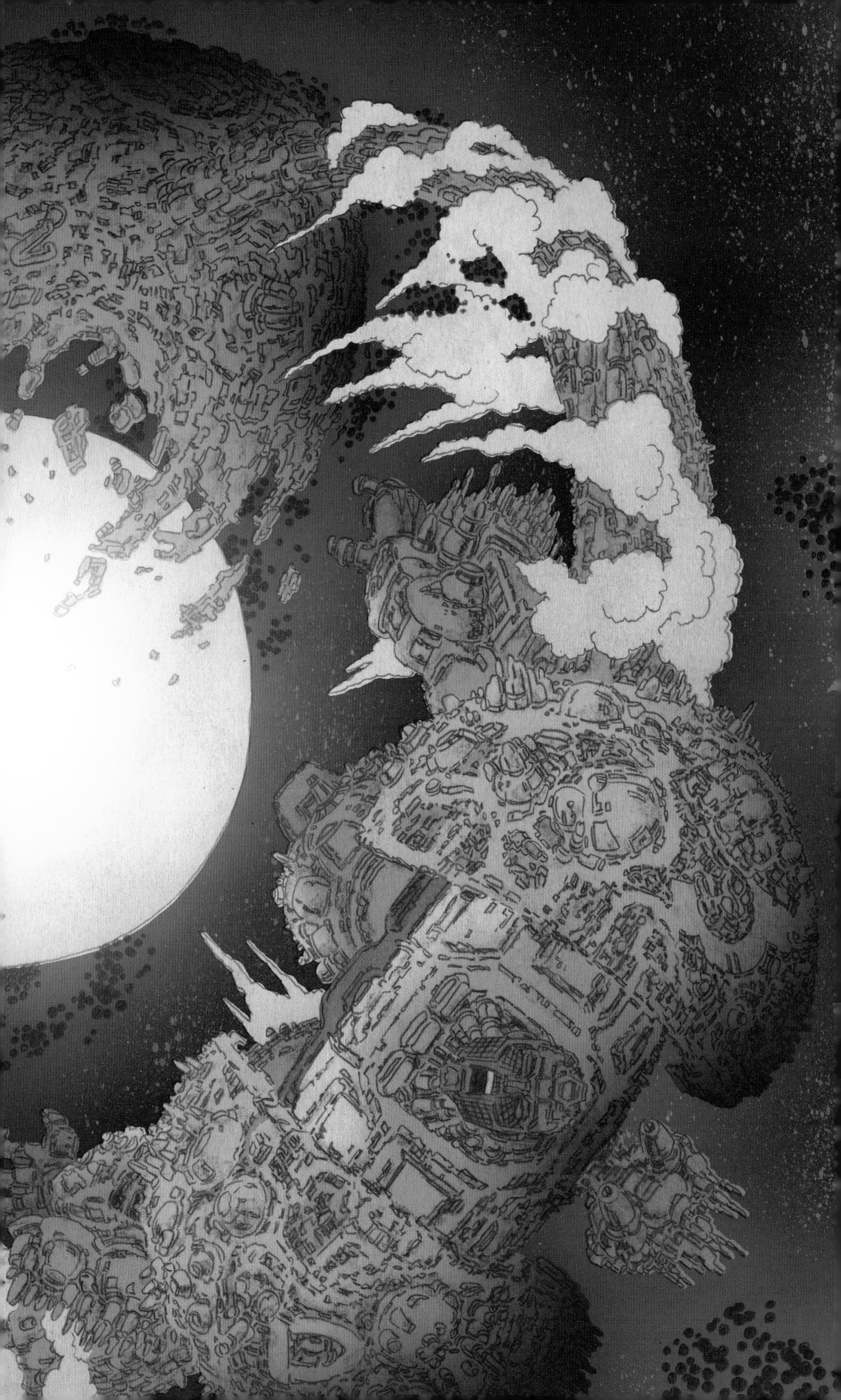

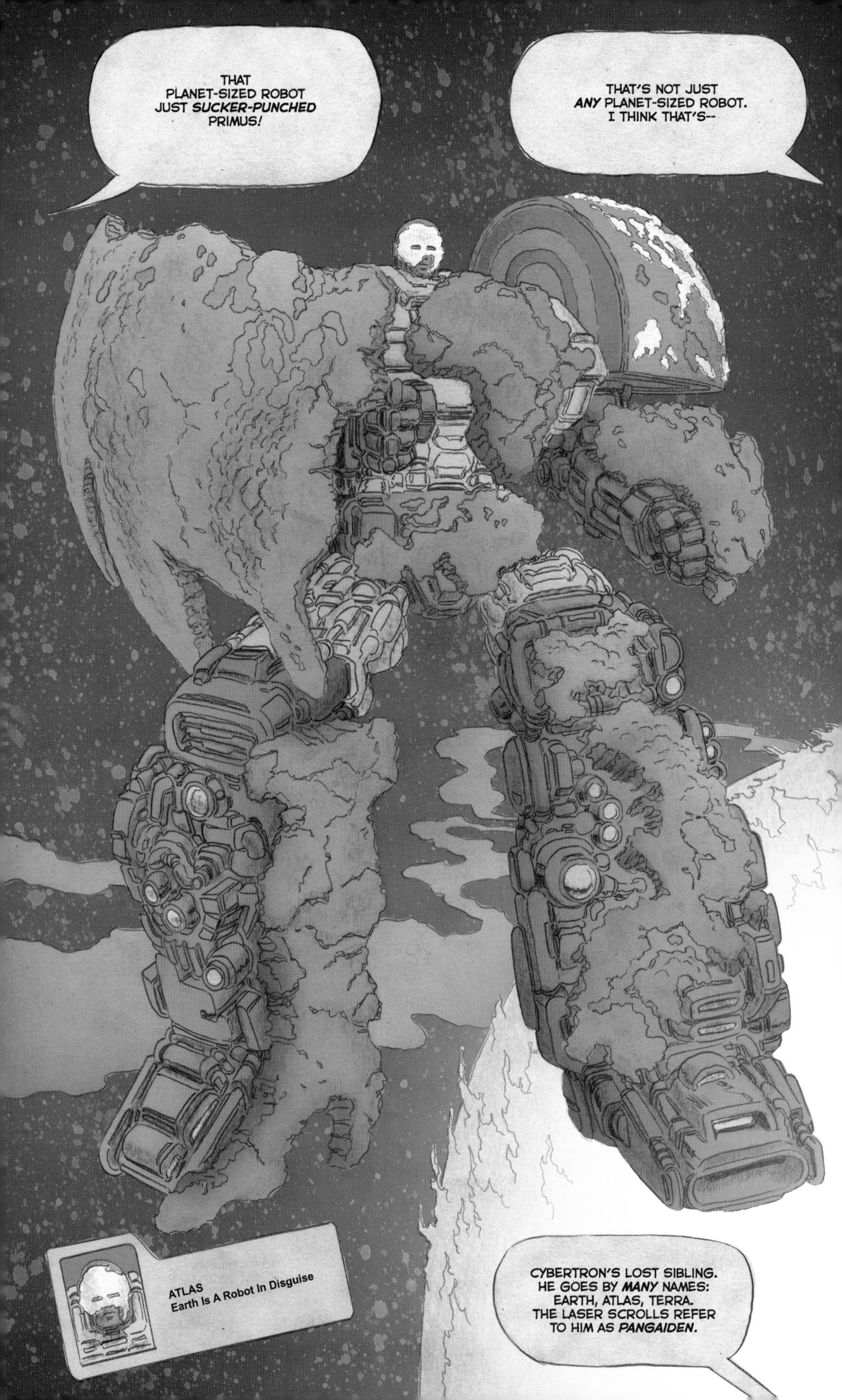
THAT PLANET-SIZED ROBOT JUST SUCKER-PUNCHED PRIMUS!
THAT'S NOT JUST ANY PLANET-SIZED ROBOT. I THINK THAT'S--
ATLAS
Earth Is A Robot In Disguise
CYBERTRON'S LOST SIBLING. HE GOES BY MANY NAMES: EARTH, ATLAS, TERRA. THE LASER SCROLLS REFER TO HIM AS PANGAIDEN.

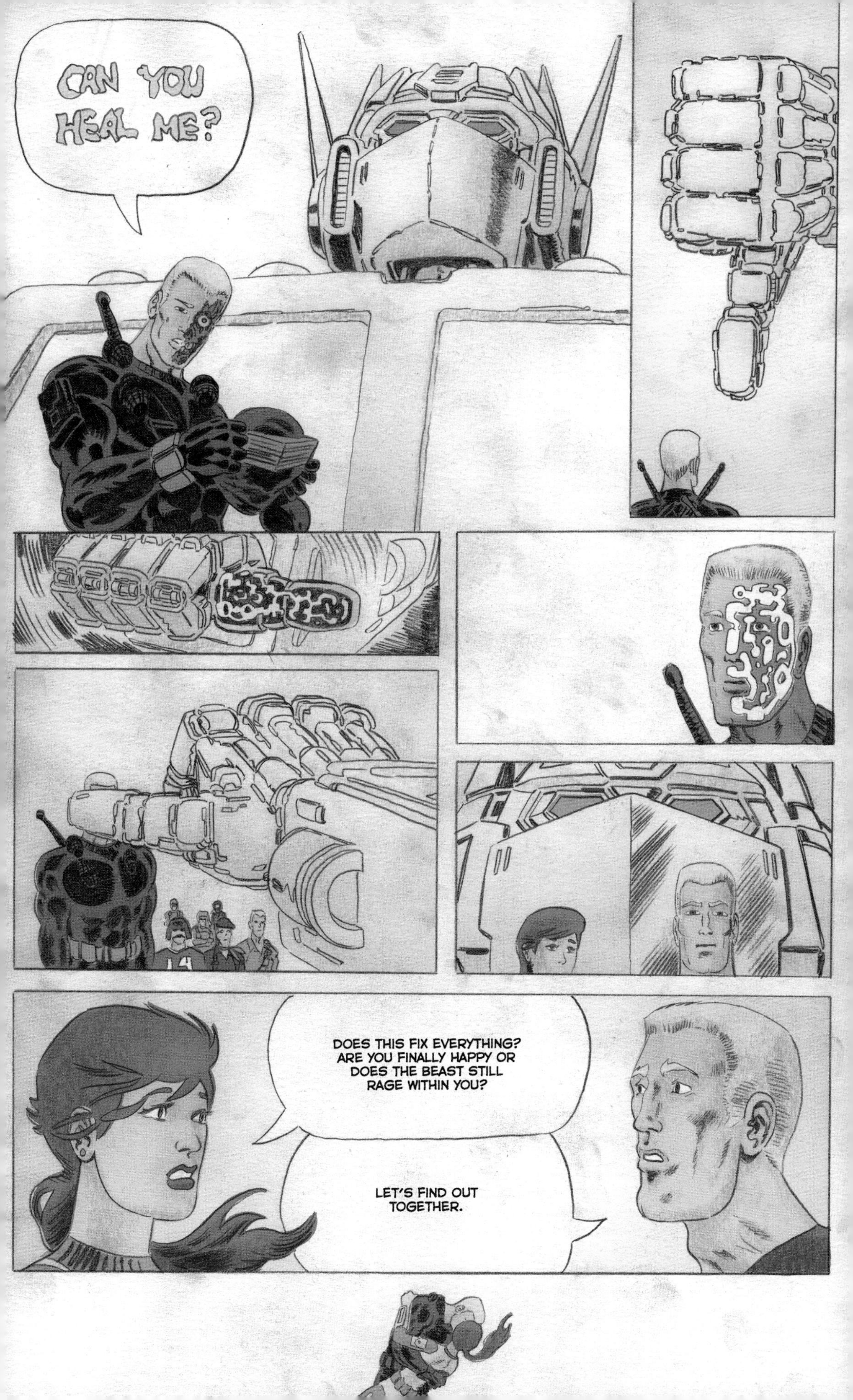
CAN YOU HEAL ME?
DOES THIS FIX EVERYTHING? ARE YOU FINALLY HAPPY OR DOES THE BEAST STILL RAGE WITHIN YOU?
LET'S FIND OUT TOGETHER.

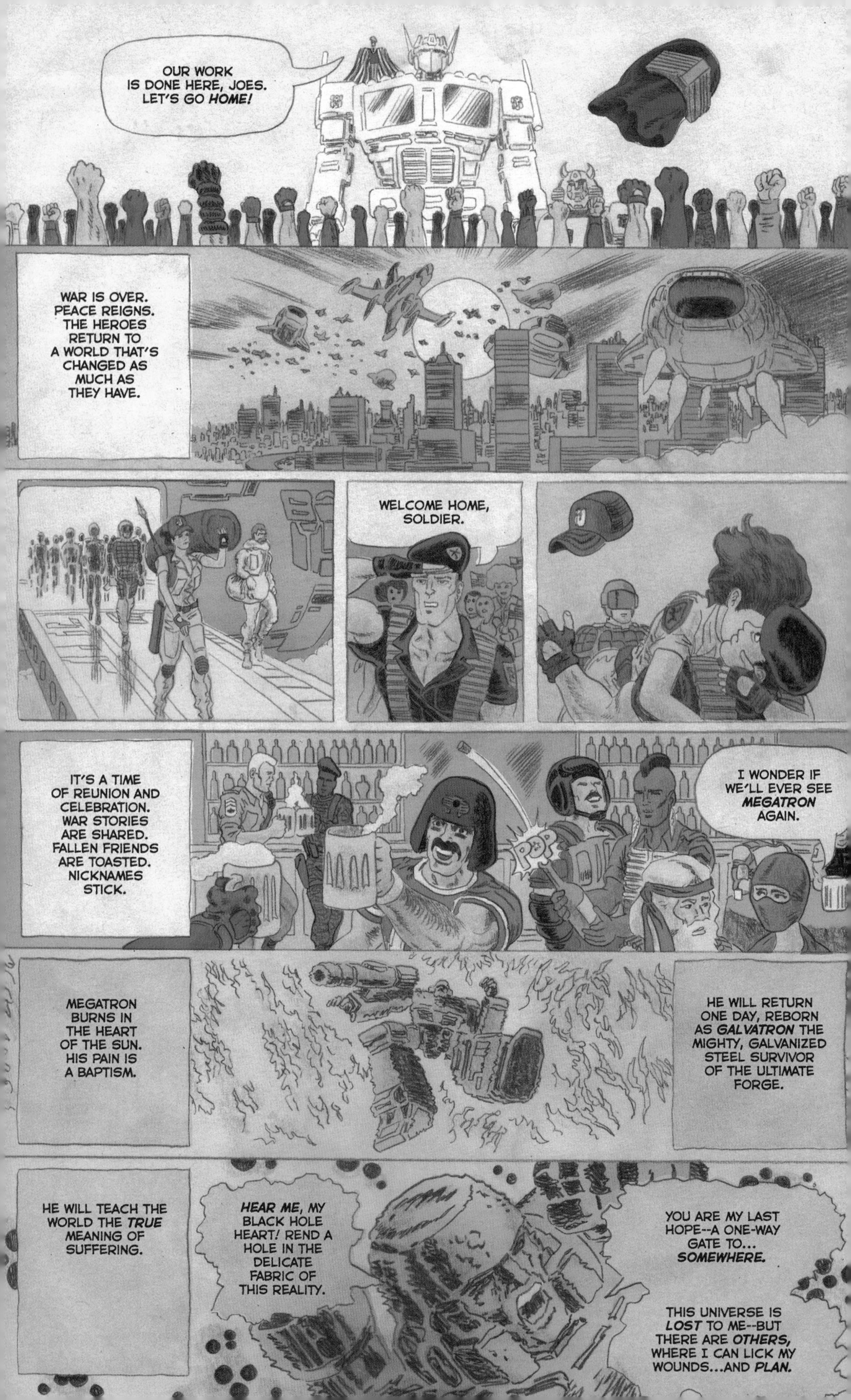

OUR WORK IS DONE HERE, JOES. LET'S GO *HOME!*
WAR IS OVER. PEACE REIGNS. THE HEROES RETURN TO A WORLD THAT'S CHANGED AS MUCH AS THEY HAVE.
WELCOME HOME, SOLDIER.
IT'S A TIME OF REUNION AND CELEBRATION. WAR STORIES ARE SHARED. FALLEN FRIENDS ARE TOASTED. NICKNAMES STICK.
POP
I WONDER IF WE'LL EVER SEE *MEGATRON* AGAIN.
MEGATRON BURNS IN THE HEART OF THE SUN. HIS PAIN IS A BAPTISM.
HE WILL RETURN ONE DAY, REBORN AS *GALVATRON* THE MIGHTY, GALVANIZED STEEL SURVIVOR OF THE ULTIMATE FORGE.
HE WILL TEACH THE WORLD THE *TRUE* MEANING OF SUFFERING.
HEAR ME, MY BLACK HOLE HEART! REND A HOLE IN THE DELICATE FABRIC OF THIS REALITY.
YOU ARE MY LAST HOPE--A ONE-WAY GATE TO... ***SOMEWHERE.***
THIS UNIVERSE IS *LOST* TO ME--BUT THERE ARE *OTHERS,* WHERE I CAN LICK MY WOUNDS...AND *PLAN.*

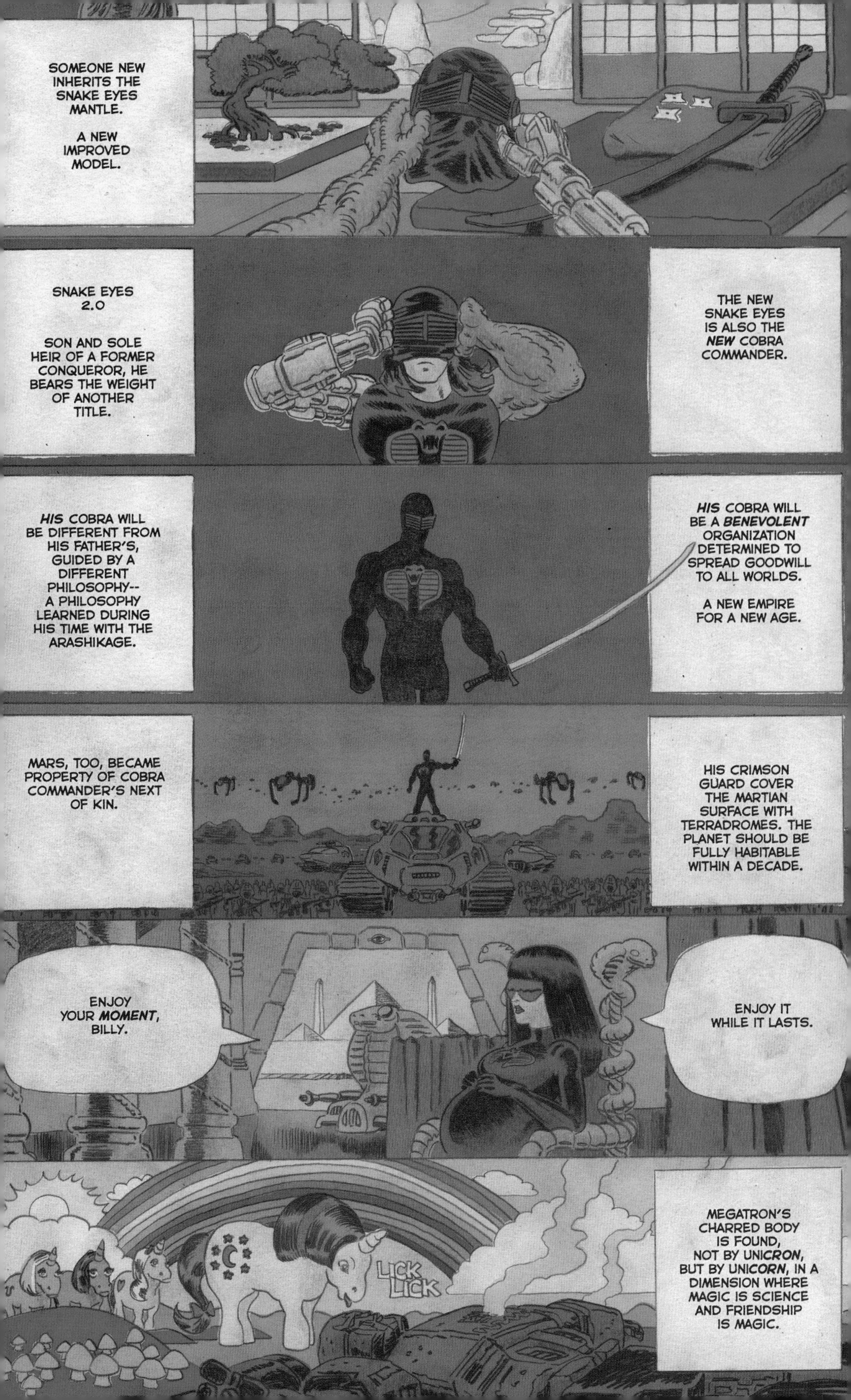

SOMEONE NEW INHERITS THE SNAKE EYES MANTLE.
A NEW IMPROVED MODEL.
SNAKE EYES 2.0
SON AND SOLE HEIR OF A FORMER CONQUEROR, HE BEARS THE WEIGHT OF ANOTHER TITLE.
THE NEW SNAKE EYES IS ALSO THE *NEW* COBRA COMMANDER.
HIS COBRA WILL BE DIFFERENT FROM HIS FATHER'S, GUIDED BY A DIFFERENT PHILOSOPHY-- A PHILOSOPHY LEARNED DURING HIS TIME WITH THE ARASHIKAGE.
HIS COBRA WILL BE A *BENEVOLENT* ORGANIZATION DETERMINED TO SPREAD GOODWILL TO ALL WORLDS.
A NEW EMPIRE FOR A NEW AGE.
MARS, TOO, BECAME PROPERTY OF COBRA COMMANDER'S NEXT OF KIN.
HIS CRIMSON GUARD COVER THE MARTIAN SURFACE WITH TERRADROMES. THE PLANET SHOULD BE FULLY HABITABLE WITHIN A DECADE.
ENJOY YOUR *MOMENT*, BILLY.
ENJOY IT WHILE IT LASTS.
LICK LICK
MEGATRON'S CHARRED BODY IS FOUND, NOT BY UNI*CRON*, BUT BY UNI*CORN*, IN A DIMENSION WHERE MAGIC IS SCIENCE AND FRIENDSHIP IS MAGIC.

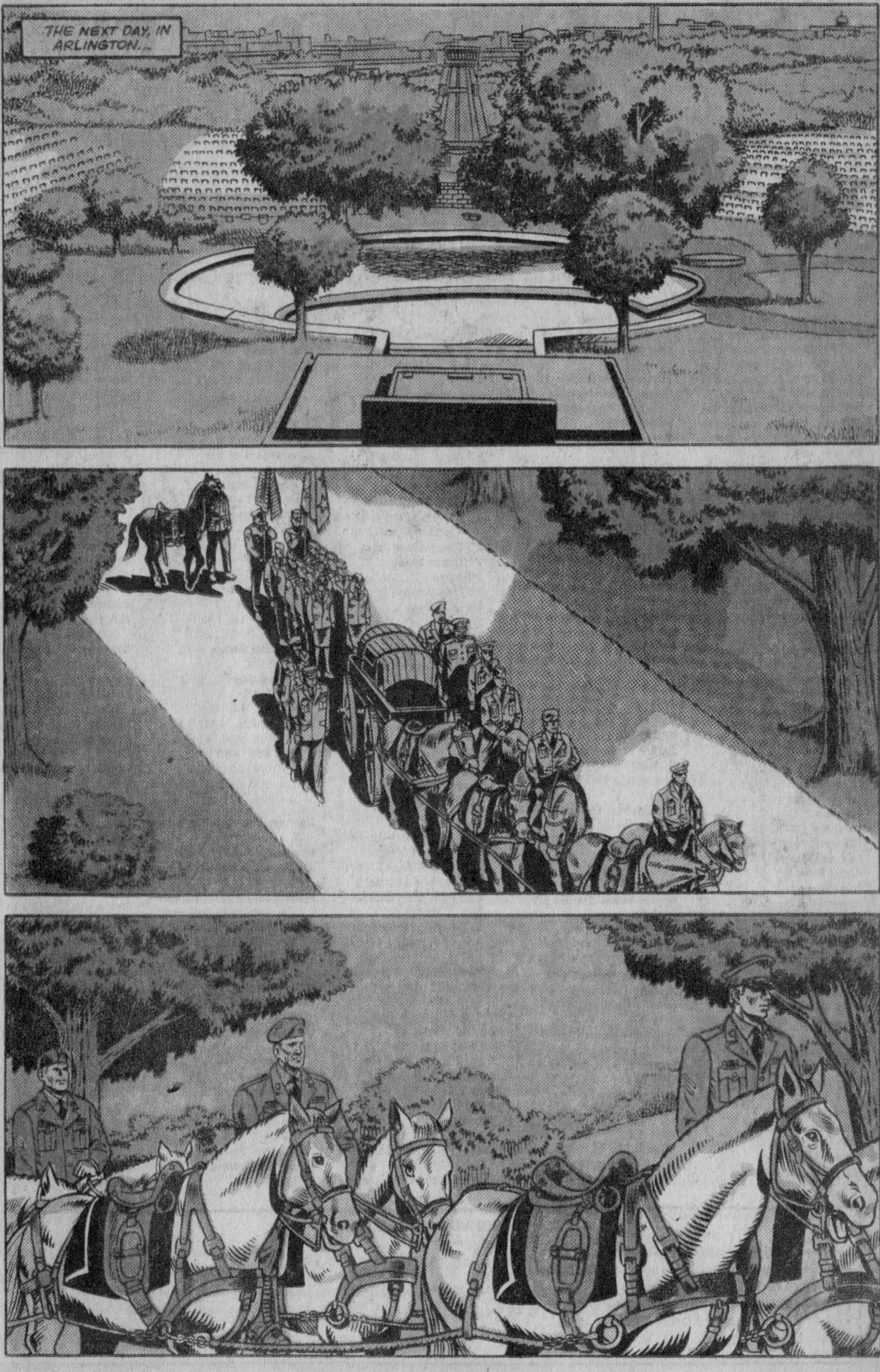
THE NEXT DAY, IN ARLINGTON...

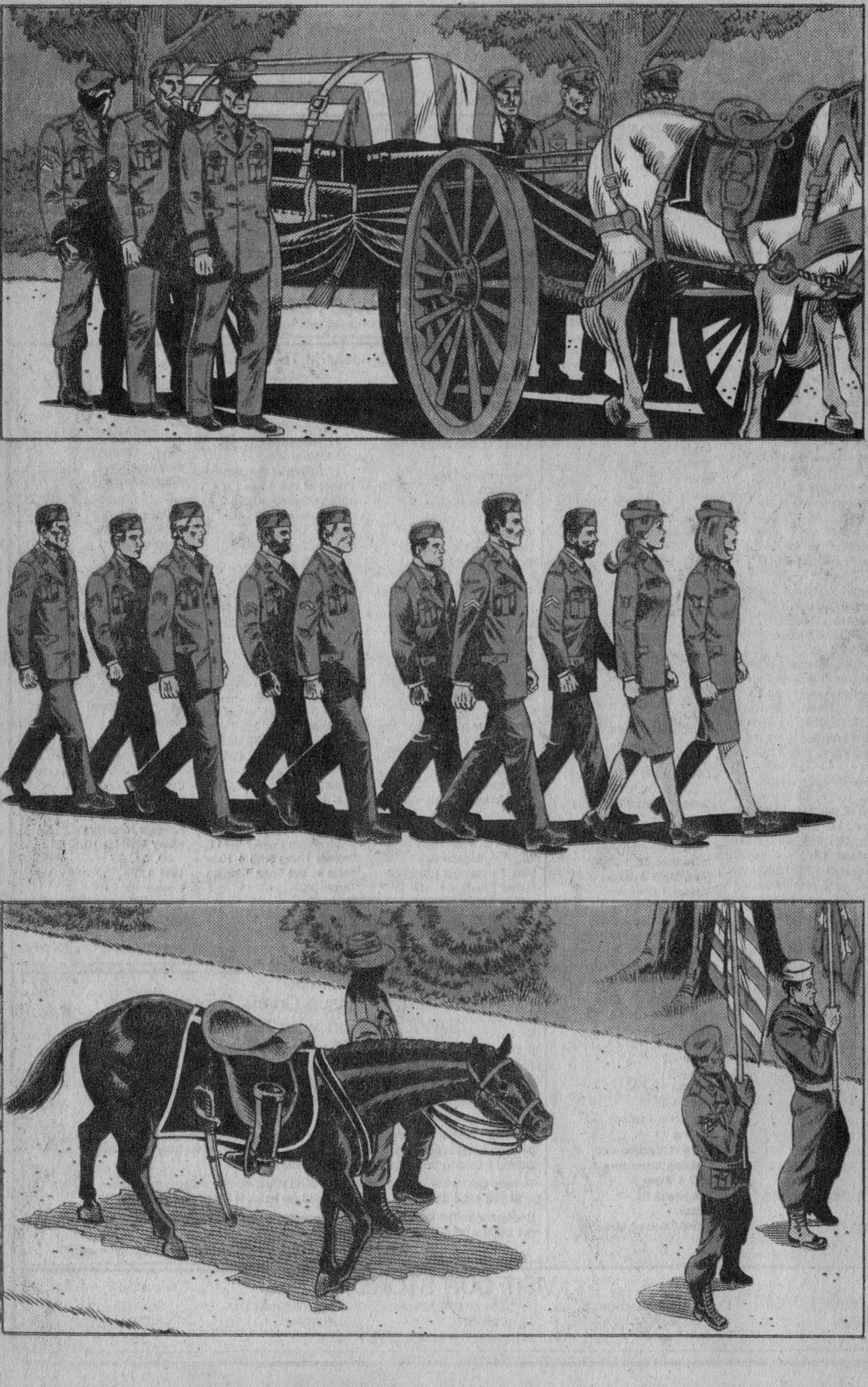

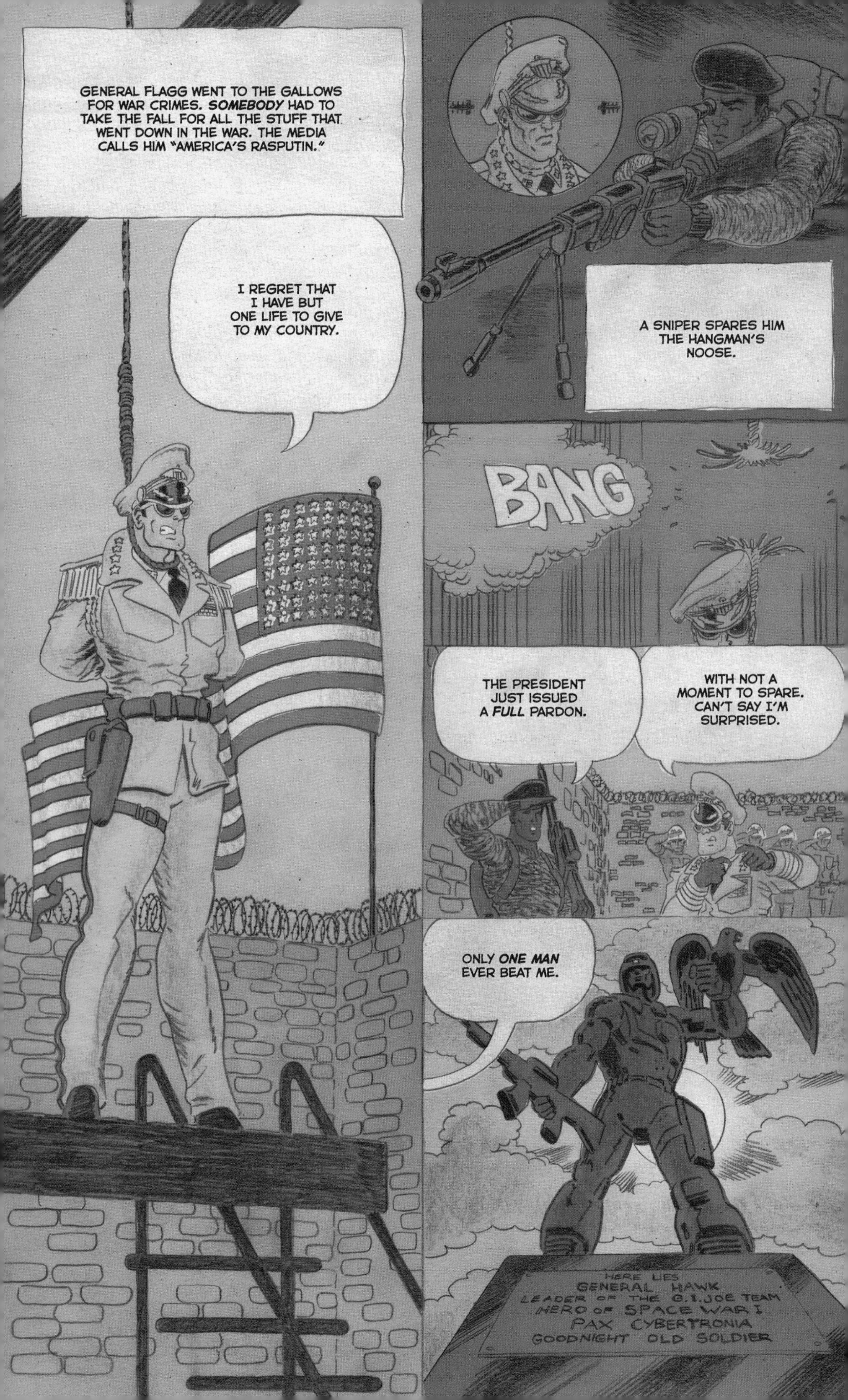
GENERAL FLAGG WENT TO THE GALLOWS FOR WAR CRIMES. SOMEBODY HAD TO TAKE THE FALL FOR ALL THE STUFF THAT WENT DOWN IN THE WAR. THE MEDIA CALLS HIM "AMERICA'S RASPUTIN."
I REGRET THAT I HAVE BUT ONE LIFE TO GIVE TO MY COUNTRY.
A SNIPER SPARES HIM THE HANGMAN'S NOOSE.
BANG
THE PRESIDENT JUST ISSUED A FULL PARDON.
WITH NOT A MOMENT TO SPARE. CAN'T SAY I'M SURPRISED.
ONLY ONE MAN EVER BEAT ME.
HERE LIES
GENERAL HAWK
LEADER OF THE G.I. JOE TEAM
HERO OF SPACE WAR I
PAX CYBERTRONIA
GOODNIGHT OLD SOLDIER

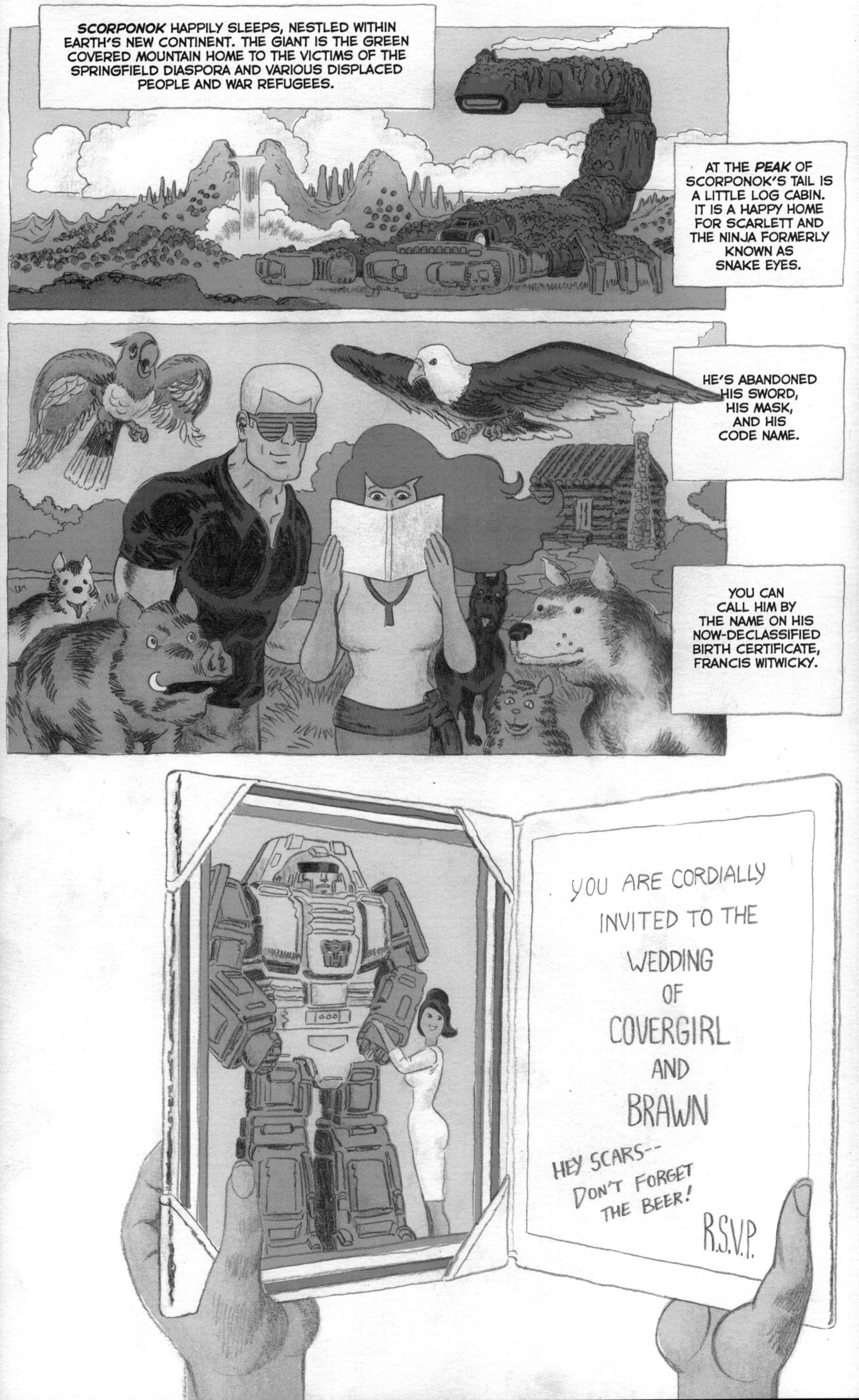
SCORPONOK HAPPILY SLEEPS, NESTLED WITHIN EARTH'S NEW CONTINENT. THE GIANT IS THE GREEN COVERED MOUNTAIN HOME TO THE VICTIMS OF THE SPRINGFIELD DIASPORA AND VARIOUS DISPLACED PEOPLE AND WAR REFUGEES.
AT THE PEAK OF SCORPONOK'S TAIL IS A LITTLE LOG CABIN. IT IS A HAPPY HOME FOR SCARLETT AND THE NINJA FORMERLY KNOWN AS SNAKE EYES.
HE'S ABANDONED HIS SWORD, HIS MASK, AND HIS CODE NAME.
YOU CAN CALL HIM BY THE NAME ON HIS NOW-DECLASSIFIED BIRTH CERTIFICATE, FRANCIS WITWICKY.
YOU ARE CORDIALLY INVITED TO THE WEDDING OF COVERGIRL AND BRAWN
HEY SCARS-- DON'T FORGET THE BEER!
R.S.V.P.

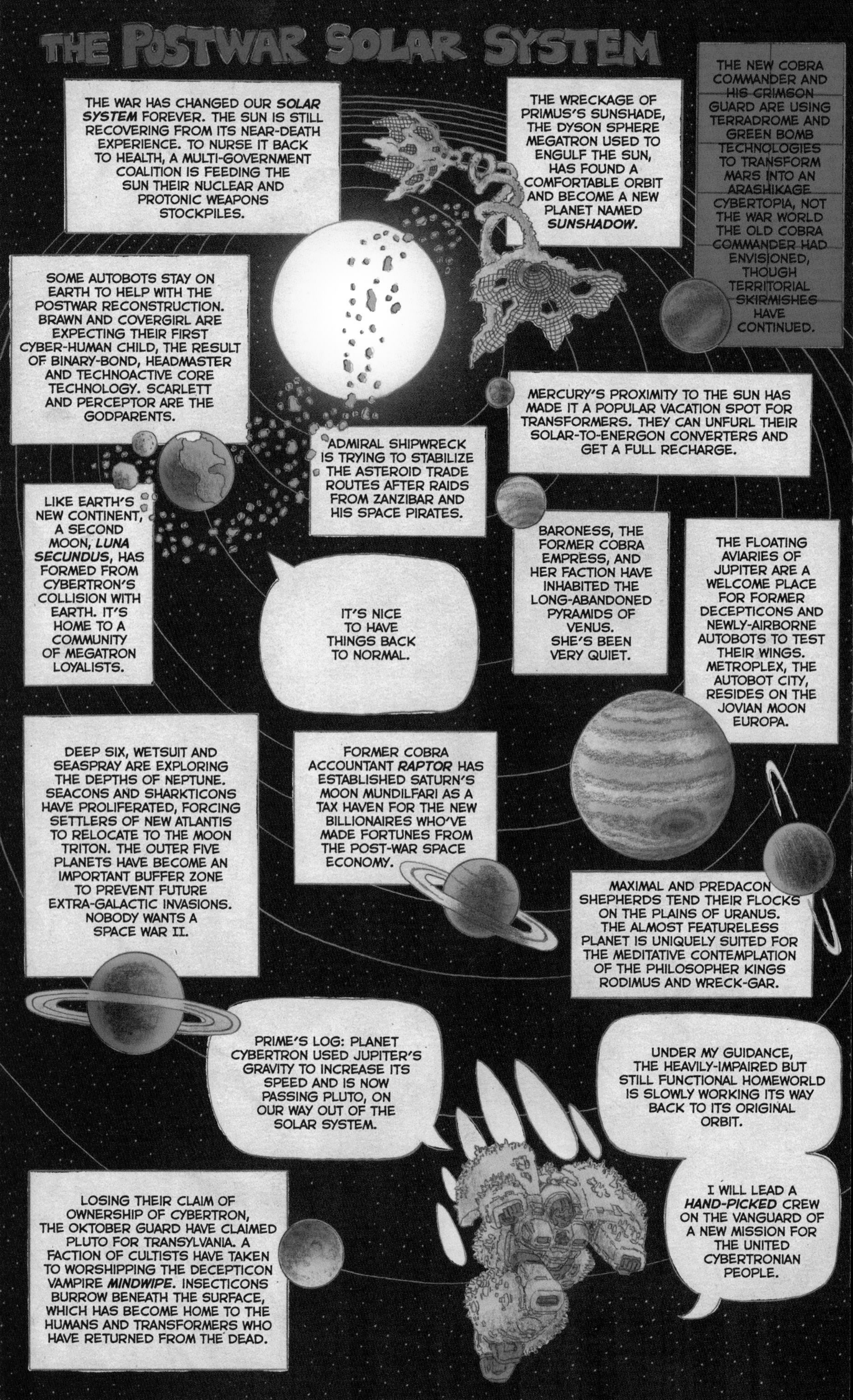
THE POSTWAR SOLAR SYSTEM
THE WAR HAS CHANGED OUR *SOLAR SYSTEM* FOREVER. THE SUN IS STILL RECOVERING FROM ITS NEAR-DEATH EXPERIENCE. TO NURSE IT BACK TO HEALTH, A MULTI-GOVERNMENT COALITION IS FEEDING THE SUN THEIR NUCLEAR AND PROTONIC WEAPONS STOCKPILES.
THE WRECKAGE OF PRIMUS'S SUNSHADE, THE DYSON SPHERE MEGATRON USED TO ENGULF THE SUN, HAS FOUND A COMFORTABLE ORBIT AND BECOME A NEW PLANET NAMED *SUNSHADOW.*
THE NEW COBRA COMMANDER AND HIS CRIMSON GUARD ARE USING TERRADROME AND GREEN BOMB TECHNOLOGIES TO TRANSFORM MARS INTO AN ARASHIKAGE CYBERTOPIA, NOT THE WAR WORLD THE OLD COBRA COMMANDER HAD ENVISIONED, THOUGH TERRITORIAL SKIRMISHES HAVE CONTINUED.
SOME AUTOBOTS STAY ON EARTH TO HELP WITH THE POSTWAR RECONSTRUCTION. BRAWN AND COVERGIRL ARE EXPECTING THEIR FIRST CYBER-HUMAN CHILD, THE RESULT OF BINARY-BOND, HEADMASTER AND TECHNOACTIVE CORE TECHNOLOGY. SCARLETT AND PERCEPTOR ARE THE GODPARENTS.
MERCURY'S PROXIMITY TO THE SUN HAS MADE IT A POPULAR VACATION SPOT FOR TRANSFORMERS. THEY CAN UNFURL THEIR SOLAR-TO-ENERGON CONVERTERS AND GET A FULL RECHARGE.
ADMIRAL SHIPWRECK IS TRYING TO STABILIZE THE ASTEROID TRADE ROUTES AFTER RAIDS FROM ZANZIBAR AND HIS SPACE PIRATES.
LIKE EARTH'S NEW CONTINENT, A SECOND MOON, *LUNA SECUNDUS*, HAS FORMED FROM CYBERTRON'S COLLISION WITH EARTH. IT'S HOME TO A COMMUNITY OF MEGATRON LOYALISTS.
IT'S NICE TO HAVE THINGS BACK TO NORMAL.
BARONESS, THE FORMER COBRA EMPRESS, AND HER FACTION HAVE INHABITED THE LONG-ABANDONED PYRAMIDS OF VENUS. SHE'S BEEN VERY QUIET.
THE FLOATING AVIARIES OF JUPITER ARE A WELCOME PLACE FOR FORMER DECEPTICONS AND NEWLY-AIRBORNE AUTOBOTS TO TEST THEIR WINGS. METROPLEX, THE AUTOBOT CITY, RESIDES ON THE JOVIAN MOON EUROPA.
DEEP SIX, WETSUIT AND SEASPRAY ARE EXPLORING THE DEPTHS OF NEPTUNE. SEACONS AND SHARKTICONS HAVE PROLIFERATED, FORCING SETTLERS OF NEW ATLANTIS TO RELOCATE TO THE MOON TRITON. THE OUTER FIVE PLANETS HAVE BECOME AN IMPORTANT BUFFER ZONE TO PREVENT FUTURE EXTRA-GALACTIC INVASIONS. NOBODY WANTS A SPACE WAR II.
FORMER COBRA ACCOUNTANT *RAPTOR* HAS ESTABLISHED SATURN'S MOON MUNDILFARI AS A TAX HAVEN FOR THE NEW BILLIONAIRES WHO'VE MADE FORTUNES FROM THE POST-WAR SPACE ECONOMY.
MAXIMAL AND PREDACON SHEPHERDS TEND THEIR FLOCKS ON THE PLAINS OF URANUS. THE ALMOST FEATURELESS PLANET IS UNIQUELY SUITED FOR THE MEDITATIVE CONTEMPLATION OF THE PHILOSOPHER KINGS RODIMUS AND WRECK-GAR.
PRIME'S LOG: PLANET CYBERTRON USED JUPITER'S GRAVITY TO INCREASE ITS SPEED AND IS NOW PASSING PLUTO, ON OUR WAY OUT OF THE SOLAR SYSTEM.
UNDER MY GUIDANCE, THE HEAVILY-IMPAIRED BUT STILL FUNCTIONAL HOMEWORLD IS SLOWLY WORKING ITS WAY BACK TO ITS ORIGINAL ORBIT.
LOSING THEIR CLAIM OF OWNERSHIP OF *CYBERTRON*, THE OKTOBER GUARD HAVE CLAIMED PLUTO FOR TRANSYLVANIA. A FACTION OF CULTISTS HAVE TAKEN TO WORSHIPPING THE DECEPTICON VAMPIRE *MINDWIPE*. INSECTICONS BURROW BENEATH THE SURFACE, WHICH HAS BECOME HOME TO THE HUMANS AND TRANSFORMERS WHO HAVE RETURNED FROM THE DEAD.
I WILL LEAD A *HAND-PICKED* CREW ON THE VANGUARD OF A NEW MISSION FOR THE UNITED CYBERTRONIAN PEOPLE.

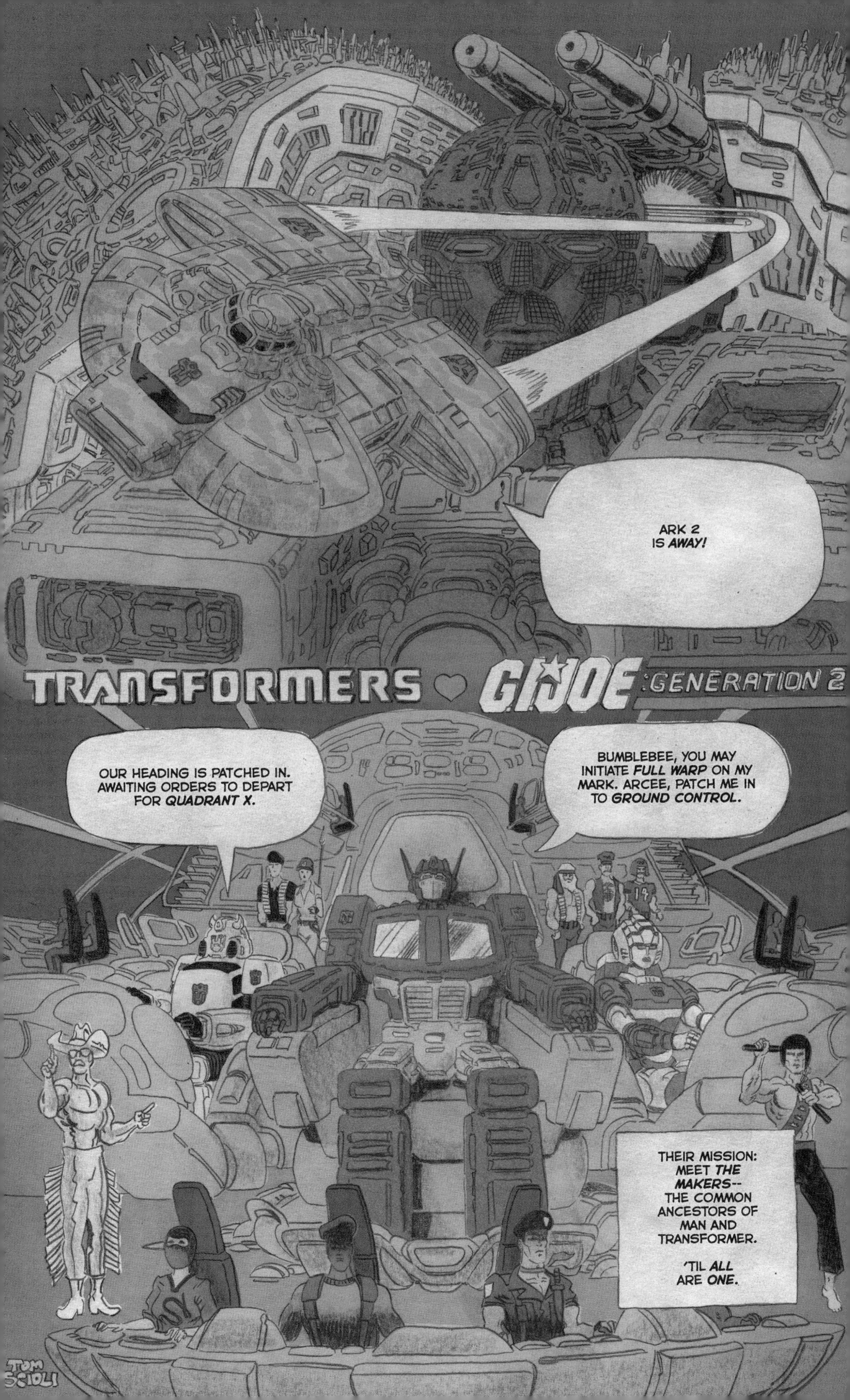
ARK 2 IS AWAY!
TRANSFORMERS ♥ G.I. JOE: GENERATION 2
OUR HEADING IS PATCHED IN. AWAITING ORDERS TO DEPART FOR QUADRANT X.
BUMBLEBEE, YOU MAY INITIATE FULL WARP ON MY MARK. ARCEE, PATCH ME IN TO GROUND CONTROL.
THEIR MISSION: MEET THE MAKERS-- THE COMMON ANCESTORS OF MAN AND TRANSFORMER.
'TIL ALL ARE ONE.
TOM SCIOLI

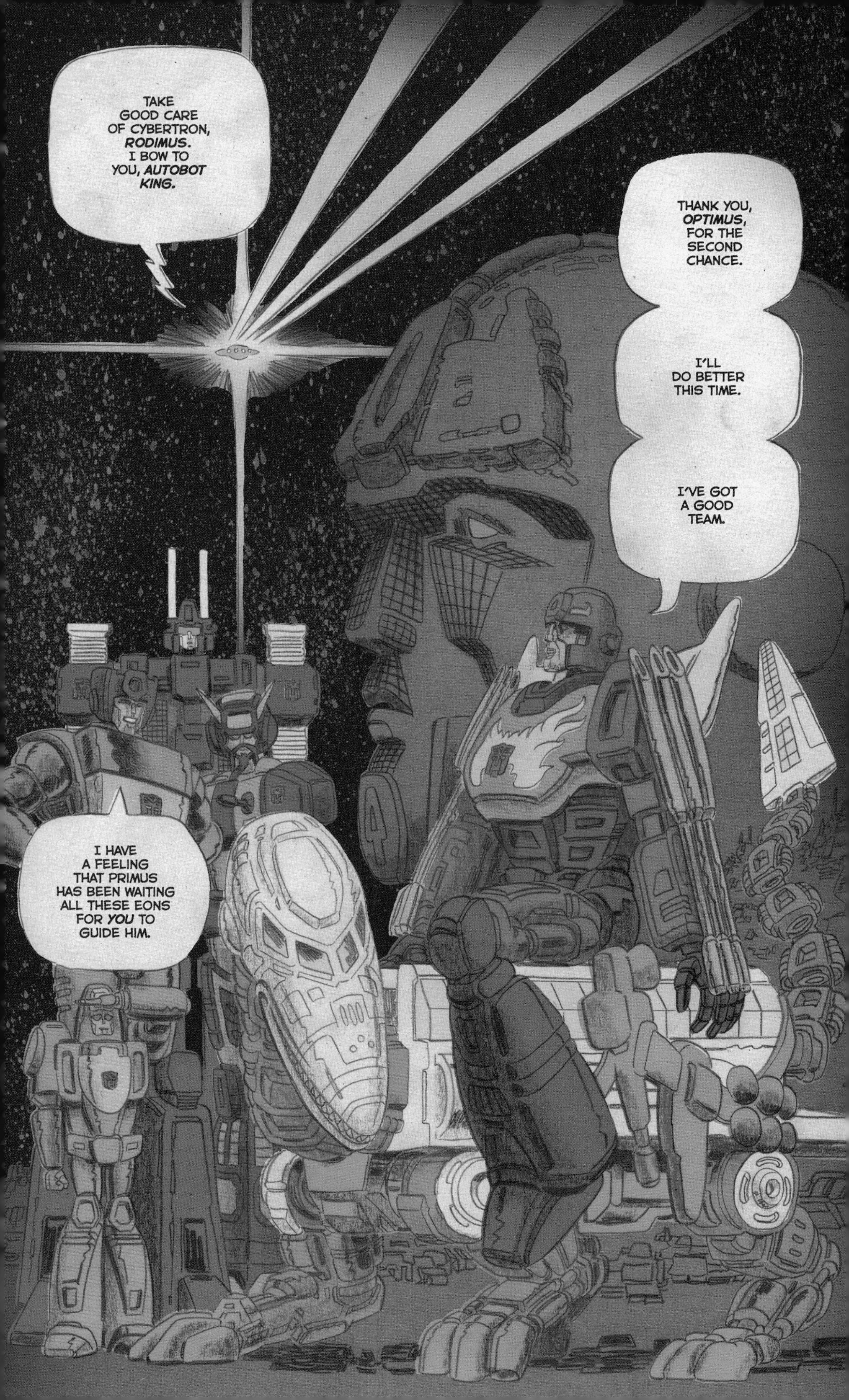
TAKE GOOD CARE OF CYBERTRON, RODIMUS. I BOW TO YOU, AUTOBOT KING.
THANK YOU, OPTIMUS, FOR THE SECOND CHANCE.
I'LL DO BETTER THIS TIME.
I'VE GOT A GOOD TEAM.
I HAVE A FEELING THAT PRIMUS HAS BEEN WAITING ALL THESE EONS FOR YOU TO GUIDE HIM.

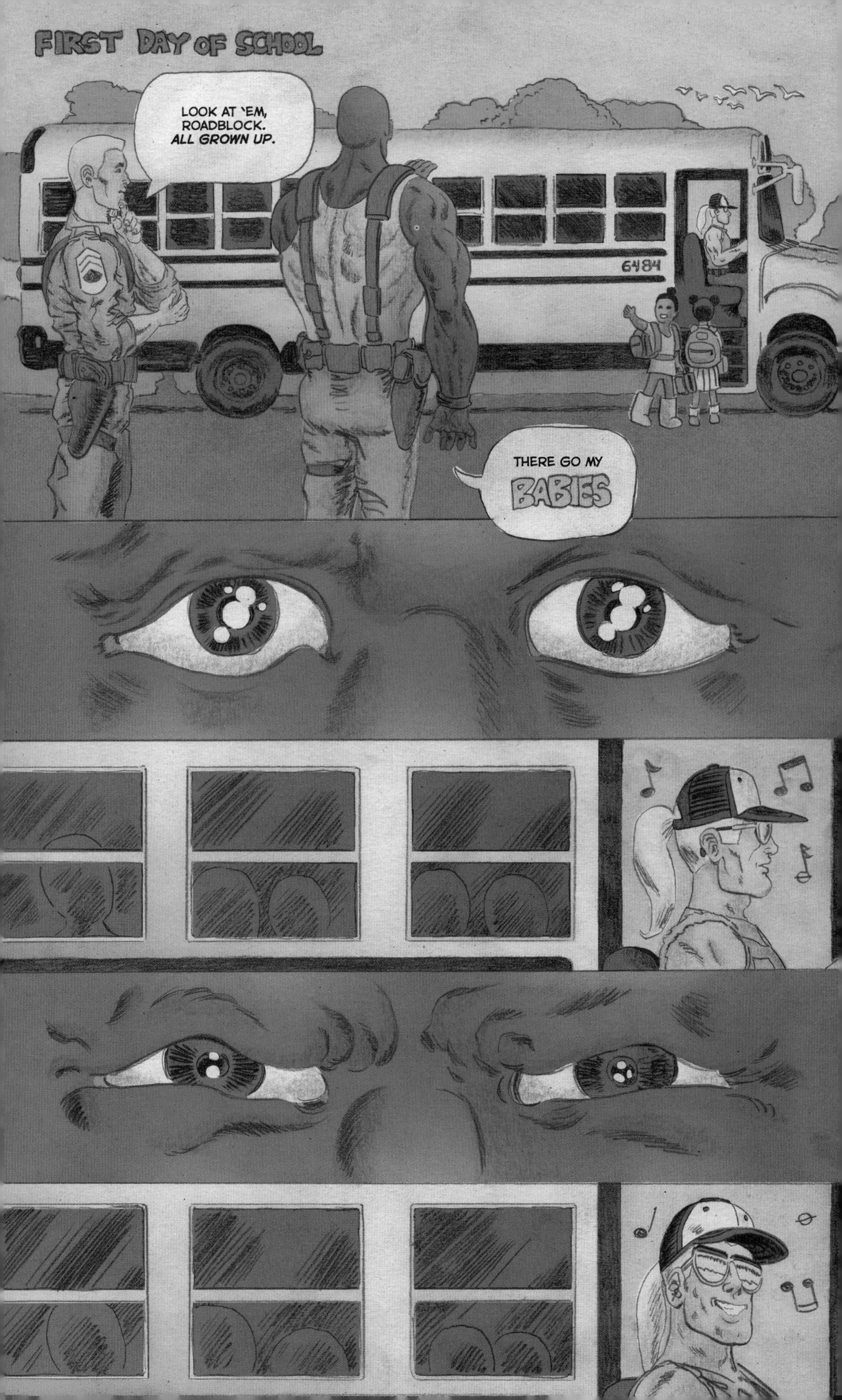
FIRST DAY OF SCHOOL
LOOK AT 'EM, ROADBLOCK. ALL GROWN UP.
6484
THERE GO MY BABIES

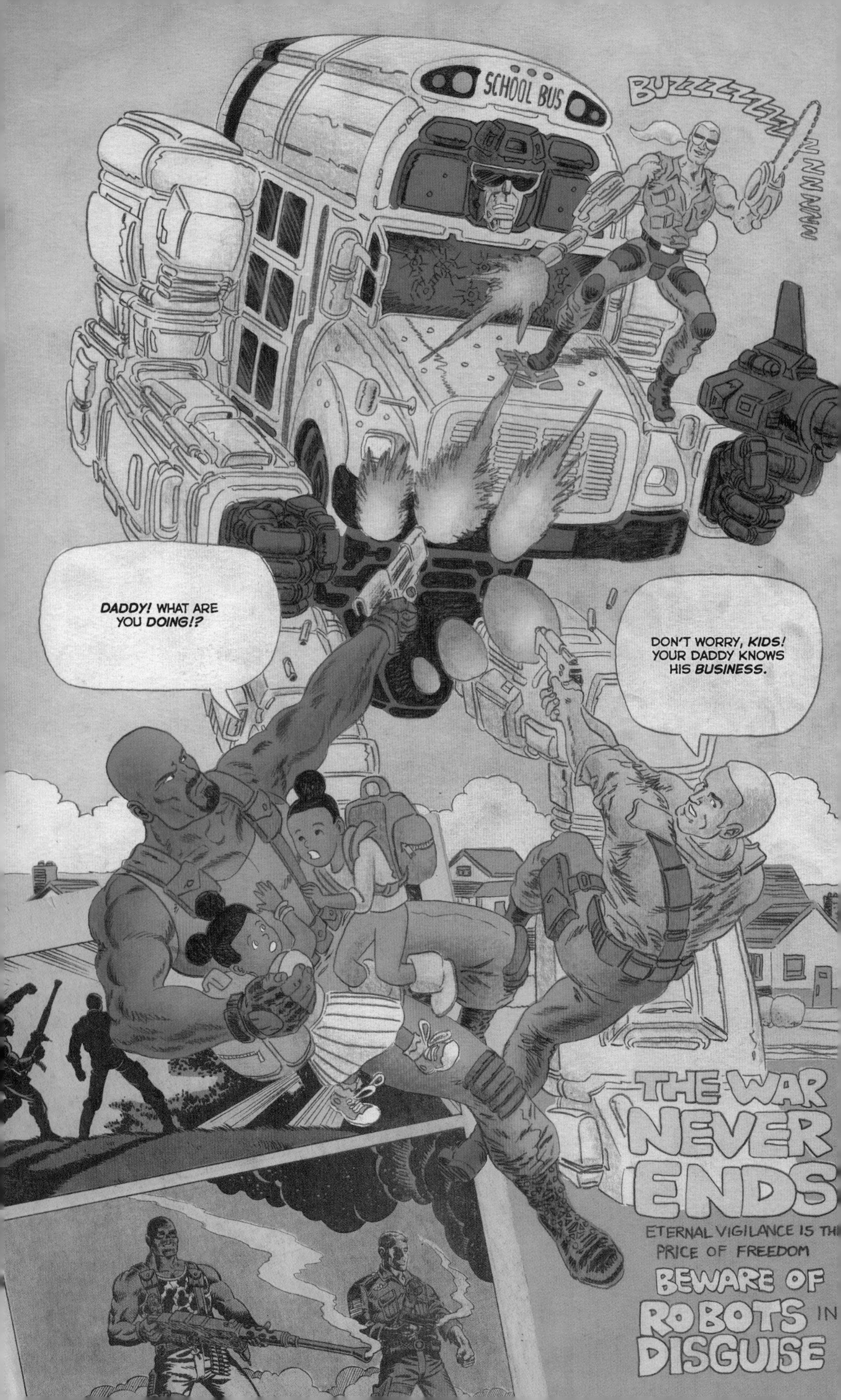
SCHOOL BUS
BUZZZZZZZZZZZZZNNNNN
DADDY! WHAT ARE YOU DOING!?
DON'T WORRY, KIDS! YOUR DADDY KNOWS HIS BUSINESS.
THE WAR NEVER ENDS
ETERNAL VIGILANCE IS THE PRICE OF FREEDOM
BEWARE OF ROBOTS IN DISGUISE

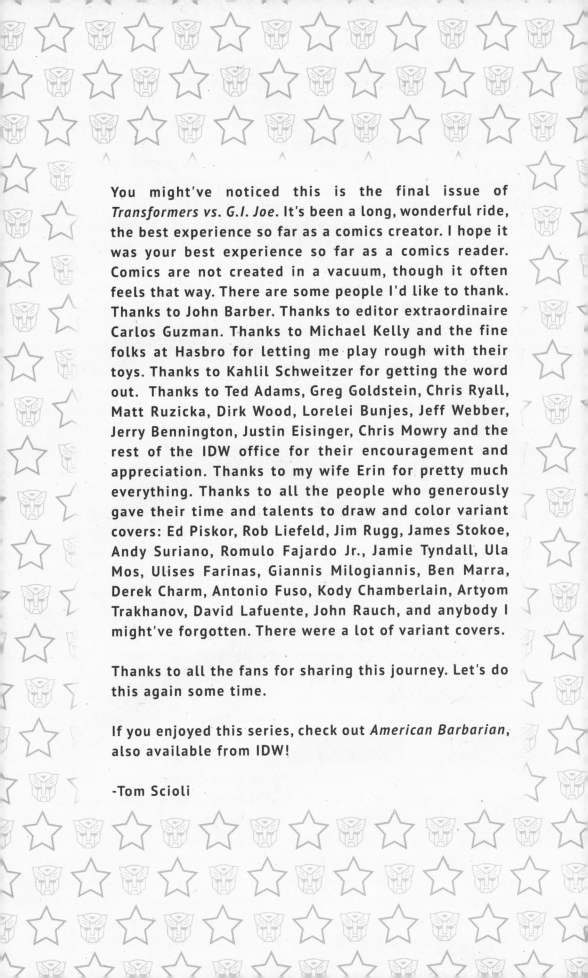

You might've noticed this is the final issue of *Transformers vs. G.I. Joe.* It's been a long, wonderful ride, the best experience so far as a comics creator. I hope it was your best experience so far as a comics reader. Comics are not created in a vacuum, though it often feels that way. There are some people I'd like to thank. Thanks to John Barber. Thanks to editor extraordinaire Carlos Guzman. Thanks to Michael Kelly and the fine folks at Hasbro for letting me play rough with their toys. Thanks to Kahlil Schweitzer for getting the word out. Thanks to Ted Adams, Greg Goldstein, Chris Ryall, Matt Ruzicka, Dirk Wood, Lorelei Bunjes, Jeff Webber, Jerry Bennington, Justin Eisinger, Chris Mowry and the rest of the IDW office for their encouragement and appreciation. Thanks to my wife Erin for pretty much everything. Thanks to all the people who generously gave their time and talents to draw and color variant covers: Ed Piskor, Rob Liefeld, Jim Rugg, James Stokoe, Andy Suriano, Romulo Fajardo Jr., Jamie Tyndall, Ula Mos, Ulises Farinas, Giannis Milogiannis, Ben Marra, Derek Charm, Antonio Fuso, Kody Chamberlain, Artyom Trakhanov, David Lafuente, John Rauch, and anybody I might've forgotten. There were a lot of variant covers.

Thanks to all the fans for sharing this journey. Let's do this again some time.

If you enjoyed this series, check out *American Barbarian,* also available from IDW!

-Tom Scioli

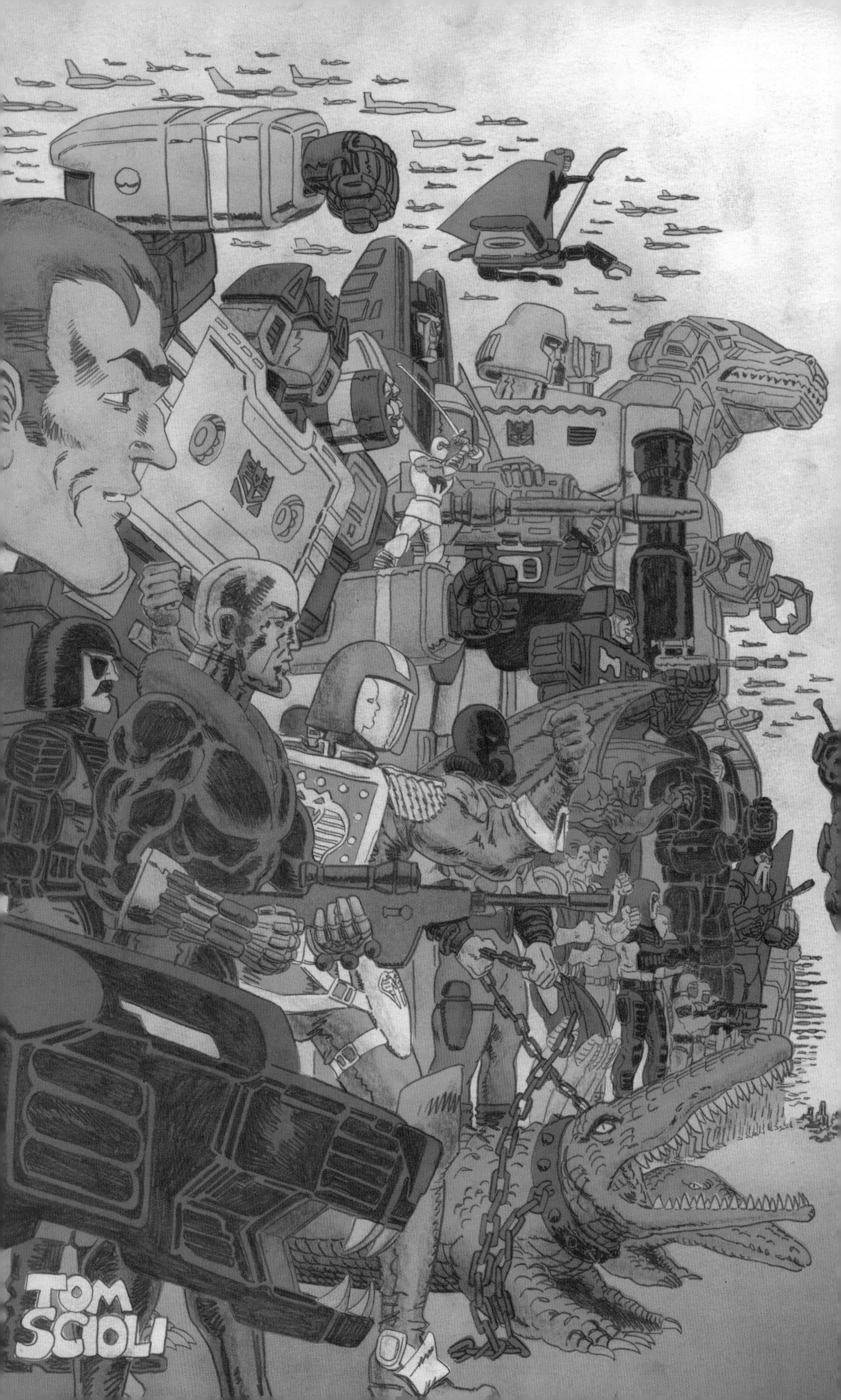
TOM
SCIOLI

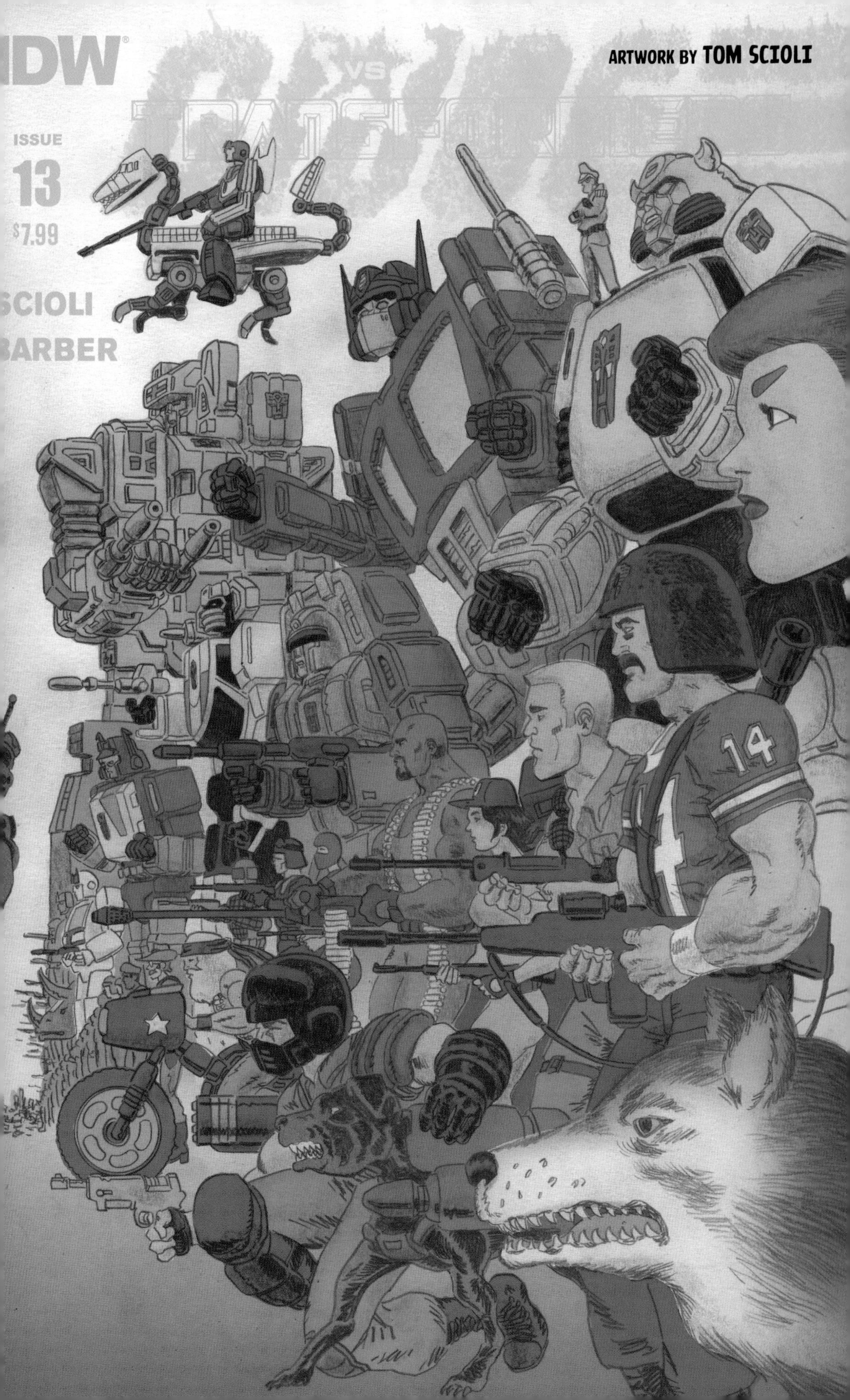

IDW
VS
ISSUE
13
$7.99
SCIOLI
BARBER
ARTWORK BY TOM SCIOLI
14

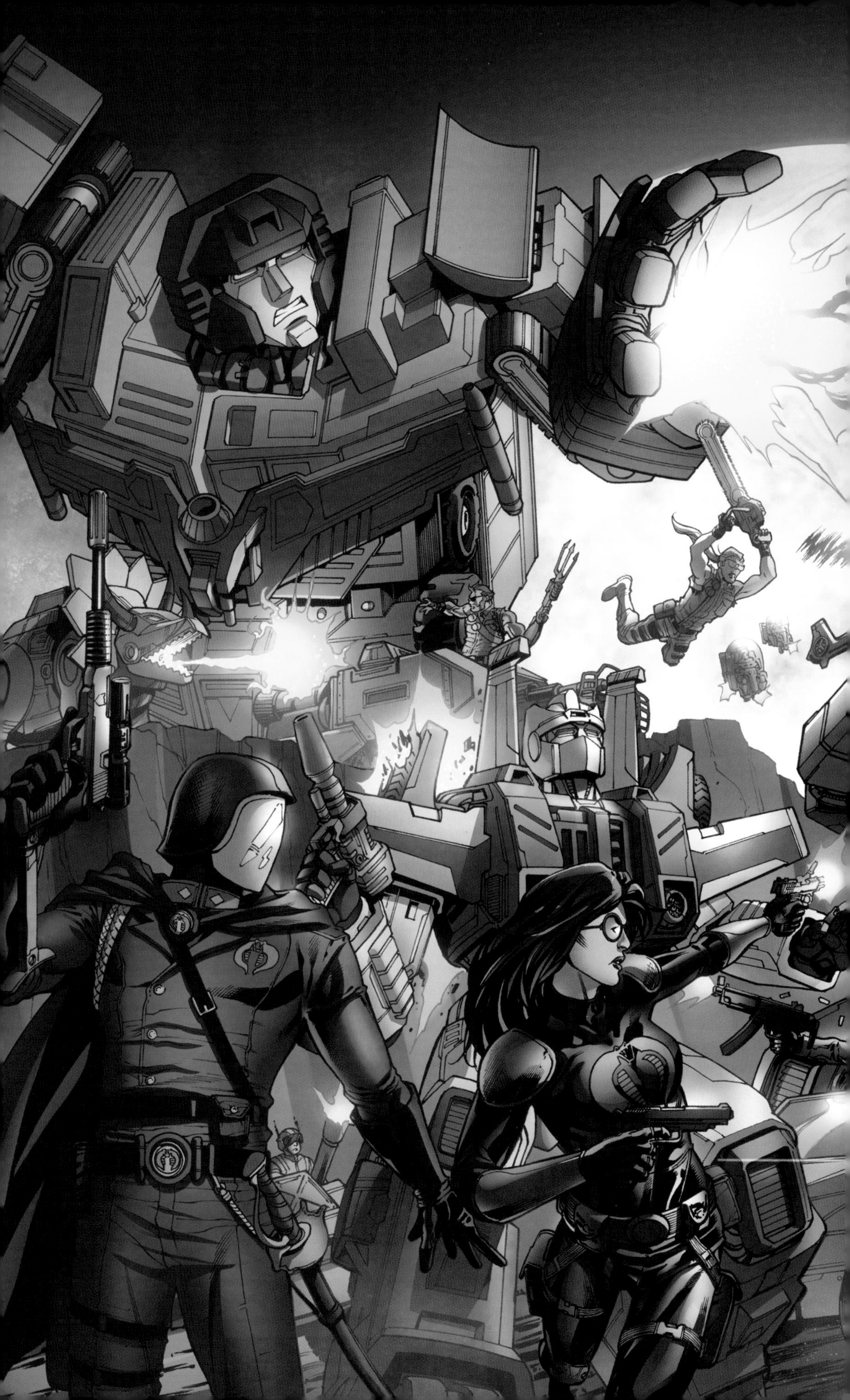

ARTWORK BY ROBERT ATKINS COLORS BY JOANA LAFUENTE

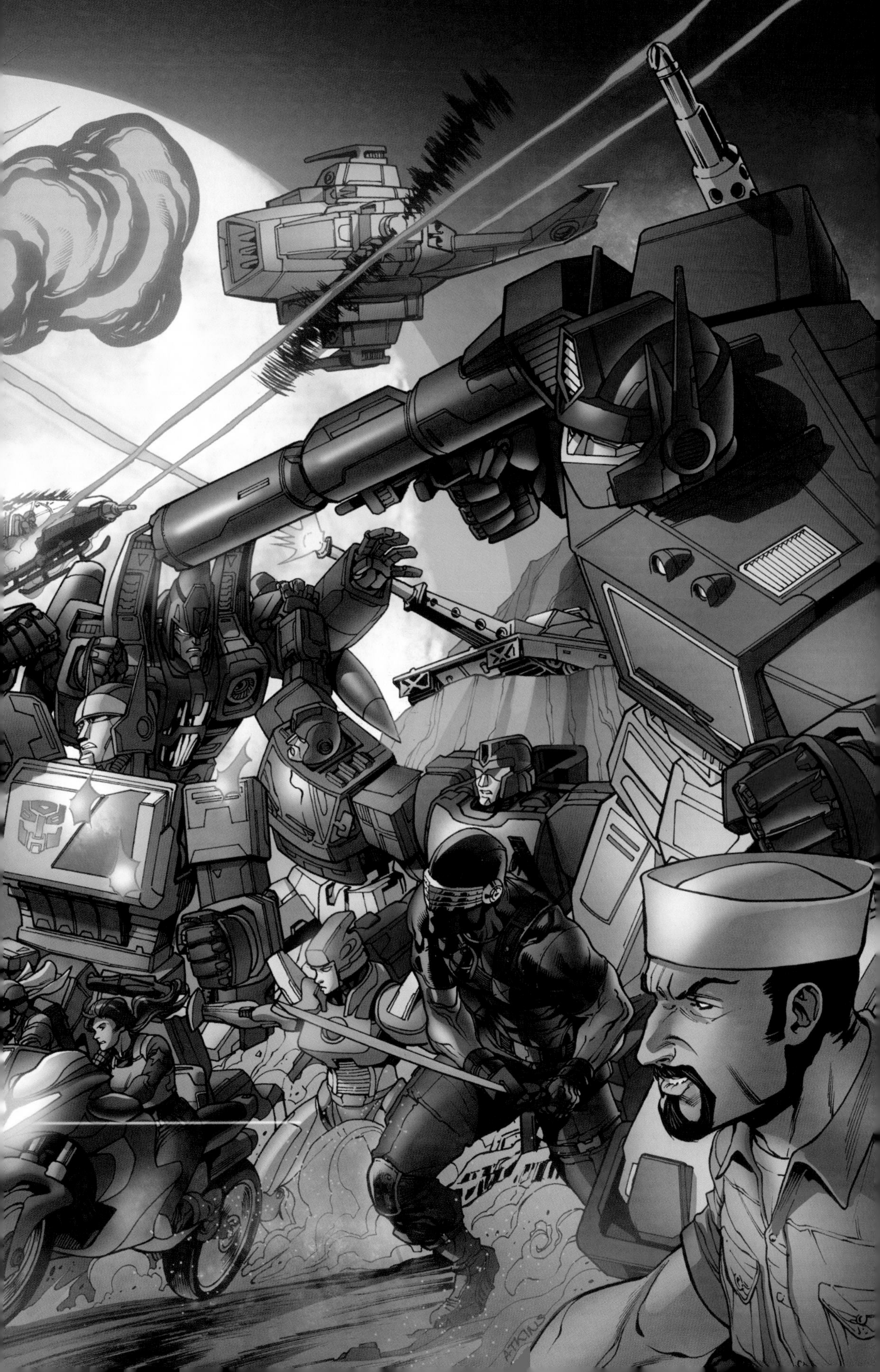

ARTWORK BY **GIANNIS MILONOGIANNIS**

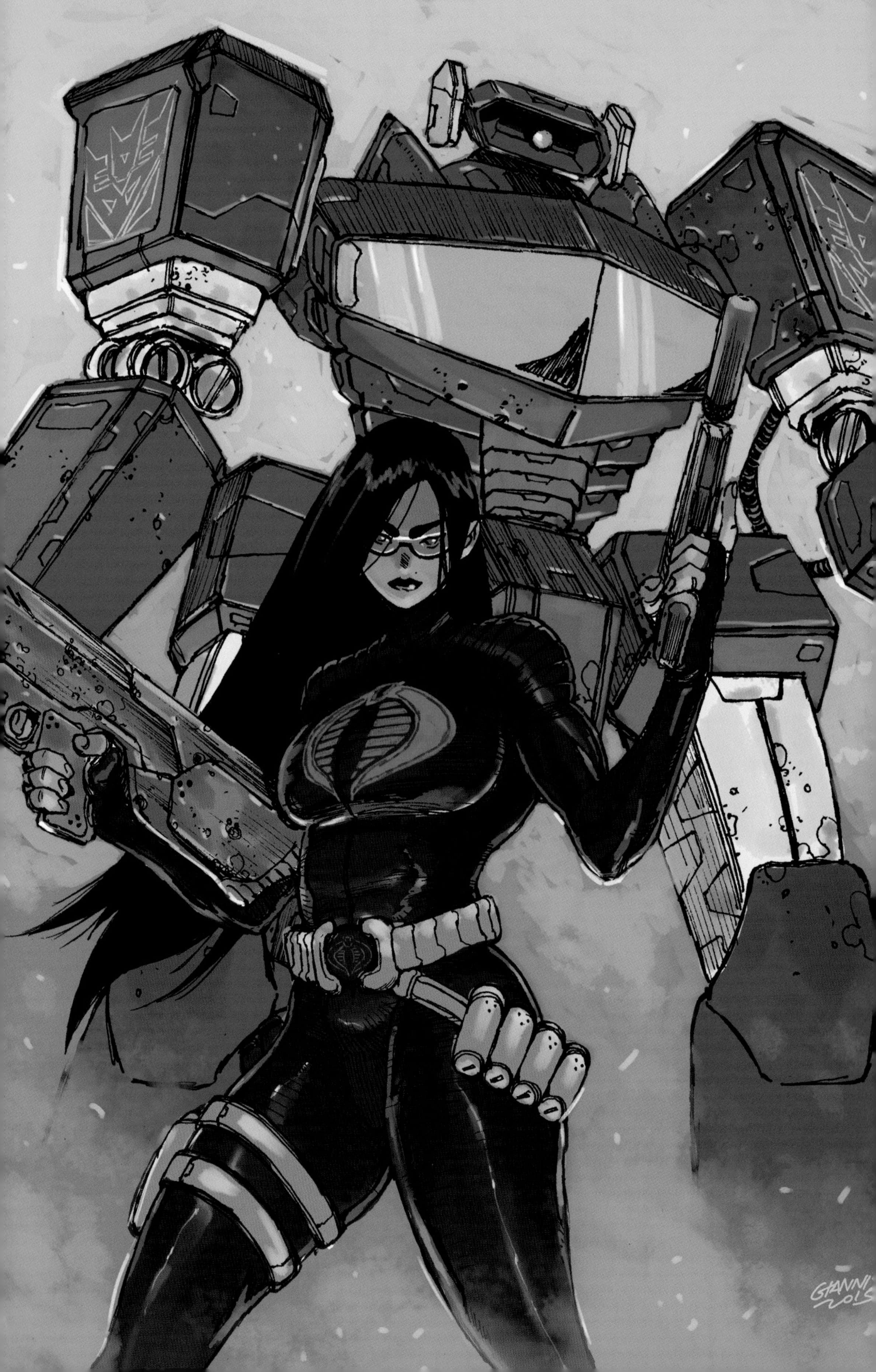

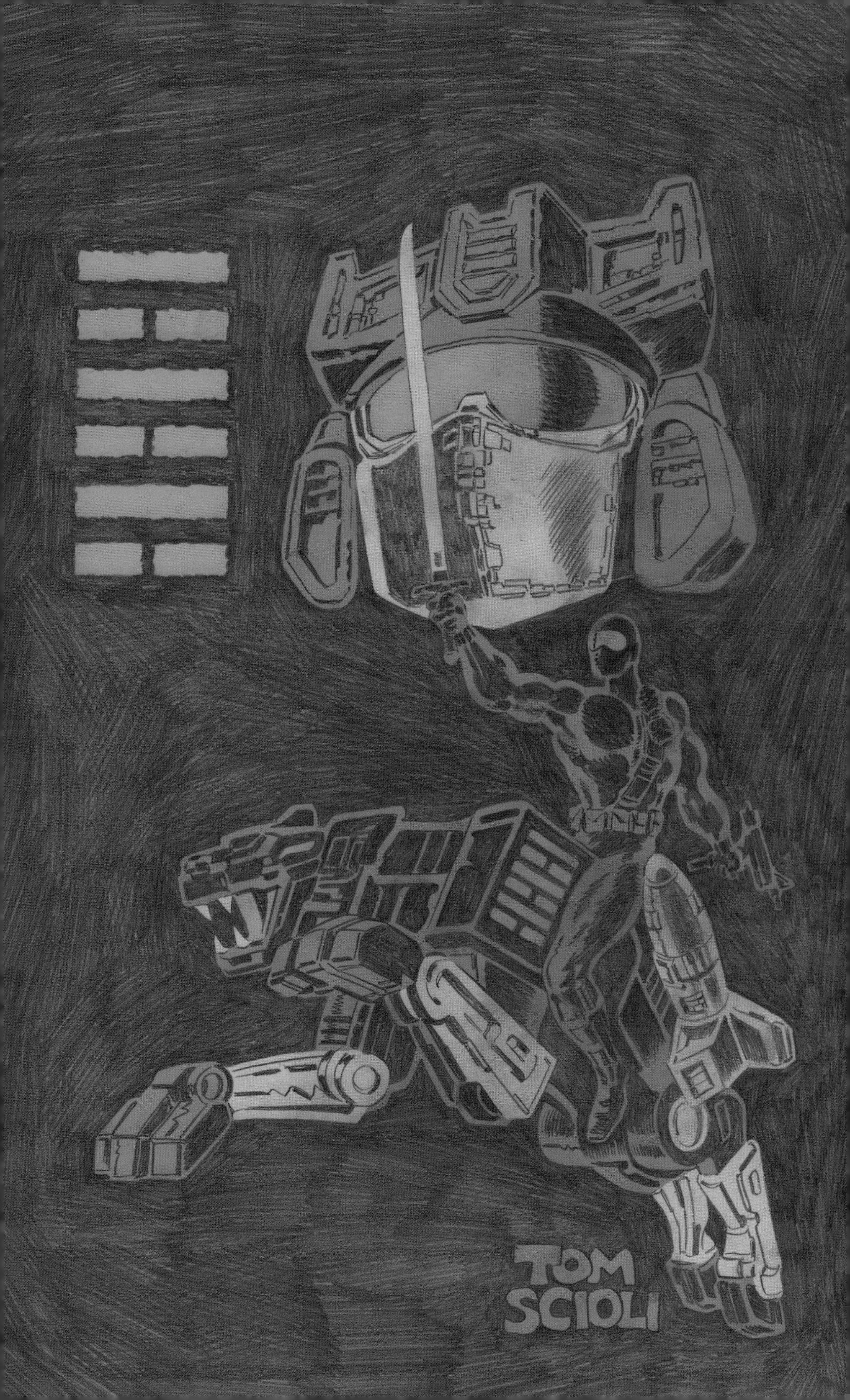
TOM
SCIOLI

BLACK CYBERTRON

BY TOM SCIOLI AND JOHN BARBER

His brother is dead.

Shockwave tries to put it out of his mind. "They always said I was the cold one." Shockwave isn't supposed to feel... he isn't supposed to feel anything.

"Emotion" was Soundwave's thing. Soundwave was the kind one with his sonorous musical voice and love of life, which were unfashionable and unbecoming a Decepticon killing machine. The only time Soundwave would lose that generous quality was when Shockwave would accuse him of "reeking of Autobot." On those occasions, Soundwave's sunny demeanor would turn dark.

"Put it aside," Shockwave tells himself, "Bury the emotion. Become the logical creature of metal and destruction you should be. Become logic."

But his brother is dead and Shockwave can't help feeling... something. He gives in a little and under his own terms. He analyzes the emotion. Anger at his placement in the hierarchy and unfulfilled dreams? Sadness over the loss of the only person he ever loved? Fear of his own mortality?

"You act like you will never die," Soundwave would often say.

Isn't that a logical intention? "The universe needs me." Dead he is of no use. Death—true death—Is a rare and shameful bird among the elite of Cybertron. Reconstruction, augmentation, and replacement of parts makes death temporary. His body is nickel and wire and silicon. The parts that decay, that break, are replaceable. Shockwave looks at the shimmering purple of the gun barrel he used to replace his own hand. True death is for the weak, the poor. It's for humans. For Autobots. For Optimus Prime. Shockwave brightens for a moment, remembering the exquisite beautiful cruelty with which Megatron executed the Autobot folk hero.

He looks past his gunhand, and refocuses his glowing monocular eye on the headless iron corpse of his brother, Soundwave.

A shattered head was not the same as a shattered hand. For Soundwave to return to the land of the living his brother would have to carry him to the land of the dead.

"You summoned us, uncle?"

Rumble enters the chamber, holding a large silver urn cradled in his right arm and the avian Lazerbeak perched on his left.

"We're going on a dark quest, my nephews. We're taking your father to Kalis."

Rumble's smirk turned into a gaping dropped jaw.

"Did you say 'Kalis'?" Hearing the dreaded word repeated, Lazerbeak lets out a piercing squawk.

"Why else would I have you gather up the scattered bits and pieces of his skull?" Shockwave found Rumble to be loutish and irksome, but occasionally his cretinous nephew displayed some tic—some slight tilt of the head, a turn of the wrist—that would remind him of his departed brother Soundwave. For a moment he'd feel a rush of goodwill towards his nephew, before he'd do something to break the brief moment of bonding.

Rumble gives the urn a shake, hearing the remains of Soundwave's head rattle.

"Carry it with the respect your father deserves."

"Yeah, yeah," sneered the cassette.

"Do as you're told, and if you keep your mouth shut, you might find yourself no longer an orphan." Soundwave had a paternal streak that was all but non-existent among the Decepticon race. His "children" were not mere tools to him. He cared for them and, in Shockwave's opinion, spoiled them.

Perhaps it was that paternal streak that made him the sole voice of caution, mercy and reason when Megatron set his sights on the planet Earth. And, maybe that's what made him lose favor in the eyes of the Deceptiking. Perhaps that's why Megatron put Soundwave's family on the frontline of the invasion Soundwave had argued against.

Of all his brother's children, why did the Joes have to get their hands on the smart cassette? Ravage the cunning cat was unique among his siblings. He'd gotten out from under Soundwave's shadow and become a force to be reckoned with in his own right, an advisor and spymaster of the utmost value to Megatron's climb to power. Now Ravage was missing in action, last seen on the late lamented planet Earth, and like Soundwave's husk, reprogrammed and working for the G.I. Joe Team.

The humans had captured Soundwave and pulled him apart, and experimented upon him. Their Coltonbolt ray had shattered his head into a thousand pieces. Which Rumble is absent-mindedly rattling in their urn.

Where was Ravage now? An acceptable loss in the destruction of Earth? Shockwave might never know what became of the feline machine.

****

Snake Eyes' grapple-gun lariat loops around the

Cybertronian cat's neck. Before long he has the Decepticat metaphorically, if not literally, eating out of his hand. Snake Eyes finds his new mount superb for traversing the meteor-scarred landscape of post EarthDeath Cybertron. Shards of that devastated planet continue to pelt Cybertron with alarming regularity. Snake Eyes knows he was lucky to escape his dying homeworld. When the long hornlike mountain of Cybertron collided with Earth, he ran towards the impact point instead of away from it. When two worlds collide, you have to decide which one will survive the impact, which one will be triumphant in the cosmic game of rock-paper-scissors, and make the split-second choice to jump ship or stand your ground. Adapt or die.

Snake Eyes is a Cybertronian now.

He relaxes his chokehold on the cybercougar's neck as its hissing changes to a motorcycle purr. Snake Eyes finds he can, with the merest shift in his weight, direct this cat, making it an extension of his will. Apparently the Hard/Blind/Soft Masters' mind control techniques work on damaged alien robot cats. Snake Eyes' mount, the size of an abnormally large horse or a small elephant, is the once-feared Ravage, a cyber-panther of deepest onyx. They are a striking pair, like the apocalyptic horseman death and his fearsome beast of burden. Like Snake Eyes, Ravage was a damaged warrior who, after multiple injuries, attempts at brainwashing and reprogramming, had seemingly forgotten exactly what he was fighting for.

Whatever side Ravage had found his sympathies on, his body belongs to Snake Eyes. The silent ninja commando had taken a moment of sentiment—or was it wry humor—to adorn the ro-beast with his brand, the blood-red morse code "dash-dot-dot-dash" of the Arashikage temple where he'd perfected his killing arts.

Snake Eyes wrenches as the cat, like its now-extinct Earth equivalent, quickly changes direction to pursue some undetectable scent, some inaudible sound and darts into the dark maw of a cave, rider and all. Snake Eyes clings close to the ro-beast and narrowly avoids another head injury on the roof of the cavern as it narrows.

The beast hisses, "I hear my father's voice... calling me to the land of the dead... calling me to Kalis."

"Callous," thinks Snake Eyes, "What a perfect name for the Cybertronian land of the dead." Perhaps a detour on the path to Trypticon is in order. He lets the bucking bronco get its wildness out before coming down hard on the reins. Snake Eyes wants to see this ro-beast's master who had supposedly conquered death itself. He can't say no to a mythic journey to the underworld, to the heart of darkness. He is Hercules riding Cerberus into the Gobot Hades.

****

The Citadel was feared by all, perhaps save Megatron. Deep under the metal ground, its reverse spires twist in a dizzying helix. It is a dark temple in a city of death, where Flame, the Autobot Apostate, performs his cursed miracles.

"Place him in the baptismal firebath."

Shockwave and his nephews obey, lowering Soundwave into the casket. Liquid-boiling and evaporating and freezing and boiling again—surges through plastisteel tubes wrapping the walls around Soundwave.

"Where is the rest of him?"

Rumble hands Flame the urn.

"You must've loved this Soundwave to have placed so much effort in the reclamation." Before Shockwave or his nephews have a chance to reply, the crimson-clad Flame snaps, "Love has no place in my domain."

Although Flame was born an Autobot, he now and forever belonged to the dark side of Cybertron. In the neglected recesses of the legendary library at the University of Iacon, he'd learned about Metatron—the Angel of Light—of whom Megatron claims to be an incarnation and Metatron's nemesis—the dark angel—Ultra Magnus, the Autobot god of death.

The ritual ends in a gout of plasma. Soundwave's body emerges whole and gleaming as if newly born, a specimen of physical perfection, but motionless. Then his right finger twitches. Then his whole hand. Then both arms, with which he raises himself to a stiff seated position. Shockwave exclaims, with a glimmer in his eye, "You're back."

After an interminable silence, Soundwave responds, but not in his sonorous basso profundo voice, but in a cold electronic monotone, what humans would use to mock Cybertronian-kind. "WHAT ARE THE PARAMETERS OF THE MISSION?"

"What?!"

Soundwave continues, "WHAT IS MY TARGET? WHAT ARE THE PARAMETERS OF THE MISSION? ONLY THEN WILL I BE ABLE TO CHOOSE THE APPROPRIATE CASSETTE AGENT AND CALCULATE THEIR PRESCRIBED OPERATION."

"Soundwave, don't you recognize me?"

"AFFIRMATIVE. YOU ARE SHOCKWAVE, SERVANT OF MEGATRON."

"I'm your brother."

"THOSE ARE EMPTY WORDS. UNAPPLICABLE. WHAT IS A 'BROTHER' TO A BEING FORGED BY UNKNOWN HANDS? WHAT ARE THE PARAMETERS OF THE MISSION?"

"Oh Soundwave, what's become of you?"

****

"So this is Callous," thought Snake Eyes.

"You're not much of a companion," hisses Ravage, "you haven't said a word all the way here."

The stygian necropolis seems abandoned, if not for some flashes and flares coming from an inverse spiraling tower hanging from the cyclopean vault above.

Even with his visor in night-vision mode, the city is cloaked in an almost supernatural murk.

A large vague shape begins moving. A tree, perhaps, swaying in the breeze. But there is no breeze, no wind in the stale air of Kalis. It's not a tree, it's a Cybertronian, heading straight for him.

Snake Eyes leans and Ravage obeys. They dash in a perpendicular away from the hulk, but are blocked by another giant. This time Snake Eyes gets a better look. It's covered with mold and rust, like an electronic zombie.

The silent Joe grabs a cylindrical grenade from his bandolier and places it in the recess behind the mechanical ghoul's knee. He's found it an effective weak spot when fighting Cybertronians, if you can reach it.

"So much for stealth," he thinks.

The blast disables the monster. It continues crawling at a much reduced, but urgent pace. As Snake Eyes and Ravage make their way further into the courtyard several more creatures emerge from the ground beneath them. Snake Eyes readies more grenades. These zombies are different from the Cybertronians he'd met. These shambling ogres are more like what Snake Eyes would call a robot, like Cobra's experimental B.A.T.s. "Robot" is an almost insulting description for the cybermen he'd come to know. Under their metallic shells, they don't seem much different than a human being, at our best and our worst. Definitely not robots. "Gobots" is the term that stuck. A half-knowing smile flashes across Snake Eyes' masked countenance. Every war has its pejorative term for "the enemy" based on the ugliest slurs near at hand. They could've done worse than being named after a blockbuster movie series. "Gobots vs. M.A.S.K." was a beloved global phenomenon, though Snake Eyes never met anybody who actually liked those films.

"If the Cybertronians are the Gobots, I guess that makes us M.A.S.K." Snake Eyes' own mask had become a second face, the one he showed the world.

A hiccup of light momentarily blinds Snake Eyes. He switches out of night vision mode. He sees a missile heading straight towards him. He and his steed weave into a mammoth avenue. He feels the warmth of the missile igniting a safe distance next to him. In the glare of the explosion, he sees who was aiming for him. Soundwave towers menacingly, looking like some kind of gleaming metallic god of destruction. He'd been repaired and restored to his full glory.

The Arashikage Ninja Commando can't help feeling jealous of the giant alien robot. If only his own cracked face could be reassembled, hammered and polished to gleaming perfection like the Decepticon's.

"Father!"

The silent Joe thinks "Soundwave? Back from the dead?" Not like before, when the robot was nothing more than a giant puppet for Doctor Venom. A mechanical marionette whose strings were pulled by the doctor. No, this is a true resurrection, but still, something is missing.

"LASERBEAK: EJECT. OPERATION: DESTRUCTION."

"He's talking about me. My destruction," thinks Snake Eyes as he fires a generous burst from his Uzi at the bird of prey erupting from Soundwave's chest.

Hearing Soundwave speak, Snake Eyes' envy diminishes. The Decepticon didn't get his voice back to the same level of perfection as his face. The Decepticon's voice was now a buzzing monotone, like autotune vocals in the pop music Scarlett would play in the old G.I. Joe barracks. But that was a lifetime away, lost with Earth itself.

Snake Eyes feels a momentary kinship with the alien. Snake Eyes remembers noting how beautiful the behemoth's voice was that day. It was just the sort of detail that would stick with Snake Eyes, who used to have a sonorous, commanding, yet melodic voice himself, or so he was told.

Snake Eyes lets fly a volley of missiles from a shoulder-mounted "gobot killer." When the smoke clears, he sees none of them were a direct hit. But they'd left their mark on the gargantuan blue Decepticon. Snake Eyes readies the next volley as his mount leaps at the stunned Soundwave.

"RAVAGE: YOU ATTACK YOUR MASTER? OPERATION: CORRECTION."

The back of his giant palm smacks the cat and rider, sending them flying in different directions. Snake Eyes softens the impact by rolling with the violent blow, converting its momentum into a surprisingly graceful backflip. Ravage hits the ground with something less than feline grace. With quick efficiency Soundwave grasps the cat by its fore and rear paws and snaps his spine with a sickening crack!

Ravage lets out a sad mewling gasp.

Forcible transformation is a blood-curdling sight for Cybertronians, but its violence is not lost on Snake Eyes either. Soundwave folds Ravage back into cassette form and slides the rectangular cartridge into his open chest plate.

"RAVAGE: INJECT. OPERATION: REPROGRAMMING."

"Together again," says a strained voice. Shockwave steps from behind a veil of smoke and places his arm on Soundwave's shoulder. Soundwave turns his head coldly toward the other Decepticon but says nothing.

"It's going to take some time for me to grow accustomed to my new role as 'the kind one.'"

CHAPTER 11 COMMENTARY
BY TOM SCIOLI & JOHN BARBER

[EDITOR'S NOTE: The views expressed in this Story Commentary do not necessarily represent the views of Hasbro and/or its subsidiary and affiliated companies. They do, however, represent the views of Tom Scioli and John Barber, so that's nice.]

PAGE ONE:
Tom Scioli: Primus, the sleeping giant face of Sub-Cybertronia, is waking up. All telecommunication on Cybertron has been non-functional since the collision with planet Earth, so Duke and Rodimus' group has been cut off from the developments going on outside. Great surprises await them when, and if, they make it to the surface.

I kind of view this "Crypt-Keeper" as a possible common ancestor of man, machine, and reptile.

John Barber: The scale is amazing here. The Joes, the Autobots, and just the huge face dwarfing all of them. You did this page before *Force Awakens* came out, but it reminds me of the composition of some of the scenes there, where the environments of old ships dwarf the heroes.

PAGE TWO:
TS: The demands of a series like this, where life exists on so many different scales has stretched conceptual and drawing muscles I never knew I had. It's been such an amazing learning experience so far.

I think about how far the characters have come, too, how much they've changed. Contrast the friendship between Duke and Mirage, with the xenophobic rhetoric between the Joes and the Autobots in their early encounters. One of the themes of this issue is growth and change and the things that spur it.

JB: This whole series... we're so far away from where we started out, story-wise. Remember when this was just some fighting in a desert for issue #0?

PAGE THREE:
TS: Springer springs into action.

Hands up, anyone in the audience who for a moment thought that was Flint, not Falcon. Falcon's character has an interesting story across the various incarnations of G.I. Joe. Duke's little brother who can't do anything right, but with potential to possibly be the greatest G.I. Joe of all. Voiced by Don Johnson in the movie.

In the DiC cartoon, he struggles with drug addiction. In short, he's a character who is complex and interesting. I wanted to delve into that relationship between Falcon and Duke. It seemed like there was a lot there to work with.

JB: Really portentous moment when Falcon pauses. Very impressive stuff, but knowing what happens next, it's interesting to read into what he's thinking about.

PAGE FOUR:
TS: '80s action movies are a big influence to this series. I had to pay homage to Schwarzenegger and Weather's bro-lock in *Predator*.

When I started working on this series, I decided that one of the rules would be to set it always in the eternal present. No flashbacks. Another rule was to throw the rules out the window, so here's a story with flashbacks and flashbacks within flashbacks.

From early on I knew I wanted one of those *Beverly Hills Cop* firing range scenes. Paper Transformer targets modeled after Soundwave, the first Cybertronian casualty of Space War I.

JB: The brotherly relationship was really important to you. Neither of us actually have brothers, do we? Probably means something. I don't know. We both had Axel Foley, that's somebody.

Great transition as the bullets punch through.

PAGE FIVE:
TS: Throw in a little Patton backdrop. There was an issue of the Hama G.I. Joe run, #82 "Weeding Out," which was a big inspiration for this issue, with Duke in no-nonsense drill instructor mode. He put the new recruits through psychological and physical torture. After massive attrition, the last few men standing were Joes. I highly recommend seeking the issue out.

I like the idea that you can have all kinds of amazing accomplishments in your civilian or military life, but that's just the basic requirement for candidacy on the Joe team. It's the best of the best of the best and everyone else can pack up and go home.

JB: That's great. It's kinda what happens when you grow up and get into real life; like—you like comics? You're the comics guy at your high school? Well, everybody in comic books was that guy or girl. Not everybody turns out to be Tom Scioli and write and draw something like this.

I love that *Patton* reference. I directly referenced it in an issue of *Transformers*, but I watched it right before I started writing the series and it really had an influence on me on the Transformers side.

TS: A flashback within a flashback to Falcon and Duke's civilian life. Part of my research for this series was immersing myself in the culture that informed G.I. Joe, like '80s cinema. The line in *An Officer and a Gentleman* where Richard Gere tells his father, Robert Loggia, "Are you afraid you're going to have to salute me?" was too good not to steal.

PAGE SIX:
TS: The haircut scene, another staple of Boot Camp cinema. *Heartbreak Ridge* and of course the scene in *Stripes* where the recruits learn they weren't required to get crew cuts.

I keep hoping Hasbro will roll out some toys based on our comic, but now I want to run through the Transformers vs. G.I. Joe obstacle course.

JB: Let's start a theme park where giant Transformers statues try to kill you.

"G.I. Joe doesn't have a dress code" is fantastic.

PAGE SEVEN:
TS: Some of this is based on the para-military terrorist training camp sequence in G.I. Joe #4 by Larry Hama and Herb Trimpe. The boot camp obstacle course is another part of the iconography of cinema at the time. It was central to films like *An Officer and a Gentleman, Heartbreak Ridge, Private Benjamin, Stripes,* a sub-motif within the larger motif of post-*Rocky* athletic contests.

I like how complicated the motivations are in this issue. Is Falcon rescuing Pvt. Pyle in the mud out of selfless loyalty? Is he doing it to spite Duke? Then there's the possibility that deliberately throwing away the record is more of a slam than beating Duke's record.

JB: That was one of the first issues of *G.I. Joe* I ever read. I was 6, and seeing this brutal training combined with the heroics was... it was morally complicated stuff at that age. I can see this playing in there—even Duke's motivations and interior are being complicated further here... so much is going on to reveal the meat of this relationship between Duke and Falcon. How much of Duke is a show here?

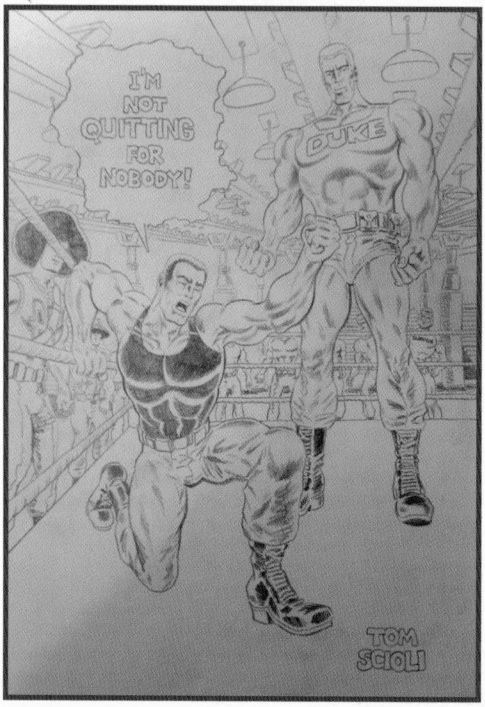
I'M NOT QUITTING FOR NOBODY!
DUKE
TOM SCIOLI

Pencils for Page 14.

PAGE EIGHT:
TS: Part of this new text, *Transformers vs. G.I. Joe*, is a reaction to an existing aggregate text of all previous G.I. Joe and Transformers stories. This is a remix/remake of a scene from *G.I. Joe: The Movie.*

The removal of firing pins was a recurring plot point in Hama's run.

JB: This was a great scene when you described this whole-cloth to me on the phone. Even better in these four panels of ultra-dense storytelling.

PAGE NINE:
TS: Quarrel was a repainted Scarlett action figure not available in the U.S.

I love the ugly depths of the sibling rivalry between Duke and Falcon. I tried to give little glimpses into their childhood, without doing an all-out Jim Henson's G.I. Joe Babies. Their implied home life has a *Wuthering Heights* vibe to it. My main goal with their dialogue during the "Extreme Fighting" scene was that their time in the ring will give them both a long overdue catharsis. Just like Duke is kind of a Schwarzenegger archetype, Falcon is kind of a Stallone. Let them settle it Rocky style.

There's something of a Cain/Abel, Jacob/Esau, Thor/Loki, Orion/Kalibak in the violent severity of their brother dynamic. In many ways it's what defined them up to this point in their lives.

JB: Yeah, your dialogue here is dead-on. I had a different set of dialogue that didn't get used—and this isn't false modesty—the comic is much stronger for it.

PAGE TEN:
TS: The combination of fighting techniques was fun to draw, a continuation of their childhood backyard brawls. I was looking at all kinds of boxing photography and old-timey pugilistic etchings.

JB: Great fighting—I love those schoolyard moments of tough guys going to watch tougher guys fighting.

PAGE ELEVEN:
TS: In boxing photography there's lights, there's darkness, and there's fluids.

JB: Searing brightness.

PAGE TWELVE:
TS: Conrad Hauser and Vincent Falcone. Brothers. Two very different, yet very similar dudes coming out of the same household. It got my wheels turning. I knew there was a story there. I just had to excavate it. It's been part of the earliest drafts of that big *Transformers vs. G.I. Joe* story treatment I'd written.

I keep looking for exceptions to the rule that for every great achiever—and the Joe team is made up of outlier super-achievers—there was some kind of trauma, some pain, that set them on that path where being best of the best was more important than anything.

Mom made him promise to take care of him, and he's been covering him for his entire life.

The red-white-and-blue ring ropes of '80s WWF.

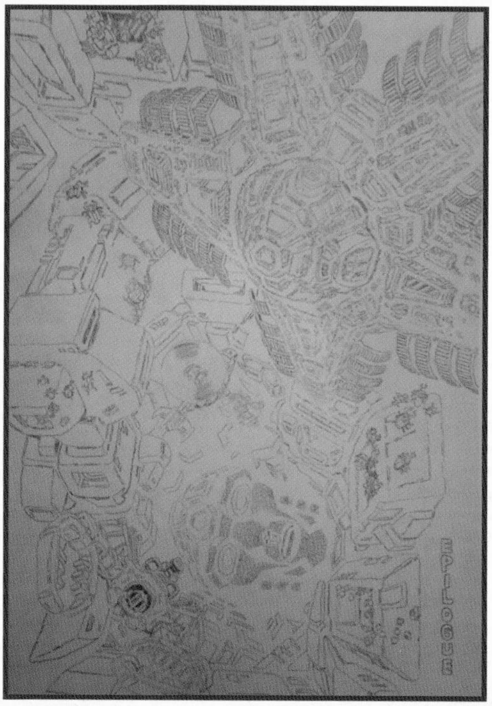
EPILOGUE

Pencils for Page 17.

JB: Every line tells a story of surprising depth and resonance. The feel of this issue is so different in such a surprising way. This whole series has been inverting expectations of what a comic like this can be, and here's a new way of doing this. In the cartoons, even really in the comics, you have a clear set-up of motivations, but this is all about "why Falcon saves Duke" which isn't... it's not a question about a shocking thing. A Joe saving another Joe. Sure, of course. But peeling back the layers, there's so much meaning.

There's an *Invisibles* issue that's all about a random guard that gets killed in an issue; there's a *WildC.A.T.s* story arc about a guy who gets shot in the knee in a previous issue. I love this kind of thing that reminds us how everything has a story.

Pencils for Pages 18-19.

PAGE THIRTEEN:
TS: I like that almost every issue of this comic is in a different genre.

I liked the idea that Falcon actually got this far in his military life because Duke had been secretly covering for him. It's possible that this is just more of Duke's psychological warfare, but if we take it as truth, then for Falcon to get good enough for G.I. Joe, it has to happen right here and right now.

JB: Yeah, that's huge. That's the most brutal thing, true or false, Duke could possibly say.

PAGE FOURTEEN:
TS: This is kind of my version of Spider-Man lifting the heavy machinery for Aunt May.

JB: Yeah. That look on Duke's face. Yeah.

PAGE FIFTEEN:
TS: Jump cut. Shipping out to Cybertron. Lt. Falcon is reborn a G.I. Joe.

JB: I love his team.

PAGE SIXTEEN:
TS: As per the genre, you've got to have the scene where the drill instructor salutes the foul-up who made good. I think the "horse apples" speech is Duke's way of saying "I love you," but don't tell him I said that.

JB: Yeah, after all that... that statement has such a deep meaning.

PAGE SEVENTEEN:
TS: Out of the flashbacks, into the eternal present. Everything, all the creepy crawly things in the depths of Sub-Cybertronia are scuttling out while they can. It's pretty small in the picture, but Mirage is holding Duke and Falcon in his hand.

JB: Woof. Remember where we left off? Good thing nothing big's going to happen.

PAGES EIGHTEEN-NINETEEN:
TS: The Earth debris dust clouds have finally parted. We see the sun for the first time in a long time. The radios are working again. Cybertron is no longer dark and silent.

JB: It certainly is not.

PAGE TWENTY:
TS: The culmination of Megatron's plan to devour the sun and superfuel Cybertron. "Tomorrow may rain, so I'll swallow the sun." Cybertron is a Transformer, too, and it's hungry.

JB: Yeah, remember talking about scale?

TS: Possible titles for next issue: Our Darkest Hour, Eternal. Midnight, The Beginning of the End.

Pencils for Page 20.

CHAPTER 12 COMMENTARY
BY TOM SCIOLI & JOHN BARBER

[EDITOR'S NOTE: The views expressed in this Story Commentary do not necessarily represent the views of Hasbro and/or its subsidiary and affiliated companies. They do, however, represent the views of Tom Scioli and John Barber, so that's nice.]

PAGE ONE:

Tom Scioli: All these giant robots, how do you make them distinctive? I like the idea that there are some Transformers who feel a protective kinship with humans. Mankind is a genuinely endangered species. I combined Defensor's whole thing with The Rescuebots. I played it like an old '80s cartoon, with all the pieces coming together. Looking through the source material, trying to find resonant bits. A robot named "Peacemaker" that turns into a gun felt like the perfect touch.

As much as this series is one big epic mega-movie, I want each issue to stand on its own. Since we're heading into the climax, it's a bit trickier, a bit more of a challenge to do that. Having the human-loving Rescuebots promise to defend mankind, then have one of the Joes return the favor at the end of the issue seemed like a nice way to bookend this chapter and build on the ongoing themes of the series.

John Barber: It's crazy to be here, so near the end, and seeing those echoes. So far away from the zero issue. The Autobots and G.I. Joe team are all willing to lay their lives on the line for each other.

PAGE TWO:

TS: I'm getting to do a lot of the scenes that I'd written way at the beginning, getting to pay off on all the different bits that were set up along the way. I imagine, before the war began, Doc and Wild Bill flew a lot of humanitarian missions together. Always thinking about the relationships between this vast community of characters. What ties them together on an individual basis. In a way, this is a workplace story, but G.I. Joe is a different kind of workplace. They share deep, harrowing experiences and create strong bonds as a result. I think Wild Bill and Doc might've even debuted in the same issue of the comic.

A creepy autopsy was on the to-do list for this series.

JB: I love getting those flashes of what life was like before. And the coloring here... so creepy, so cool. And—and—is that a happy ending? Maybe?

PAGE THREE:

TS: Terrordromes figured heavily in the earliest drafts for the series, back when G.I. Joe was more of an intergalactic task force. They were habitats called Terradomes manufactured by the M.A.R.S. Corporation, an integral part of space colonization.

JB: That's right... early on, you had the idea of starting off with this super-high-tech G.I. Joe team. The Terrordromes are a great fit for Cybertron.

TS: Cobra Commander looks like a Pac-Man ghost in panel two.

There's the interim "Fred" version of Cobra Commander impaled. There's only room for one Cobra Commander. It's amazing how many issues the Fred version of Cobra Commander lasted. It was the era of New Coke. I liked the Fred version. It was an interesting path from a storytelling perspective: remove the villain of the series and replace him with a reader-identification character. The moments where Fred would bluff his way through various scenes were genuinely tense.

Cobra Commander has such a great entourage. G.I. Joe as a brand started with such uniformity, but evolved into such a bizarre psychedelic phantasmagoria by the end of the '80s.

JB: That stuff was bonkers when it came out, at least I remember it being pretty crazy, but here it feels like it's just catching up to you. Like, I don't even question those guys being here.

Also, there's a weird juxtaposition where "Fred" almost looks like he's perched on Cobra Commander's arm, just for a second—like the back of his head is a visor and he's some kind of robot parrot—and then the image resolves itself and the file card locks it in. Cobra Commander does not mess around.

PAGE FOUR:

TS: This is where Transformers go when they die. I like the idea of surprising the reader on every page turn. This plays on the old comics a little bit. In the old series, Optimus was trapped, for way too many issues, inside a video game. You have the Tron riff.

I like the idea though, that the Transformers afterlife isn't entirely separate from our afterlife. Maybe they're the same thing. Transformers and Joes alike become stray electrical impulses and this is where they find themselves. You have the baggage you bring with you from the mortal plane. Grimlock is having a hard time letting go.

JB: One—the colors here are incredible. Literally like no other comic. Two—pulling in the grids from the old packaging and the wire-frame-looking grids on the characters is genius. And three...

TS: Kremzeek, in the cartoon, was a product of its time: *Gremlins* combined with a computer virus. Kremzeek as a metaphysical figure was one of the earliest things I had in mind for the series. As the series climax approaches, these early notions are finding their place. Finding purpose and lending gravitas to the various strange and neglected characters in the source material is a very enjoyable part of the job.

JB: I have very little recollection of Kremzeek but when I saw this, I got a wide smile on my face.

PAGE FIVE:

TS: Time for some unmaskings. I was highly unsatisfied with every single unmasking in the original G.I. Joe series. All those masks promised so much and delivered very little. It's sort of in the nature of masks. I'm trying to think of examples where what was under the mask was remotely as cool as the mask itself. That was the challenge I set for myself: give these characters some cool faces so when the masks come off, you fall out of your chair.

It's a shame it took this long for Cobra Commander and Serpentress to have a scene together. They have a real chemistry. They look good together, too.

JB: I love the chair. What's he reading?

The trick with the masks is that the mystery is so much more resonant than the revelation.

Plus—Cobra Commander's eye holes on the penultimate panel...

PAGE SIX:

TS: Again, I did a lot of thinking about what these characters look like under their masks. I wanted the face underneath to be delightful, unpredictable, and to tell its own story. I wonder if there is an example of a really good mask reveal in fiction. Snake Eyes, post-surgery Baroness, Cobra Commander, Destro in the old comic were all let-downs. Darth Vader under the mask was okay, I guess, but still a let-down. Boba Fett was lame. I thought Kylo Ren was a good way of approaching the problem and just saying, "underneath all these masks is a face." It can be argued that the best option is to just never show what's under the mask, like *V for Vendetta*. I don't agree.

So here is the gauntlet thrown. I think this issue has the top three under-the-mask reveals of all time.

The glasses dug into her face during the plane crash in issue #0. The glasses-shaped scar makes her "read" as the Baroness. I modeled the rash on Serpentress' face on the poor flexographic printing on my copy of *G.I. Joe ARAH* #44, by Larry Hama, Rod Whigham, Andy Mushynsky, George Roussos, and Joe Rosen. Issue #44 was a key issue for *Transformers vs. G.I. Joe*, because it's the first and only appearance of the Creeper Bomb, which ended up playing a vital role in this series.

JB: It's easy to say "it's more powerful to leave it to the reader's imagination." It's harder to actually make it something that pays off. The Kylo Ren scene was great. You knew who was under the mask, you know what Adam Driver looks like, but the reveal was still powerful because it played against the trope. It's just a guy. Unlike Boba Fett, like you said. I agree 100%. There, you knew it was just a guy, and revealing it was just a guy was... there was no twist to it.

Here, though—he's a snake! And Baroness reminds me a little of that Kirby drawing of Victor Von Doom with no mask, and just a single scar. It's not that bad. I like the reveal a lot here.

And, man, the composition of the tendrils reaching out from the faces to the missile with the snake chair, composed symmetrically unlike the three-quarter view when Serpentress entered the room on page 5, and the discarded masks in the shadows of the tendrils. The geometry of the room changes—I mean, I think it can make sense but the angle changes the interpretation—with the embrace and kiss.

I like that she's taller than him. I thought for a second it might be the heels, but they've both got heels.

PAGE SEVEN:

TS: More afterlife action. Joining the giant faces of the Matrix— as seen in the cartoon—is something you must earn. Not all Primes become part of the Matrix.

I've been waiting to use Bludgeon, the Skeleton Samurai, repurposed as an angel of death.

The ghosts that reside in the Autobot Matrix... some of the old Transformers episodes were my introduction to the ideas of Carl Jung. I wouldn't call any of those episodes a masterpiece, but a lot of desperate creativity was funneled into those cartoons.

JB: "Me Grimlock... speechless!" is beautiful. This reminds me of this Conan comic book/record I had as a kid where Conan led the people to heaven but couldn't enter. I think another book did a similar thing, too.

PAGE EIGHT:

TS: Scarlett and Snake Eyes. Scorponok and Fortress Maximus. Those crazy kids.

Snake Eyes has replaced Galen as Fortress Maximus' binary-

bond partner. Scarlett has replaced Zarak as Scorponok's. Regime change, coups and deposed dictators abound.

A lot of the stuff on this page came from a prose story I was writing for issue 11. I felt it merited inclusion in the body of the comic instead. I combined Fortress Maximus' Master Sword, from the Japan-only Transformers series *SuperGod Masterforce*, with the Master Sword from *The Legend of Zelda*. Now it's the souls of Snake Eyes' Ninja Masters that inhabit it.

JB: The tongue ramps. I got nothing here, but tongue ramps. So beautiful.

PAGE NINE:

TS: This is a moment, maybe the heart of the issue. Scarlett gets to see what's under Snake Eyes' mask. I think they're both afraid of how she'll react.

In the original series, characters would get nauseous when they'd see Snake Eyes' face.

JB: That seems kinda cruel a reaction. This is such an amazing layout. Ten panel page. That last look on Scarlett is so enigmatic, too.

PAGE TEN:

TS: Here it is. The one we've all been waiting for. And, for the first time since issue #0, Snake Eyes speaks.

PAGE ELEVEN:

TS: Megatron's turmoil. "Uneasy lies the head that wears a crown." It's not easy being King of the Universe. He's haunted by the ghosts of the Matrix. They're intruding into his meditations. Grimlock is a very recent addition to that pantheon and he's not so high-minded and aloof to be above revenge.

Some *Evil Dead*-style, fighting-your-own-hand action.

JB: Yeah! And it's great to see Grimlock doesn't just get peace within the Matrix. It's a new front to attack Megatron. After last page, I feel like you've really captured the idea of these strands getting drawn together. The first issues especially had a feeling of going in different directions. Sometimes it seemed random.

WHAT GOOD IS YOUR PLANT-BOMB IF IT NEVER REACHES ITS TARGET?

Page 15, Panel 2 from *G.I. JOE: A REAL AMERICAN HERO* #44

But you had that plan you'd put together in the beginning, and as much as things deviated, there was enough where it all started to pull back together, and here—pages 10 and 11, specifically—it seems like everything's coming into place. The end of this series is going to be about things converging.

PAGE TWELVE:

TS: Be a man, Metroplex. Tough love. He's been starfish-shaped since Megatron first became Ruler of Cybertron. Cowed and humiliated, like so many of his fellow Autobots, in a state of shock, unable to transform. Rodimus tried to command him to transform back in issue #5. Now the whole crew is chiming in, plus peer pressure from his fellow robot cities Scorponok and Fortress Maximus.

Check out Metroplex's guns.

JB: Nice. And those three together, fantastic. Bye, starfish Metroplex.

True story: I went to the Hasbro offices in Rhode Island last week, and before I left, my daughter was sad I was going. I said "do you know where I'm going? I'm going to a place where they make toys!"

And Ava replies, "Do they make starfish toys?"

So I stumble, and I say, "Well, they make Disney Princesses and *Star Wars* and *My Little Pony* and *Transformers* and Marvel Super Heroes. They make all kinds of great toys."

Ava says, "Tell them they should make starfish toys."

So Hasbro... ball's in your court.

PAGE THIRTEEN:

TS: Joes and Autobots—Jotobots—make a show of force. Their numbers, when assembled, are far larger than anyone would've predicted. They are the disenfranchised.

JB: Amazing page. The scale, the scope, the detail, the faces... Does it get any bigger?

PAGES FOURTEEN-FIFTEEN:
JB: YES IT DOES!

TS: Megatron commands Primus to form a Dyson Sphere (The Sunshade) around the sun. This is a *Lord of the Rings* moment. The city-sized robots are the Ents.

With the big forcefield, this almost looks like a still from the cartoon. The only double-splash page in an issue full of double-splash moments.

JB: I was at Hasbro when this came in and even on my phone, this is an enormous moment.

PAGE SIXTEEN:

TS: Blaster broadcasts the code to shut down Trypticon's forcefield at maximum volume. What that code sounds like is up to each reader, but good luck not hearing "In Your Eyes."

Now they can finally pelt Trypticon with green bombs like they wanted to in issue #2.

PAGE SEVENTEEN:

TS: Metroplex vs. Trypticon.

Wild Bill rides again.

Now that Metroplex is back on his feet, there's no stopping him.

JB: I love that first pair of panels. Metroplex's punch is great, but there's so much else going on—Blaster's cassettes, the incoming Decepticons. Then Metroplex punching through Trypticon... so great.

PAGE EIGHTEEN:

TS: Cobra Commander, once again, is the spoiler, the wild card. He has a masterful sense of timing.

Doctor Venom is wearing the S.N.A.K.E. armor, projecting his Creeper-controlling signal.

JB: The storytelling in the last two panels is beautiful.

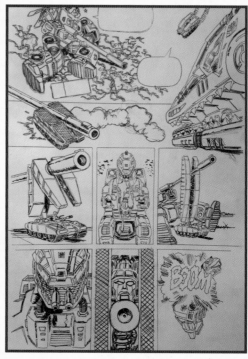

Pencils for Page 19.

PAGE NINETEEN:

TS: Defensor gets the favor returned. Steeler and the bridgelayer to the rescue. I've been wanting to do something cool with the bridgelayer tank from day one.

JB: And this is a really cool thing. The bridgelayer was a great one-note toy. Like, it looks really industrial and cool but the thing it does is so weird and passive. Now, holding a giant gun named "Peacemaker" so a combiner can aim it at a mile-tall robot tyrannosaurus is even cooler than letting the MOBAT cross a stream without getting wet.

PAGE TWENTY:

TS: As early as issue #1, we talked about clipping panels here and there from old G.I. Joe and Transformers comics. I finally got around to doing it. "I'm late." This one is from *G.I. Joe ARAH* #14, by Larry Hama, Mike Vosburg, Jon D'Agostino, Joe Rosen, and C. Scheele.

I also cut and pasted lines from the bible here, too.

JB: I think that was the book I was thinking of with that Conan thing earlier.

TS: The future is predicted, the coming of a Cobra Emperor. The true Serpentor. The line from *Rosemary's Baby* is a perfect note to end the issue on.

CHAPTER 13 COMMENTARY
BY TOM SCIOLI & JOHN BARBER

[EDITOR'S NOTE: The views expressed in this Story Commentary do not necessarily represent the views of Hasbro and/or its subsidiary and affiliated companies. They do, however, represent the views of Tom Scioli and John Barber, so that's nice.]

PAGE ONE:
TOM SCIOLI: This was a page I started working on back before the series began. I knew it was a moment I wanted. Transformers are very awe-inspiring at this angle.

JOHN BARBER: Amazing way to start the issue. That kind of scale is surprisingly hard to pull off—or, anyway, you don't see it every day.

PAGE TWO:
TS: Starscream has changed into a jet and is taking the Joes for a ride as Hawk cleaves the cockpit with his tomahawk. Wild Bill has been transformed by his technoactive cube implant into a superhuman man-machine hybrid. This issue was such a pleasure to work on. There's an excitement and momentum when you're starting a project and when you're ending one. It made me really glad I did all that preparation work in the beginning, so when I got to the end, I had the confidence of knowing all the pieces would fit together.

JB: That second panel, perfectly set up by the first and betraying no extraneous detail. Everything you need as a reader is there, and everything there is what you need. I'm going to sound like the Chris Farley show here. We talked about these last few issues at a good length, but that was a couple months ago, and then here it comes and every instant is better than what you'd told me or whatever little bit I contributed.

PAGE THREE:
TS: In the old comics, it was established that Destro and Hawk are each others' equivalent, setting them up forever as nemeses. The stage of their final battle is the mirrored disco surface of Megatron's head. Doctor Venom is wearing S.N.A.K.E. armor, minus the helmet.

JB: Another epic shot. Destro showing up in those original comics is what really kicked the series into high gear. The first year was good, but the second year was great.

PAGE FOUR:
TS: The first panel echoes Hawk and Destro's climactic battle from issue #16 of the original G.I. Joe: ARAH comic. It was a last-minute decision to include the original panel in the background. I'd been sampling from old G.I. Joe and Transformers comics to such great effect, that it made sense to use it to underscore the timelessness of Hawk and Destro's never-ending battle. In an earlier draft, Hawk says something about how they've been doing this forever. Destro tells Hawk he has no concept of what forever is.

JB: It's cooler the way the sampled art tells that, freeing the dialog to focus on the tomahawk. That sampling is fascinating to see—I was thinking a lot about it as you did this issue. It's such a unique thing here, where this isn't pulling a panel out and sticking it on a computer screen, or something—it's way more musical. We both grew up in the era of samples in music and video, but it's never really carried over to mainstream comics, which is sort of weird because it's one of the places that's clear of legal issues...

TS: It's been fun pairing characters from both franchises. I like the alchemy at play. Serpentress looks good paired with Laserbeak, as does Lady Jaye and Swoop, the dinobot pterodactyl.

PAGE FIVE:
TS: I'm fascinated with the interchangeability of Duke and Hawk. I gave Hawk white hair, which makes him a little more Lee Marvin. Hawk's snake impalement echoes Duke's "death" in the G.I. Joe animated movie.

JB: And the fight in Prophet #8, which I'm sure I mentioned before.

TS: Venom operates without anaesthetic.

JB: Tom, I'm not sure he's a good doctor.

PAGE SIX:
TS: Duke picks up where Hawk left off, as if it were meant for him all along. Megatron's head functions as a netherworld separate from the ongoing battle, but part of it, too. It's the Arena of Sport.

JB: That interchangeability is another fascinating piece. Some fans haaaaaaaaaate Duke. Others hit the series at the right age where he's the "main guy." Either way—great fight scene.

PAGE SEVEN:
TS: Lots of final battles and Revelations, with a capital "R," in this Robot Ragnarok. As metal as it gets.

JB: The action goes to slow motion and then you just can't wait to turn the page and find out what that shattered gem means! At least, I can't wait.

PAGE EIGHT:
TS: What's under the mask? Goodbye, Destro.

Mini-Megatron! Finally! Been waiting for the right moment for him to show up.

JB: He's like your Ewoks, but he gets stepped on.

PAGE NINE:
TS: Clearing up the mystery of "Who Shot Hawk?" in issue #1. And, due to popular demand, a flashback to Hawk and Storm Shadow's issue #5 bathroom brawl.

JB: We were so young back then. Both thens.

PAGE TEN:
TS: The death of Hawk followed by the death of Doctor Venom. Kwinn threatened to make Doctor Venom swallow a grenade in the old comic.

You met Mini-Megatron, now meet Mega-Megatron. I modeled his look after the movie Megatron which always looked to me like a junk pile of angry scrap metal.

JB: That thing with Kwinn and the grenade always stuck with me. Big combiner Megatron is awesome. There was a thing in the Transformers comics where Megatron had to fight all the other Decepticons combined—now here he is. Wait, wait, I have a good one here: "My god—it's full of cars."

Thank you, thank you; you'll all miss my contributions.

PAGE ELEVEN:
TS: Psychedelic interlude. Scarlett/Zkarlett goes into the matrix, via the dream machine brainwave scanner. She becomes Scarlett in the Sky with Diamonds. This is a war fought on two fronts, the physical and the metaphysical. Optimus' rebirth required a physical and a spiritual component. Ultra Magnus revived the Prime physically, but he would've been a mindless zombie, a true robot, without the return of Optimus's soul. For that we can thank the Goddess Queen of Scorponok.

I've enjoyed depicting these neon landscapes.

JB: That art effect is so cool, and the actual drawing so beautiful. Is that how Prime sees himself or how the afterlife sees him?

PAGE TWELVE:

TS: One of the great starships of science fiction, The Decepticon Flagship *Nemesis*. Early in the development for this series, I'd planned a much larger role for Shipwreck, but with such a large cast, some characters get lost in the shuffle. I'll make it up to you in 2025, Admiral

JB: I think that works, getting back to him after a long time away.

PAGE THIRTEEN:

TS: The Return of Planet Earth! Planet Earth is such a great playground. So many story possibilities.

JB: Tell that to the vocal section of Earth-hating Transformers fans!

PAGE FOURTEEN:

TS: The Atlas Protocol. We get to see what the earthbound Joes were up to the past few months, especially Flint who got less screen time than Shipwreck. Cameo by the Tucaro from *G.I. Joe* #32.

JB: Aw! I didn't realize that's who it was!

PAGE FIFTEEN:

TS: Part of the fun of working on an established property is that you have tremendous resources at your disposal, the collective creativity of the years of work that went before. I tried to use that to its fullest. This is maybe the most recent bit. 200+ issues in, Larry Hama's G.I. Joe is a beautifully baroque, still-unfolding mythology. A year or two ago he did a story where the Joes find a secret Pit under The Pit. In it was a giant eyeball. That bit was too good not to use here to introduce Atlas.

The Earth is a giant Transformer that takes orders from General Joe Colton.

JB: I love that you're pulling from the current stuff. It's amazing to have Larry Hama still writing G.I. Joe in 2016!

PAGE SIXTEEN:

TS: Snake Eyes. The wild card. The character whose actions seem to be dictated by a roll of the dice.

JB: One of the difficulties with Snake Eyes, I think, is that while he's super-cool he's also super-unapproachable. He's not like a character like Wolverine or Batman who are hyper-competent but you get in their head. Everybody takes Snake Eyes' silence to be part of the persona—no first-person narration or thought balloons—but while that really seems like the only course of action, it distances the reader. I love how you lean into that, and really play that up. Larry did, too, I think (I say "did" as the original Snake Eyes is currently dead in Larry's comic) but you've pushed it to the fore.

PAGE SEVENTEEN:

TS: Billy: could he be the one to bring unity to the cosmos? Billy's had a rougher time than anybody in this series and he's still going strong. He's a fighter. In the old comic, he led the Springfield resistance movement at the age of 11. Cobra Commander is so insecure, so threatened by his son, he doesn't see that he is in many ways the perfect heir to the throne. They have their father/son battle to the death. Storm Shadow makes sure Snake Eyes gives them some room.

JB: I love imagining the fight without the backgrounds. So cool. It draws me in so much.

PAGE EIGHTEEN:

TS: I had so much fun putting together this "Megatron Lives" collage. Literal pastiche.

JB: Yeah, that is lovely.

PAGE NINETEEN:

TS: The death of Storm Shadow. He gives one of those *Lone Wolf and Cub* sword-through-the-chest death rattle soliloquies.

JB: When somebody finally stabs me to death, I hope I have one-tenth that level of composure.

PAGE TWENTY:

TS: Cobra Commander's exploding helmet bites him on the ass. The death of Cobra Commander. We should've promoted the body count on the cover like issue #109 of *G.I. Joe: ARAH* with its bright yellow "Body Count: 7 and Climbing" blurb. We should've done one of those "who will die?" floating head covers. Or better yet a "who will live?" cover!

JB: We still can! At least as I type this. As you read this, reader, we cannot.

I always loved the plastic explosive thing with the helmet, but when I first read that, I think my dad had to explain why that didn't just solve Duke's problems. Now it finally does.

PAGE TWENTY-ONE:

TS: Somebody was going to drive through somebody's eye in this series. Ultra Magnus does the honors.

JB: With the movie cast assembled around him. And an AWESOME G.I. Joe group shot, for good measure.

PAGE TWENTY-TWO:

TS: Ultra Magnus vs. Megatron.

JB: And the Matrix opens!

PAGE TWENTY-THREE:

TS: I didn't have the proper Optimus Prime toy when I was a kid, but I did have Ultra Magnus—which re-used the Optimus Prime toy but painted all white. I wondered what the connection was between these two characters. I wondered why resplendent-in-white risen Christ Optimus was inside of Ultra Magnus.

"The Return of Optimus Prime" in the TV series was a pretty big deal to me. It was teased on commercials. It was pretty close to the end of the TV series and my connection to it, but for a time, it was a parallel modern sci-fi mythology with infinite potential.

JB: That same thing took James Roberts and Alex Milne in *More Than Meets the Eye* to another take on that guy-inside-Magnus thing—which actually led to a new character, Minimus Ambus, inside Ultra Magnus' current toy. It's cool to see that original Ultra Magnus toy inspire a lot of stories.

PAGE TWENTY-FOUR:

TS: Starscream taking the opportunity to be wormy.

JB: I just love this page. "I was talking to the Matrix." That's our Starscream!

PAGE TWENTY-FIVE:

TS: The Matrix as football, betting fumbled and intercepted back and forth. Whoever gets it gets possession of Cybertron.

PAGE TWENTY-SIX:

TS: Bumblebee is the ever-loyal retainer. Wild Bill has basically become a demi-god. I wanted some of the human characters to ascend to cyberdeification.

JB: And it takes us all the way back to issue #0!

PAGE TWENTY-SEVEN

TS: Primus' feeding frenzy cannot be stopped. Even Optimus is unable to get him to release the sun.

JB: The twisting around where it's not Unicron eating a planet, it's Primus eating the sun, and all that entails...

PAGE TWENTY-EIGHT:
TS: Starscream is such a worm.

I modeled General Flagg after Larry Hama, who started with issue #1 of G.I. Joe and continues writing it to this day. I studied his work very closely for this series.

JB: And following through on a very long set-up to get there.

PAGES TWENTY-NINE AND THIRTY:
TS: Interplanetary Sucker Punch!

JB: Nothing more can be said.

PAGE THIRTY-ONE:
TS: In one of our earliest conversations about this series, we talked about doing this, making Earth the ultimate Transformer. It seemed impossibly audacious back then, but turns out to be a perfectly natural progression for the series. It's the apotheosis. We talked about doing this and then dropping the mic.

JB: Yeah, I know that's a thing I wanted to do forever, but you came to it independent of me. It's amazing that we actually got here. "Pangaiden" is my favorite name.

PAGE THIRTY-TWO:
TS: I was reading Akira, fell asleep on the couch, then woke up and wrote this sequence, which was not in the original script. It's such a magical moment that you can't imagine the series without it.

JB: Yeah... the thumbs down, and after everything that's happened, it seems like that's going to be a real thumbs down.

PAGE THIRTY-THREE:
TS: Like Lord of the Rings, our fantasy war epic has a series of endings and epilogues with a cast of thousands. It's really nice to be able to do this in the medium of comic books where abbreviated, rushed and often nonexistent denouements are the norm.

JB: I loved seeing these pages coming in.

PAGE THIRTY-FOUR:
TS: Billy carries on two traditions: he's the new Snake Eyes and the new Cobra Commander. Baroness bides her time. An interplanetary Game of Thrones war of succession between Mars and Venus is foreshadowed.

I couldn't leave the Ponies out of this Hasbro crossover.

JB: Assuming it's actually in this printed comic, that is the greatest thing ever, Tom.

PAGES THIRTY-FIVE AND THIRTY-SIX:
TS: You can't beat the funeral scene from G.I. Joe: ARAH #22, so I didn't even try, adhering to Wally Wood's axiom "Never draw anything you can copy, never copy anything you can trace, never trace anything you can cut out and paste up." Add to that, "never draw anything you can scan from an old comic."

This sequence was modeled after JFK's funeral.

Once I was in cut-and-paste mode, I was looking for moments from Todd McFarlane's G.I. Joe: ARAH issues to use so we could put McFarlane's name in the credits. There wasn't anything that fit the story, though.

JB: You'll have to wait for Spawn vs. Punisher.

The funny thing for me is I was picking up G.I. Joe: ARAH here and there for the first 20 issues—I had the treasury of #1, a 3-pack with some issues, a paperback with some, a couple issues here and there—definitely not #19, which was referenced every issue because it was a massive attack on the Pit and the death of a bunch of characters. But #21 and onward I read. So this funeral was from the first issue with any words on my very long streak of regular G.I. Joe-reading.

PAGE THIRTY-SEVEN:
TS: Flagg at the gallows. Even wars have laws and Flagg broke every one of them. But his contingency plans within contingency plans make him unbeatable, except in one instance. General Hawk got to be the untarnished, celebrated, venerated war hero, not him.

JB: Flagg stayed pretty cool, though.

PAGE THIRTY-EIGHT:
TS: I modeled this epilogue page after the final page of Frank Miller and Chris Claremont's Wolverine graphic novel.

JB: Aw! I didn't catch that, either. That's awesome.

PAGE THIRTY-NINE:
TS: The postwar solar system. This could be the setting for a great massively multiplayer RPG. Even though this is the last issue, I kind of wish somebody would take this new world, ripe for exploration, and run with it. With this series we've created a living, breathing universe with a past, present, and future that extends in every direction.

JB: This is really something, here. Great coda.

PAGE FORTY:
TS: Optimus is a trailblazer at heart. He's restless, a better wartime leader than peacetime leader.

JB: Love the Ark 2's paint. Manages to reference G.I. Joe: ARAH and Transformers: Generation 2.

PAGE FORTY-ONE:
TS: Rodimus is the opposite. He's a great peacetime leader. He's, sensitive, intelligent, curious, vulnerable, and collaborative. Perhaps there's a reason Primus looks like him.

JB: Cybertron's in good hands.

PAGE FORTY-TWO:
TS: The excellent film G.I. Joe: Retaliation highlights Duke and Roadblock's domestic life, as played by Channing Tatum and Dwayne "The Rock" Johnson respectively. Life is back to normal. This is kind of like a Freddy Krueger ending.

JB: That is the greatest mash-up anybody's done.

PAGE FORTY-THREE:
TS: The way you end a story says a lot about authorial intent. That's a wrap!

John, it's been a pleasure.

JB: Tom, getting to be a small part of this, and to get to know you through this comic, has been a singular highlight of my life. This comic... it's been an honor you let me into this. I love this thing so much, and I'll miss it, and miss working with you, but I know—from you, the best is yet to come!

TOM SCIOLI is a Pittsburgh-based comics maker, educator and historian. His past works include the Xeric-winning *UnMortals: The Myth of 8-Opus*, the Eisner-nominated *Godland*, and the webcomics *Final Frontier, Satan's Soldier* and *Mystery Object*. He is currently the artist and co-writer of *Transformers vs. G.I. Joe*.

JOHN BARBER is just happy to be included here. He's written the second-most Transformers comics of anybody, and currently writes the *Transformers* ongoing series (usually with Andrew Griffith on art), *Action Man* (Paolo Villanelli drawing), and co-writes *Back to the Future* (with Bob Gale; Marcelo Ferreira on art) and *Revolution* (with Cullen Bunn, Fico Ossio drawing), which has even more Hasbro characters getting mad and becoming friends. Here, he was lucky to get to watch Tom Scioli do his magic.

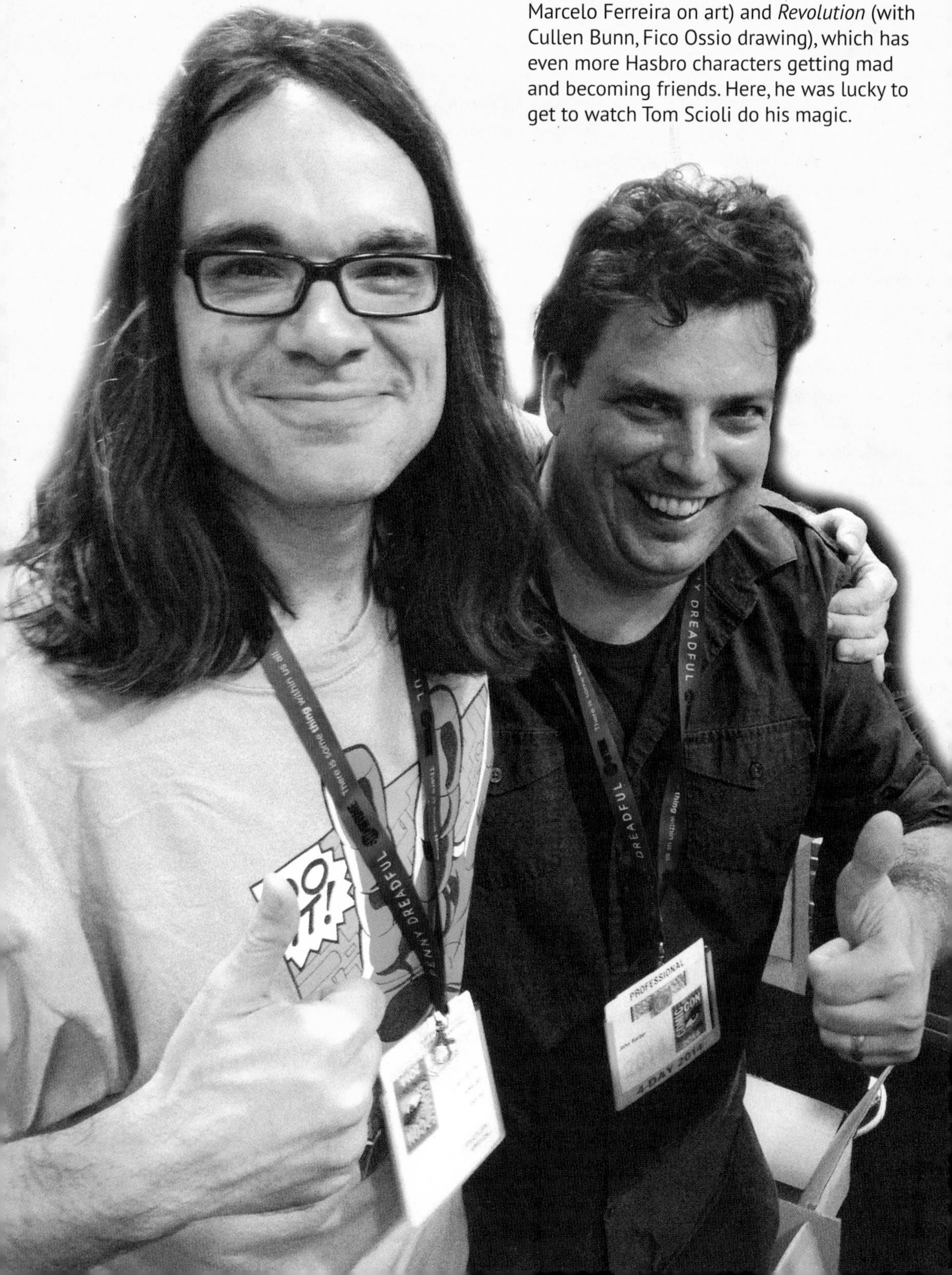
PROFESSIONAL